Half Moon Rising

CHORAL MUSIC FROM MAINLAND CHINA,
HONG KONG, SINGAPORE AND TAIWAN

COMPILED AND EDITED BY JOHN WINZENBURG

SATB AND PIANO

EIGENTUM DES VERLEGERS · ALLE RECHTE VORBEHALTEN
ALL RIGHTS RESERVED

PETERS EDITION LTD

A member of the EDITION PETERS GROUP
LEIPZIG · LONDON · NEW YORK

John Winzenburg

Dr John Winzenburg is an associate professor of music at Hong Kong Baptist University, where he conducts the Cantoría Hong Kong and the HKBU Choir. Winzenburg also regularly appears as conductor with the Hong Kong New Music Ensemble. His groups have distinguished themselves at international competitions, major venues around China and through novel performance events in Hong Kong. Winzenburg is active internationally as clinician, lecturer, adjudicator and scholar. He spent the 2004–5 school year as a Fulbright Doctoral Fellow at the Central Conservatory of Music (CCOM) in Beijing after earning graduate degrees in orchestral and choral conducting from the University of Iowa and University of Minnesota. His research on Chinese-Western fusion compositions and new Chinese choral music have earned him a growing list of contributions in international publications, including *Perspectives of New Music, Twentieth-Century China, Asian Music, CHIME* and the *Journal of the Central Conservatory of Music*, and for Palgrave Macmillan and The University of Michigan Press. Winzenburg began studying Mandarin while earning his BA in East Asian Studies in the 1980s. Since then, he has worked and studied in various parts of China and Japan for more than sixteen years.

Project manager: David Blackwell
Music origination: New Notations London
Text layout: Moira Roach

Peters Edition Limited
2–6 Baches Street
London N1 6DN

sales@editionpeters.com
www.editionpeters.com

This collection © 2015 by Peters Edition Ltd, London

ISMN 979-0-57700-908-7

All rights reserved. No part of this publication may be reproduced, stored in a retrieval system or transmitted in any form or by any means, electronic, mechanical, photocopying, recording or otherwise, without the prior written permission of the publisher.

Contents

Introduction iv

Mandarin Chinese Diction/Mandarin Pronunciation Guide ix

Ban Ge Yue Liang Pa Shang Lai | Half Moon Rising   Xinjiang folksong, arr. Cai Yuwen 2

Ba Jun Zan | Magnificent Horses   Fantasy on a Mongolian folk tune, arr. Yang Hongnian, ... 6
　　　　　　　　　　　　　　　　adapted and arr. Jing Ling-Tam

Cha Shan Qing Ge | Tea Mountain Love Song   Guizhou folksong, arr. Chen Tscheng Hsiung 16

Diu Diu Dang Ah | Old Train Song   Taiwan Yilan folksong, arr. Chien Shan-hua 29

Dui Hua | Antiphonal Flower Song   Anhui folksong, arr. Shi Jin Bo 43

Gai Tau Hong Mei | Street Calls   Leong Yoon Pin 54

Ge Lao Huan Ge | Happy Song of the Gelao   Gelao folksong, arr. Zhou Zhengsong 62

Hong Dou Ci | Red Bean Poem   Liu Xue'an, arr. Hwang Yau-tai 69

Ken Chun Ni | Cultivating Spring Soil   He Lüting 76

Kuai Le De Ju Hui | Happy Reunion   ancient tune of Sun Moon Lake, arr. Chuan-Sheng Lu 82

Lok Sui Tien | Rainy Days   Hakka folksong, arr. Toh Ban Sheng 92

Mo Li Hua | Jasmine Flower   Jiangsu folksong, arr. Chen Yi 102

Mu Ge | Shepherd's Song   Eastern Mongolian folksong, arr. Qu Xixian 108

Pao Ma Liu Liu Di Shan Shang | Horses Run on the Mountain   Xikang folksong, arr. Zhao Yushu 115

Qing Chun Wu Qu | Dance of Youth   Uyghur folksong, arr. Wang Luobin, ... 125
　　　　　　　　　　　　　　　　choral arr. Wang Shiguang

Ru Meng Ling | Like a Dream   Richard Tsang 136

Seui Diu Go Tau | Under the Mid-Autumn Moon   Chan Kai-Young 147

Shui Guang Lian Yan | Ripples Glisten Away . . .   Chen Yihan 159

Shui Xian Hua | Narcissus Flower   Chinese folksong, arr. Lin Sheng-shih 172

Tin O O | Dark Clouds   Northern Taiwan children's song, arr. Tsai Yu-Shan 177

Xiao He Tang Shui | Flowing Creek   Yunnan folksong, arr. Ma Shuilong 185

Xiao Huang Li Niao | Little Oriole   Mongolian folksong, arr. Chan Hing-yan 192

Yang Guan San Die | Parting at Yangguan Pass   ancient Chinese tune, transcribed 203
　　　　　　　　　　　　　　　　by Xia Yifeng, arr. Wang Zhenya

Yi Wang | To Forget   Hwang Yau-tai 217

Introduction

China's new international stature is stimulating interest in all its cultural forms, old and new. Chinese choral music is a more recent yet vibrant addition to these forms, as until a century ago choral singing was relatively rare in China. Now, throughout Chinese communities everywhere — from Mainland China to Hong Kong, Taiwan, Singapore, Malaysia and beyond — it has become an everyday experience in school activities, ceremonies, concerts and festivals. New Chinese compositions and arrangements, like the title song of this collection, have been central to the growing choral culture.

When Cai Yuwen arranged *Ban Ge Yue Liang Pa Shang Lai* (Half Moon Rising) for chorus as a student at the Shanghai Conservatory in 1953, there were few unaccompanied Chinese choral works as models. Western music had only begun to take root in China from the 1920s, and choral music was still relatively new to the country. But due to its subtle combination of folk forms and Chinese language in the choral idiom, Cai's arrangement was selected for performance at the Conservatory's 1953 graduation concert, and in the same year received a silver medal at the Fourth World Festival of Youth and Students in Bucharest.

Cai's work was heard as 'new' at that time because of the way it blended styles from China's ethnic Han majority and Uyghur minority with Western musical language. In fact, such new sounds have become a hallmark of Chinese composers in all regions over the past century. 'New Chinese Music' refers to all types of vocal and instrumental works written from the early twentieth century that combine Western and Chinese musical traits, originally for the purpose of 'modernization'. Centring on musical interaction, they frequently include extra-musical features of Chinese culture like poetry, calligraphy and painting.

Chinese choral music has evolved within this larger national framework by adopting the pillars of Western choral music, which had not been central to the Chinese tradition before 1900. Most fundamental was the initial adoption of divided SATB voices. It also modelled itself on small- and large-scale genres like part songs and cantatas for its repertoire. And along with Western structures, harmony and texture, it has increasingly embraced the *bel canto* vocal aesthetic. Equally important, however, has been the purposeful inclusion of Chinese traditions as a fundamental principle. The Chinese choral repertoire is noteworthy for its wealth of folksongs used either directly or indirectly, and is also marked by extensive variety of regional music and texts. Mandarin is the national language and is most frequently used for singing Chinese choral works, but many are performed in regional dialects, representing different ethnicities and geographical regions. Chinese vocal genres also reflect social traditions through arrangements of ballads, work songs and mountain songs. And traditional singing styles are used, for example in works that employ folk embellishments.

Chinese choral music has thus become a meeting point of regional, national and international forms. Like Chinese music as a whole, these forms have interacted over the past 80 years alongside major historical movements. Through often turbulent decades, the choral repertoire has developed in three main styles: Chinese folk tunes set to Western Classical-Romantic musical language; works with heightened emphasis on Chinese folk styles and Western/Soviet Romantic influences; and expanded regional, vocal and musical styles. These three categories form the basis for the works included in this collection. In many ways, they correspond to major points in modern Chinese history.

Chinese composers first began studying Western music in the decades up to 1949. For them, musical features of the Western Baroque, Classical and Romantic periods were regarded as 'new' because they represented paths toward 'modernization', necessary to strengthen China against various outside threats (see *Ken Chun Ni*). In this early stage of Chinese choral music development (early- to mid-century), composers typically set Chinese folk tunes or composed tunes with Chinese texts in a Western Classical-Romantic idiom. Texts could involve various social/political themes, lyrical/historical subjects or religious content, but their Chinese musical content was frequently limited to the use of folk tunes or implied folk styles (as in *Shui Xian Hua* and *Hong Dou Ci*). The melodies were framed in Western tonal harmony with moderate degrees of chromaticism, and were most often accompanied by piano until groups developed to perform *a cappella* works after 1949.

From the late 1940s many composers stepped up their efforts to capture a more recognizable Chinese sound in their choral works with more traditional music content. Folk tunes or folk styles became central to the overall arrangements, rather than simply being framed within functional harmony (see *Dui Hua* and *Pao Ma Liu Liu Di Shan Shang*). Instead, the harmony was often based on the pentatonic scale itself. Triads were built from the melodic pitches that comprised this scale, but they did not as strictly adhere to a tonic-dominant-tonic pattern. Folksongs remained a major foundation for choral arrangements, but vocal lines were more reflective of regional traditions (see *Kuai Le De Ju Hui*). Other aspects of Chinese history, poetry and even instrumental traditions were also important source materials. Choral music in this style included both accompanied pieces and an expanding body of unaccompanied works.

In the People's Republic of China cultural policies were similar to those in Soviet countries, where composers pursued international socialist principles by praising home-grown traditions. Alongside folk styles, many compositions tended towards later Romantic harmonies, expansive melodies and dynamic-textural variety. Chinese choral compositions of this type employed texts with strengthened nationalistic elements capturing an imaginary Chinese 'essence', especially from the countryside or history (see *Mu Ge*). The Soviet musical influence was especially visible during the close Chinese-Russian relationship of the early People's Republic, and new Chinese works were written in martial fashion (for large choral forces at high dynamic levels) to extol the virtues of the new socialist motherland. China had its own 'classical' forms as well. Vocal forms might first be represented by Chinese opera, but instrumental works could also serve as source materials for choral music. Accompanied works sometimes saw the piano mimicking the original Chinese instrument within heavily Romantic language (see *Yang Guan San Die*).

Since the late 1970s Chinese choral literature has ranged ever more widely, especially as many Chinese composers have received training in modern Western techniques, sometimes abroad. This third Chinese choral style embodies the amalgam of individual approaches, and is marked by much regional variety, experimentation and compositional originality. Different Han majority and non-Han minority traditions are highlighted according to the work (see *Xiao Huang Li Niao*), and while still often scored with Mandarin texts, works are frequently performed in regional and local dialects, as for example *Mo Li Hua*. Pieces now employ varying balances of Chinese-Western, folk-classical-popular and traditional-experimental languages in their compositions. On the one hand, they reach far back into China's long history, recreating classical poetry with new musical inflections (see *Ru Meng Ling*); on the other, they use an array of local traditions as sources of experimentation, including vocal effects and harmonic variety (see *Gai Tau Hong Mei*).

One sign of expanded regionalism is found in the rich body of works written outside Mainland China. Especially since the 1980s, due to migration and political-ideological differences, some composers have drawn from indigenous traditions to assert local identity instead of or alongside pan-Chinese nationalism. Taiwan choral repertoire is especially pronounced in this respect. While Mandarin was the official language in Taiwan from the end of the Second World War, the greater attention given to local Taiwanese culture from the late 1980s has resulted in choral works that have gained international recognition, as, for example, *Diu Diu Dang Ah* and *Tin O O*.

This third choral style of expanded regional, vocal and musical character has flourished in recent decades across Chinese communities. Contemporary works can be highly experimental, exploring musical and vocal styles in greater depth (see *Shui Guang Lian Yan*). Even as musical exploration expands, we see a common reliance on aural-visual 'markers' that are central to new Chinese choral music. One frequent marker is the pentatonic folk melody embedded into the harmonic foundation. Another is the hybridized Chinese-Western vocal delivery of works performed in folk styles and local dialects (see *Seui Diu Go Tau*). Choirs in different Chinese regions have varying degrees of exposure to folk traditions. Many Mainland Chinese choirs will perform folk arrangements with a heavily 'nasalized' tone or local timbre, using scores with numbered notation instead of Western staff notation. But many, if not most, in Taiwan, Singapore, Hong Kong and Mainland urban-coastal areas now embrace the *bel canto* aesthetic as their main approach to choral training, with only an imaginary sense of older Chinese folk or regional timbres.

Despite varying social and political systems among different Chinese communities, wider choral trends show them moving in parallel directions. The emergence of compositions, publications and ensemble participation by singers of all ages, regions and musical backgrounds reflects China's rapidly developing appetite for group vocal expression of its regional and ethnic traditions. After the initial appearance of choral music in the mid-twentieth century, the growing middle class in all regions has led to a surge in interest in choral singing by people wanting to participate in group music-making. Increased training of conductors, composers and vocalists, both locally and with students going abroad, has rapidly advanced the quality of Chinese choirs. Greater international exchange has taken place via choir tours and festivals, and new Chinese compositions and arrangements are often written for those events (see *Lok Sui Tien*). Furthermore, we see a significant development in the private or unofficial publishing industry, due to far greater market and governmental openness (especially in the Mainland) than in the past.

The repertoire is now developing further as Chinese choral culture reaches out to different parts of the world, and as choirs on all continents look for opportunities to share in its music. At a recent festival in Argentina, for example, I presented a series of workshops on Chinese choral music to local participants, while a university choir from southern China performed to a wildly enthusiastic South American audience. Yet despite a growing interest in performing Chinese pieces, non-Chinese choirs often face similar apprehensions: How can they find suitable pieces to perform? How can they sing texts in Mandarin and other dialects with appropriate vocal styles? How can they access background information on arrangements and folk traditions?

Half Moon Rising

This collection offers choirs everywhere a step-by-step approach towards accessing, understanding and performing Chinese choral music. It offers a representative group of works from different periods and composers of the past century, providing a historical perspective of China's adoption of the choral form. It also introduces a broad range of regions, styles and dialects to show China's rich multiplicity. The difficulty level of the collection is largely medium-easy to medium in order to enhance accessibility for choirs with little or no Chinese background. For this reason, it features some of the most commonly performed works that highlight traditional Chinese and Western Romantic styles. An entire body of contemporary repertoire rich with experimental techniques is also evolving and will no doubt merit further attention in the future.

The format for this anthology combines hard copy and online media, for convenience, depth and practicality. The book contains a general Introduction and Mandarin Pronunciation Guide for basic historical background and easy reference for singing the Mandarin pieces, which form the majority of the collection. It also contains scores in transliterated syllables with non-singing English translations underneath the corresponding musical staves. Unaccompanied works include piano reductions to facilitate the learning process. Each score is preceded by an introduction with useful information on composers, folksongs, texts, choral settings and performance notes, followed by literal, word-for-word translations. It should be noted that pronunciation for sung Chinese sometimes differs from daily conversation. In this volume, transliterated song texts and titles generally appear as they are to be sung. The Chinese-character song titles appear in either complex or simplified form according to their original scoring. And transliterated composer names — where surnames are usually listed first, followed by given names — generally follow the manner in which they are copyrighted or more commonly appear in international publication.

The online support includes a general Pronunciation Guide for the main Mandarin dialect, along with individual detailed written and aural guides for each work in their respective dialects. It also contains further background and support materials to enhance rehearsal preparation. Each Pronunciation Guide contains the original Chinese characters followed by their corresponding Romanized syllables, International Phonetic Alphabet, literal translation and 'poetic', non-singing translation. The process of transliterating Chinese song texts for publications is still in its infancy and no single authoritative source yet exists for phoneticization. This online guide systematically approximates sung Chinese syllables for the extended collection.

This anthology represents one of the first attempts to publish a collection of modern Chinese scores in English from the various regions inside and outside of China. The task has not been easy: Chinese choral music has emerged alongside a century of monumental change, and differences in social and political systems continue to present both challenges and opportunities. The preparation of scores and background materials has required intensive effort in researching, collecting and editing sources not easily located around the various territories. Completing copyright agreements across different legal and cultural boundaries has been one major accomplishment of this work. With the completed anthology, however, choirs can experience first-hand the great vocal, musical and cultural variety that now exists within a common Chinese choral framework.

Acknowledgements

I would like to offer my profound gratitude to all those who have helped bring *Half Moon Rising* to fruition. First, I extend a special note of thanks to my editor David Blackwell and research assistant Amanda Liu for their tireless, detailed efforts over many, many months. Thanks also to Leona Cheung and Lisa Lin for their punctual assistance in score and text preparation, and to colleague Helan Yang for valuable advice on database and archival research. Members of my student ensembles Cantoría Hong Kong and the Hong Kong Baptist University Choir have exerted much effort in providing numerous sample recordings, for which I am grateful. My gratitude also goes to Zhang Boyu and Lin Chun-Lung for the important liaison support they provided, as well as Chris Tam for his work on many of the sample recordings. Sincere thanks to the colleagues and staff at Hong Kong Baptist University who have helped make this project possible. A number of other professional colleagues made substantial contributions regarding repertoire compilation, background information and editing advice, including Lesley Chan, Chen Yun Hung, Grace Chiang, Dorathy Kong, Esmond Lim, Lukas Nickel, Jo-Michael Scheibe, Toh Ban Sheng and Wang Ying-fen. I also appreciate the various conductors and choirs who contributed recordings for online excerpts and the sample CD. I remain deeply indebted to Thomas Lancaster and William LaRue Jones for their past support and encouragement in linking conducting and scholarly endeavours.

This collection depended upon the positive response of numerous composers and arrangers, as well as their family members, many of whom had limited previous contact with the international publishing world. I am gratified that they and their works can gain further exposure to choirs worldwide. I would like to add a final note of thanks to everyone at Edition Peters, whose collective commitment has been instrumental in seeing this project through to success.

John Winzenburg
Hong Kong Baptist University

Mandarin Chinese Diction

Mandarin Chinese is the language most widely spoken or understood across Mainland China, Hong Kong, Singapore and Taiwan. It is also the most common for singing Chinese choral repertoire. Two-thirds of the pieces in this anthology are sung in Mandarin (see the introductions to each piece). The following is a brief guide for Mandarin singing diction and has been made for choral singers with little or no Mandarin background. Some spoken syllables have been modified for choral singing. Refer also to the online Pronunciation Guides for Chinese characters, phonetic transcriptions and recordings, literal translations and notes for all works and languages in the collection.

Written Chinese
- Written Chinese is a pictorial rather than phonetic language of pictograms called 'characters'.
- Each character is made up of individual strokes and multi-functional sections called 'radicals'.
- Mainland China and Singapore use 'simplified' characters with fewer strokes.
- Hong Kong and Taiwan use traditional or 'complex' characters with more strokes.
- Tens of thousands of characters exist — adults normally read several thousand in daily life.
- Characters are usually used alone or in two-character combinations.

Spoken Mandarin Chinese
- Each Chinese character is spoken with only one syllable.
- Spoken Mandarin has four main tones: high, rising, low rising, falling; plus a neutral tone.
- Tones are generally not used in choral singing and do not need to be learned for this collection. Practise speaking the text on a monotone, as tones can actually hamper choral preparation.
- Various Romanization systems exist for transliterating Mandarin. Pinyin is the most common system (see table overleaf) and is used in this collection.
- Mandarin is spoken with different accents in different places.

Choral singing in Mandarin Chinese

Singing in Mandarin is sometimes different from speaking, and choral pieces are often sung differently by choirs in different Chinese regions. There are multiple styles of singing Chinese pieces due to the increasing adoption of Western *bel canto* techniques. As well, a conservatoire style of Chinese folk singing has developed that combines regionalized traditional idioms with a generalized national folk sound alongside *bel canto* elements. Chinese choral singing thus has many overlapping influences, and text delivery depends on the context.

No definitive system yet exists for transcribing Mandarin into the International Phonetic Alphabet (IPA). Numerous discrepancies exist among published linguists, choral and voice scholars and composers alike. This is due to slight differences between mouth, lip and tongue positions of Mandarin sounds and the most familiar IPA symbols used for speaking and singing Western languages. For example, the [ɿ] and [ʅ] symbols were created to represent specific Mandarin 'i' sounds and are not officially recognized as IPA, while official IPA symbols like [ɨ], [z̩] and [ʐ̩] are also used for these but present limited accuracy for singing. The following guide is intended to approximate Mandarin singing diction. It uses standard singer's IPA symbols whenever they can reasonably represent the Mandarin sounds, introduces a small number of less familiar IPA symbols that can effectively represent special Mandarin sounds, while balancing detailed accuracy with limitations of diction training and preparation time. Its purpose is to offer choirs a fair approximation of syllables within a manageable scope of time and effort.

Mandarin Pronunciation Guide

Letter	Pinyin Spelling & Position	IPA	How to Pronounce	English Approximation
a	a as simple vowel final	[a]	same as English	ah or father
	ai as diphthong final	[ai]	sustain [a] & shorten [i]	eye or tie
	an as nasal final	[an]	sustain [a] & enunciate [n]	John
	ang as nasal final	[aŋ]	sustain [a] & enunciate [ŋ]	encore or conga
	ao as diphthong final	[au]	sustain [a] & shorten [u]	how
b	b as initial consonant	[b]	same as English	boy
c	c as initial consonant	[ts]	tongue tip touches just behind the upper front teeth; aspirated	cats
	ch as initial consonant	[tʃ]	tongue tip curls backward & its bottom touches mouth roof	China
d	d as initial consonant	[d]	same as English	dog
e	e as simple vowel final	[ɤ]	mouth open with slight 'smile' of [e]; flat tongue slightly raised in back; raised soft palate	combine her-huh
	ei as diphthong final	[ei]	sustain [e] & shorten [i]	hey or pay
	en as nasal final after w	[u(ə)n]	lips form [w]; sustain [u] and slip in [ə] just before [n]	wunderkind or junta
	en as nasal final after b, ch, f, g, h, k, m, p, r, s, sh, z, zh	[ən]	sustain [ə-ɤ] & enunciate [n]	between hunt-junta
	eng as nasal final	[əŋ]	sustain [ə-ɤ] & enunciate [ŋ]	combine lung-learn
	er as sliding final	[ər]	curl the tongue inward & slightly release the jaw as the sound slides	flower
f	f as initial consonant	[f]	same as English	food
g	g as initial consonant	[g]	same as English hard g	go
h	h as initial consonant	[h]	same as English	how
i	i as simple vowel final	[i]	same as English long e	knee
	i as semi-vowel final after z, c, s	[ɿ]	short buzzed continuation — resonate vocal folds on preceding consonant	Godzilla/ principal/possible
	i as semi-vowel final after zh, ch, sh, r	[ʅ]	long buzzed continuation — resonate vocal folds on preceding consonant	Grrr! or germ/chirp/ shirt/measure
	ia as diphthong final	[ia]	shorten [i] & sustain [a] glide vowels	neon or diablo
	ian (& yan) as nasal final	[iɛn]	shorten [i], sustain [ɛ] & enunciate [n]	yen or niente
	iang as nasal final	[iaŋ]	shorten [i], sustain [a] & enunciate [ŋ]	Bianca
	iao as triphthong final	[iau]	shorten [i], sustain [a] & shorten [u]	meow or miaow
	ie (& ye) as diphthong final	[iɛ]	shorten [i] & sustain [ɛ] glide vowels	liaison
	in as nasal final	[In]	sustain [I-i] & enunciate [n]	between tin-teen
	ing as nasal final	[Iŋ]	sustain [I-i] & enunciate [ŋ]	sing-seeing
	iong as nasal final	[iɔŋ]	shorten [i], sustain [ɔ-ʊ], enunciate [ŋ]	Jung
	iu as triphthong final	[iou]	shorten [i], sustain [o] & shorten [u]	polio
j	j as initial consonant	[dɕ]	similar to zh [dʒ] but tongue tip is forward & blade touches mouth roof	jeep
k	k as initial consonant	[k]	same as English	kind
l	l as initial consonant	[l]	same as English	loud

Letter	Pinyin Spelling & Position	IPA	How to Pronounce	English Approximation
m	m as initial consonant	[m]	same as English	may
n	n as initial/final consonant	[n]	same as English	known
	ng as final consonant	[ŋ]	same as English	sing
o	o as simple vowel final	[ɔ]	same as English	for
	ong as nasal final	[ɔŋ]	sustain [ɔ–ʊ] & enunciate [ŋ]	Jung
	ou as diphthong final	[ɔu]	same as English	know
p	p as initial consonant	[p]	same as English	pay
q	q as initial consonant	[tɕ]	similar to ch [tʃ] but tongue tip is forward & blade touches mouth roof	between cheats or cheese-tsetse-fly
r	r as initial consonant	[r]	tongue tip curls backward & touches mouth roof	rouge
s	s as initial consonant	[s]	same as English	soft
	sh as initial consonant	[ʃ]	tip of tongue curls backward & its bottom touches mouth roof	shoe
t	t as initial consonant	[t]	same as English	tie
u	u as simple vowel final after consonants other than j, q, x, y	[u]	same as English	too
	u as simple umlaut vowel after consonants j, q, x, y	[y]	form lips for [u] & tongue for [i]	German ü for Günter
	ua as diphthong final	[ua]	shorten [u] & sustain [a] glide vowels	suave
	uai as triphthong final	[uai]	shorten [u], sustain [a] & shorten [i]	quite or why
	uan as nasal final after consonants other than j, q, x, y	[uan]	shorten [u], sustain [a] & enunciate [n]	swan
	uan as nasal final after consonants j, q, x, y	[yɛn]	shorten [y], sustain [ɛ] & enunciate [n]	Ewan or between you-ye went
	uang as nasal final	[uaŋ]	shorten [u], sustain [a] & enunciate [ŋ]	wonky
	ue as diphthong final	[yɛ]	shorten [y] & sustain [ɛ] vowels	you ate or ye went
	ui as triphthong final	[uɛi]	shorten [u], sustain [ɛ] & shorten [i]	Duane or way
	un as nasal final after consonants other than j, q, x, y	[u(ə)n]	lips form [w], sustain the [u] and slip in [ə] just before [n]	wunderkind or junta
	un as nasal final after j, q, x, y	[yn]	sustain [y] & enunciate [n]	German Günter
	uo as diphthong final	[uɔ]	shorten [u] & sustain [ɔ] glide vowels	quote
ü	ü as simple umlaut vowel final after consonants l, n	[y]	form lips for [u] & tongue for [i]	German ü for Günter
w	w as initial semi-vowel	[w]	as in English	want or won't
x	x as initial consonant	[ɕ]	as English 'sh', but flatten & raise your tongue blade near mouth roof	between she-see
y	y as initial semi-vowel	[j]	as in English	yours
z	z as initial consonant	[dz]	tongue tip touches the upper-lower front teeth opening — unaspirated	Godzilla or odds
	zh as initial consonant	[dʒ]	tongue tip curls backward & its bottom touches mouth roof	judge

Ban Ge Yue Liang Pa Shang Lai | Half Moon Rising

Ban Ge Yue Liang Pa Shang Lai is based on a folksong from the Uyghur ethnic music tradition in northwestern China. It serves as one example of Han Chinese culture mixing with minority and Western cultures in its new choral repertoire. **Language**: Mandarin.

Arranger

Cai Yuwen (1921–2012) was born in Guangdong province of southern China, and as a youth was exposed to its local musical forms. Like most Chinese of his generation, Cai's career was affected by the war period of the 1930s and 1940s. He earned a Bachelor's degree in engineering in 1943, but continued his musical training during and after his university studies. He studied Chinese theatre music in Hong Kong in 1947 and during the Civil War joined an arts troupe on the side of the communists, writing revolutionary songs. Cai received national recognition in the 1950s due to the international success of *Ban Ge Yue Liang Pa Shang Lai*.

Folksong

Though Cai's primary interest was in his native Guangdong music, *Ban Ge Yue Liang* is a folksong of the Uyghur ethnic group in China's northwest Xinjiang province. The Uyghurs have their own spoken and written Turkic language, and their main religion is Islam. Xinjiang has long been a region of trade and cultural exchange among travellers of the Silk Road, and Uyghur music in many ways sounds similar to Middle Eastern music styles. *Half Moon Rising* is a playful nocturne on a love theme. Its simple melody is characterized by the 'bended' notes (consecutive lowering and rising *portamentos* by half-steps) that occur at various points, as well as the coquettish 'yi la la' refrains. The tune became known to Han Chinese largely via Wang Luobin — one of the mid-twentieth-century Han Chinese who collected folksongs from the Uyghurs and other ethnic minority groups. He notated and translated *Ban Ge Yue Liang* into Mandarin based on his interaction with the singer Ha Daer in 1939.

This setting

Cai's choral setting arose from an undergraduate composition course at the Shanghai Conservatory in 1953. Western music was becoming more common in China at that time, but even as students learned the Western musical language, musicians like Ling Yinghai, Cai's professor at the Conservatory, were placing great emphasis on utilizing China's ethnic traditions, often by arranging folksongs. Cai found great inspiration in this tune, and his arrangement found favour because of the various ways in which he harmonized the bended melody, as well as the shifting textures and contrasting middle section. His arrangement was selected for performance at the conservatory's graduation composition recital, and in the same year was performed at the Fourth World Festival of Youth and Students in Bucharest, where it received a silver medal.

Ban Ge Yue Liang was among the earlier Chinese arrangements for unaccompanied chorus. From the Western choral perspective, it is important to understand that little or no choral tradition existed in China before 1900, so the seemingly simple concepts in Cai's arrangement represented relatively new sounds. Winning an international prize in a Western art form helped earn the choral piece and Cai great recognition in China. Due to its love theme, it was not published right away, but it was later published in the former Soviet

Union (in Russian) and China. The love theme adversely affected Cai during the Cultural Revolution (1966–76), but the song has since been frequently published and performed by choirs around China.

Performance notes

This piece should be performed in a *legato* style with the 'yi la la' refrains given a subtly flirtatious character. Pay special attention to the dynamics, both within and between verses, and keep the sound focused at the softer dynamic levels after bar 15. Phrases are generally four bars in length, so if you choose to breathe every two bars, try to minimize interruption of the phrase.

As part of the graceful style, the diphthongs on 'yue liang' need an appropriate balance between individual vowel articulation and glide between vowels. Be careful not to accent 'me' in bar 5 of verse 2. Give firm articulation to the initial consonants in 'Qing ni ba na kuai da kai' from bar 9 in both verses, to bring out the character of this phrase. The word 'reng' ('to toss') in bars 18 and 22 has a highly characteristic sound in Mandarin, and its phonemes match the playfulness of the love theme. Chinese performance practice thus often has choirs go immediately to the 'ng' of that word as a kind of text painting, sometimes with a slight scoop from underneath the pitch.

Literal translation

1.
Ban ge yue liang pa   shang lai,   yi la la pa   shang lai,
Half a moon to climb up to come, (vocable) to climb up to come,

zhao zhe wo di gu niang shu zhuang tai, yi la la shu zhuang tai.
shining on my girl   dressing table, (vocable) dressing table.

Qing ni ba na sha chuang kuai da kai,
Please you have that screen window quick to open,

yi la la kuai da kai, yi la la kuai da kai,
(vocable) quick to open, (vocable) quick to open.

Zai ba ni na mei gui zhai yi duo, qing qing di reng xia lai.
Then have you that rose to pick one petal, gently   to throw down to come.

2.
Ban ge yue liang pa   shang lai,   yi la la pa   shang lai,
Half a moon to climb up to come, (vocable) to climb up to come,

wei shen me wo di gu niang bu chu lai? Yi la la bu chu lai?
why   my girl   not out to come? (vocable) not out to come?

(Second half repeats from verse 1)

Ban Ge Yue Liang Pa Shang Lai
半个月亮爬上来
Half Moon Rising

Xinjiang folksong
arr. Cai Yuwen

1./2. The half moon is rising,   e la la, it is rising,

1. shining on my girl's dressing table,   e la la, dressing table.
2. why won't my girl come out?   E la la, why not come out?

1./2. Please open up the window quickly,   e la la, open it quickly,

© Wang Luobin and Cai Yuwen. Reproduced by permission.

5

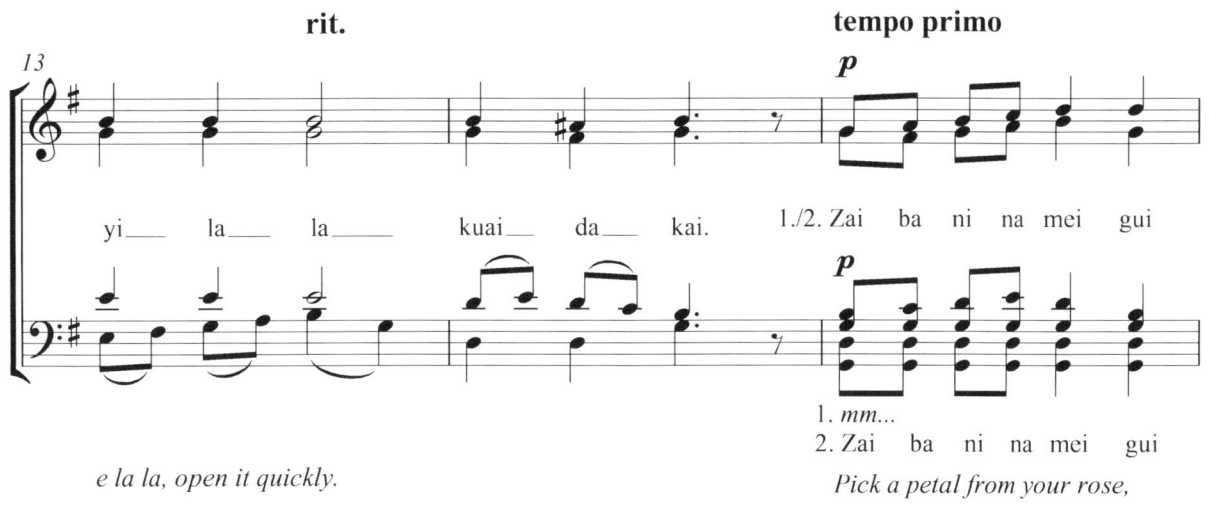

e la la, open it quickly. *Pick a petal from your rose,*

and gently drop it to the ground.

Pick a petal from your rose, *and gently drop it to the ground.*

Ba Jun Zan | Magnificent Horses

Magnificent Horses is an arrangement for chorus, *erhu* fiddle or flute, and sleigh bells of the Chinese choral work *Ba Jun Zan*. It uses vocables to mimic horse rhythms and shouts of the horsemen on the Mongolian grasslands. **Language**: Vocables.

Arranger

Jing Ling-Tam is a professor of vocal studies at the University of Texas-Arlington. She has been highly active as a clinician and guest conductor of all-state and honour choirs around North America and is also a frequent workshop presenter and juror at international conferences and choral festivals. Ling-Tam previously worked with the Fort Worth Opera Association for sixteen seasons, and for over a decade she was on the summer faculty at the American Institute of Musical Studies in Graz, Austria.

Folksong

Magnificent Horses is an example of contemporary cultural interaction within China and beyond. It is adapted from *Ba Jun Zan* by Beijing arranger-conductor Yang Hongnian, itself a Mandarin arrangement of a work by Mongolian composer Se Enkhbayar, who grew up in China's Inner Mongolia region. Traditional Mongolian song themes focus on the grasslands and animals of Mongolia and the nomadic lifestyle of its people. Mongolians have long had a close relationship with the short, stocky horses that they depend on for daily life, and songs have often been sung in their honour. Like China in general, Inner Mongolia did not have a choral tradition in the Western sense until the past century, and choral versions of songs were originally modelled on a traditional style of folk singing, with texts glorifying Mongolia's horses of the past, as chronicled in the life of the thirteenth-century emperor Genghis Khan.

Magnificent Horses keeps the spirit of those versions, combining melodic and stylistic fragments of Mongolian music. The repeated long-short-short rhythms mimic the sound of running horses. The score includes some of the numerous types of embellishments used in Mongolian singing, and also characteristic are the sustained high notes, especially at the ends of melodic phrases and in the final bars of this piece.

This setting

Jing Ling-Tam published *Magnificent Horses* in 1998, removing the text of the original work and adding a solo instrument and sleigh bells to create a highly accessible arrangement for groups everywhere. The addition of a solo instrument matches the Mongolian folk style of using traditional Mongolian instruments, such as the horse-head fiddle, to accompany folksongs. Scored here for the two-stringed Chinese *erhu* fiddle, the part may also be played by the Chinese or Western flute.

This arrangement is in four main sections plus a coda. The first seven bars are introductory, then bars 8–18 form an intermediary second section that continues the atmosphere from the introduction. The two main melodic phrases at 19–27 form the third section, and their repetition with the added sopranos and altos forms the fourth. The coda begins with the final build-up at bar 30.

While basic phrases, gestures and melody from the previous versions remain in this setting, they are substantially rewritten. The solo instrument adopts both choral and tenor solo lines from the original, while certain musical gestures have been removed or reassigned to different voice parts, for example, the baritone solo here was previously sung by the soprano section as a countermelody to the tenor soloist. Certain grace-notes, slurs and melodic motion have also been rearranged. Most notably, whereas the Chinese version ends *pp* following a four-bar *decrescendo*, *Magnificent Horses* builds to a *ff* climax at the end.

Performance notes

This piece is heavily atmospheric and contains constantly shifting dynamics and textures. Prepare these carefully in relationship to each other and to the dramatic motion as a whole. As indicated by the arranger, singers should sustain the 'ng' sound of the 'ding' syllables and not the vowels. When grace-notes occur on the same pitch as their primary note, articulate them as if they are on separate pitches. Carefully consider the *f* dynamic at bar 8 in relation to the *mf* level at bar 17 (both times). Monitor the choral-instrumental dynamic at 23 so that the baritone solo can come out freely. There, the baritone soloist should articulate grace-notes brilliantly and energetically without losing the overall sense of line. The solo instrument should separate the trill from the figure on beat 4 of bar 28. The soprano C♯ in bar 38 is optional.

Pay close attention to balance between voices and instruments as it varies between sections and within the repeated section. The solo instrument needs to be audible in relation to the voices, especially when doubled by the sopranos. It also needs to be heard in the harmonic sonority of the final three bars. The dynamic level of the sleigh bells will greatly depend upon the size of the choir and strength of the vocal forces. It should always be energized, but soft enough to allow for audibility of the flute and voice parts.

Ba Jun Zan

八 骏 赞

Magnificent Horses

Fantasy on a Mongolian folk tune
for Erhu/Flute, Sleigh Bells and SATB choir

arr. Yang Hongnian
adapted and arr. Jing Ling-Tam

A separate part for Erhu/Flute is available to download at www.editionpeters.com/halfmoonrising

© 1998, JEHMS Inc., A Division of Alliance Music Publications Inc. Reproduced by permission.

Cha Shan Qing Ge | Tea Mountain Love Song

Cha Shan Qing Ge is a Taiwan choral arrangement of a folksong from the mountainous tea-growing region of Guizhou province. Accompanied by piano, it tells of a tea-picker's fondness for her beloved who works in a nearby tea forest. **Language**: Mandarin.

Arranger

Chen Tscheng Hsiung first graduated from the National Taiwan Academy of Arts before studying conducting and theory-composition at the Mozarteum Musik Akademie in Salzburg. After returning to Taiwan in the late 1960s, Chen wrote various arrangements of Chinese works, and from the mid-1980s he conducted the Taipei Chinese Orchestra. In 1991 he was appointed conductor of the Taiwan Symphony Orchestra. Chen also established the Taiwan Youth Orchestra and taught at some of Taiwan's most prestigious universities. He continues to work in both Western and Chinese music around Taiwan and internationally as guest conductor, clinician and adjudicator.

Folksong

The southwestern province of Guizhou is a mountainous area famous for its numerous minority groups and their diverse folk music, and also for its tea. The wide range of its folk music comes from its ethnic variety. Numerous festivals are held by the different ethnic groups each year, at which folksongs are sung. Among the main genres, each Guizhou group has 'drinking songs', while love songs, including the mountain songs, are also important because of the landscape of Guizhou.

Images abound of tea-pickers dressed in different ethnic garbs working the green hillsides, and it is from this backdrop that the *Tea Mountain Love Song* appears. Different melodies exist under this title in China; this particular tune originated in Guizhou and became well known in Taiwan. The pentatonic melody is in two parts: the first part (in the slow introduction) starts low and rises; the second part (in the Moderato middle verses) has a unique, angular contour, starting high and descending. It is stated in four varying two-bar groups and is characterized by its rhythm of nine short notes followed by a tenth long one.

In contrast to some of the other folksongs in this volume, the text of this folksong is highly poetic and extensive in the manner of *Yang Guan San Die*. Sung in five text verses, the first verse acts as a declamatory refrain. The other verses are strophic and describe the tea plantation surroundings, the warm Guizhou climate and the tea-pickers' innermost feelings.

This setting

Chen Tscheng Hsiung published *Cha Shan Qing Ge* in a set of Chinese folksongs arranged for piano and mixed choir in 1982. Its dramatic, slow introduction and postlude frame four inner verses. In the introduction the piano paints the image of mountain slopes with its long descending run. The internal verses are in $\frac{6}{8}$ metre at a Moderato dance tempo. This metre is not frequently found in traditional Chinese music, but here it conveys the tea-picker's discovery of young love. In the first Moderato verse at bar 15, all voices sing homophonically, with the soprano melody describing the path to the Tea Mountain pavilion. The second verse at 25 has the treble voices singing a two-part canon to describe the boisterous character of the tea-picking girls. The third verse is introspective and slow; here the tenors sing of the young lover's secret sentiments. The fourth verse is lively again to represent the hope for mutual feeling. In this manner, Chen's varied arrangement reflects the different moods and thoughts that are captured in the original text verses.

Performance notes

This work depends upon good interaction between the choir and piano. A number of the piano figures are scenic, for example the descending right-hand gestures in bars 1–2, while the middle verses provide more of a dance accompaniment. Pianists should play the slow introduction and postlude with earnestness and restrained tempo. Play rolled chords with determined continuity but bringing out each pitch, and carefully align chord changes with those in the choir. Don't rush the two-bar introductions to each of the Moderato verses — be sure to anticipate the tempo of the next choral entry. Left-hand downbeats at 1, 3 and 53 need resolute articulation, and the final G minor chord of bar 62 needs to be audible amidst the sustaining choir.

The downward choral *portamentos* of the introduction and postlude are idiomatic of Chinese folksongs. They should be light and not exaggerated, with the two primary notes unstressed and weight briefly added during the *portamento*. Sopranos should de-emphasize the grace-notes at bars 10 and 60, gradually adding weight to the primary C pitch after it is secured. Give special attention to the fast-moving text at bar 50, keeping lips and cheeks loose. Review the online Pronunciation Guide so that the tongue position is clearly distinguished between certain related, initial consonants, like 'cha' and 'qing', 'xin' and 'shang', and 'zao' and 'cai'. Special Chinese vowels on 'ren', 'he' and 'biao' also need close attention.

Literal translation

1.
Cha ye qing ye, shui ye qing ye,
Tea to be (also) fresh ah, water to be (also) fresh ah,

qing shui shao cha xian gei xin shang di ren,
clear water to boil tea to offer to give to beloved of person,

qing ren shang shan ni ting yi ting,
lover to go up the mountain you to stop one to stop,

he kou qing cha biao biao wo di xin.
drink a mouthful of fresh tea to represent my of heart.

2.
Shang gang di xiao lu tong dao cha shan ting,
Up the hill of small road leads to tea mountain pavilion,

shi tou cai de liang jing jing,
stone to step on so shiny,

ni song zou duo shao feng yu di ye wan,
you give away how many stormy nights,

ni ying jie duo shao can lan di li ming.
you welcome how many splendid dawns.

3.
Zao chen cai cha zou chu liao men,
Morning to pick tea to go out from the door,

zong yao kan yi kan wo di xin shang ren.
always to want to look at my beloved one.

Huang hun hou ta shang hui jia di xiao lu,
Dusk after to tread on to return home of small road,

reng yao wang yi wang ni gao da di shen ying.
still to want to look forward to your tall big of figure.

4.
Wo mo mo di xiang ya, qiao qiao di wen,
I silently to think ah, secretly to ask,

ni jia xiang you mei you zhe yang di cha lin?
your hometown to have or not to have this kind of tea forest?

Cha lin li you mei you cai cha di da jie?
Tea forest within to have or not to have to pick tea of big sister?

Da jie li you mei you ni xin ai di ren?
Big sister within to have or not to have your beloved of person?

5.
Wo gao sheng di chang ya, di sheng di wen,
I loudly to sing ah, softly to ask,

wo di cai cha ge ni ai bu ai ting?
my to pick tea song you to love or not to love to hear?

Zhe ge sheng xiang bu xiang ni jia xiang di qu diao?
This singing voice to resemble or not to resemble your hometown of tune?

Cai cha nü xiang bu xiang ni xin ai di ren?
To pick tea girl to resemble or not to resemble your beloved of person?

Cha Shan Qing Ge
茶 山 情 歌
Tea Mountain Love Song

Guizhou folksong
arr. Chen Tscheng Hsiung

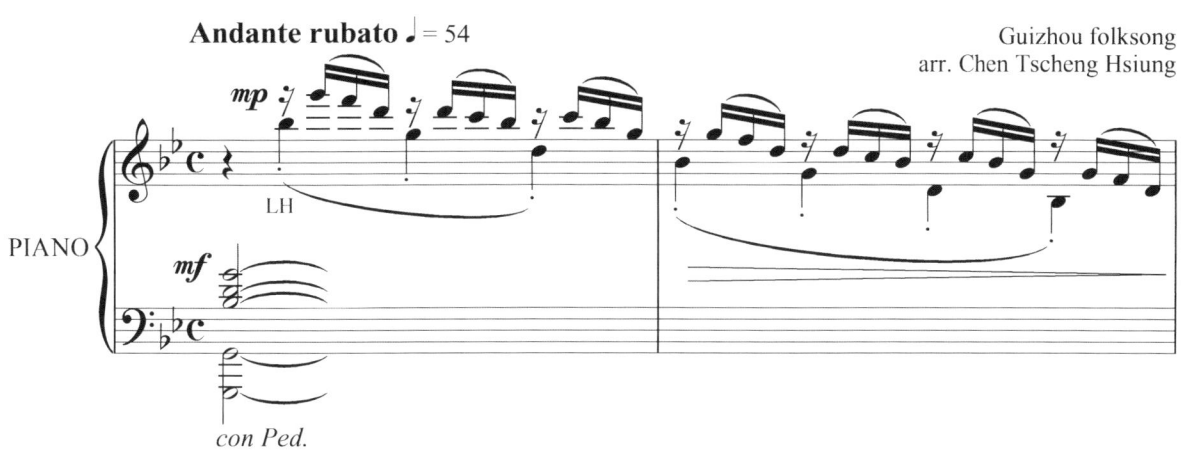

S.: Cha ye qing ye,
A.: Cha ye qing ye,
T.: Cha ye qing ye,
B.: Cha ye qing ye,

Oh, the tea is so fresh and the water so clear,

© 2015 by Peters Edition Ltd, London

shui ye qing ye,___ qing shui shao cha___ xian gei

shui ye qing ye,___ qing shui shao cha___ xian gei

shui ye qing ye,___ qing shui shao cha

shui ye qing ye,___ qing shui shao cha___ xian gei

I made tea with fresh water to give

xin shang di ren,___ qing ren shang shan ni ting yi ting,

xin shang di ren,___

xin shang ren,___ qing ren shang shan ni

xin shang ren,___

to my sweetheart, my dear, please take a rest when you go up the mountain,

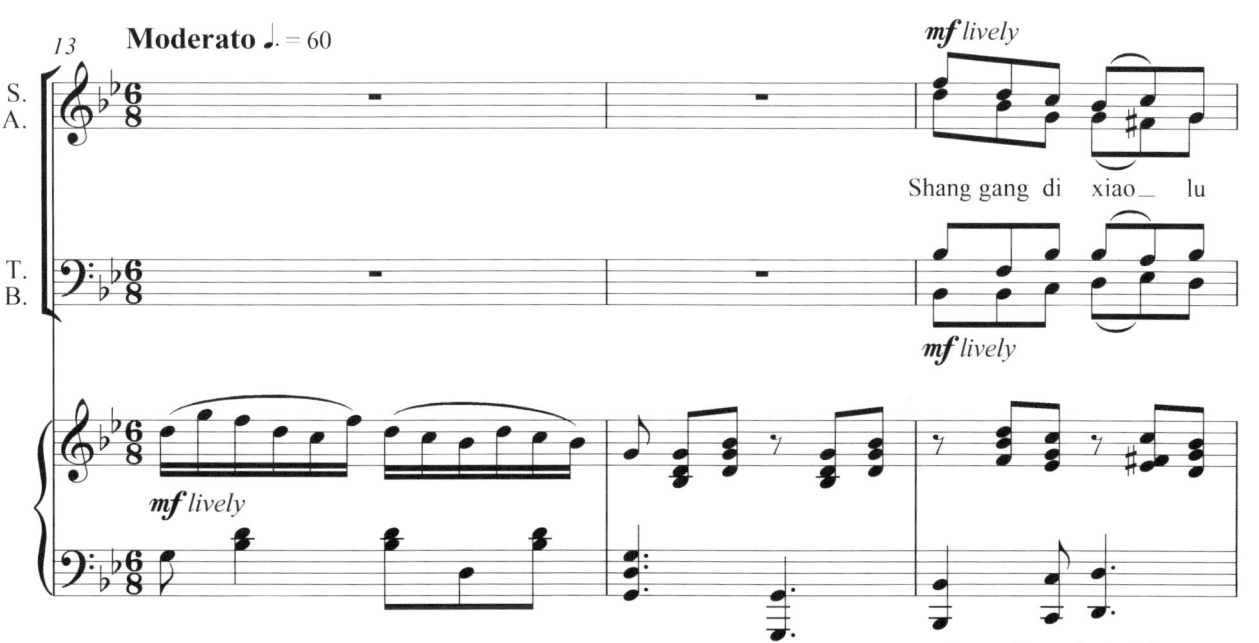

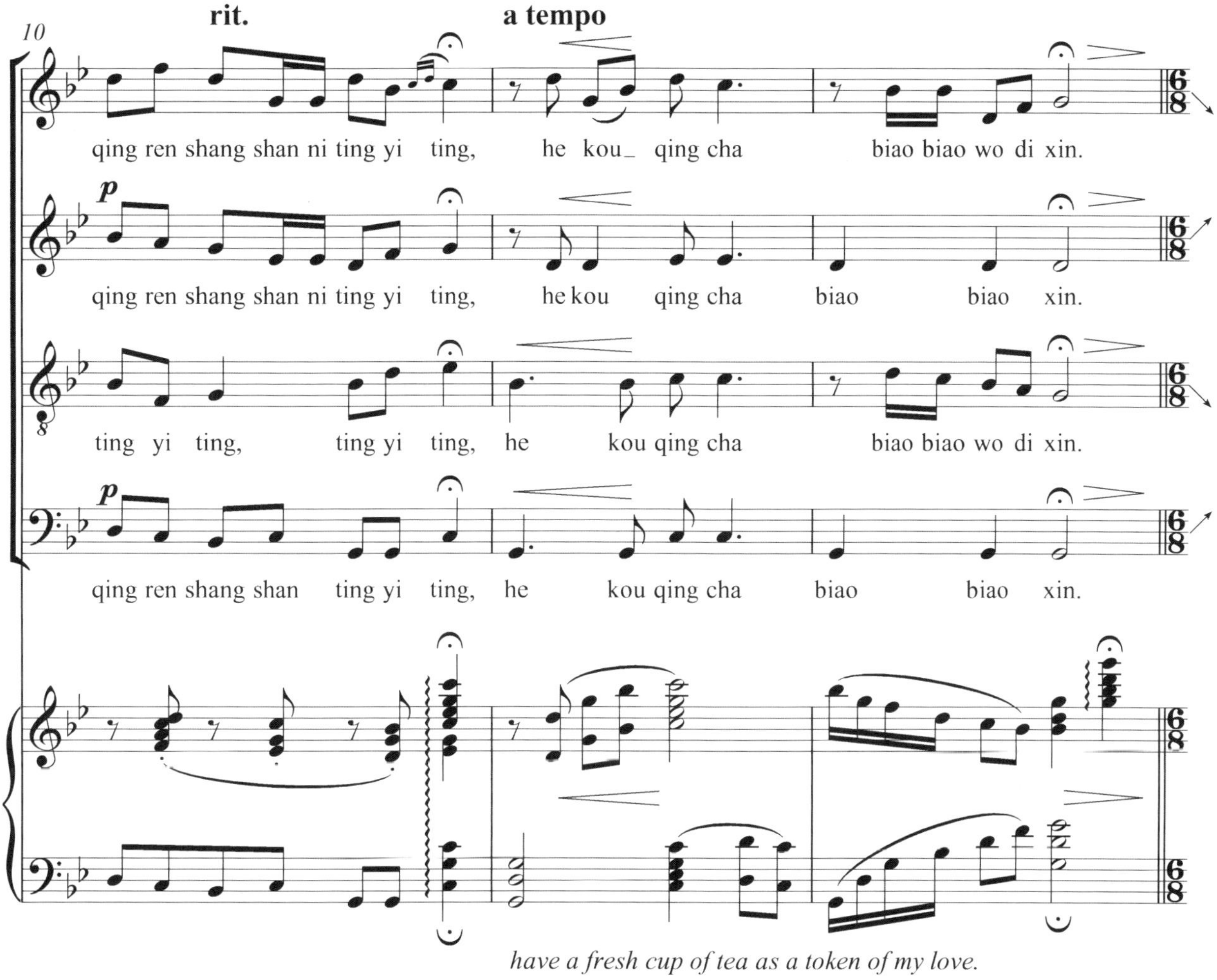
10
rit.
a tempo
p
qing ren shang shan ni ting yi ting, he kou_ qing cha biao biao wo di xin.
qing ren shang shan ni ting yi ting, he kou qing cha biao biao xin.
ting yi ting, ting yi ting, he kou qing cha biao biao wo di xin.
qing ren shang shan ting yi ting, he kou qing cha biao biao xin.
have a fresh cup of tea as a token of my love.

13
Moderato ♩. = 60
S.
A.
T.
B.
mf lively
Shang gang di xiao_ lu
The path on the hill leads

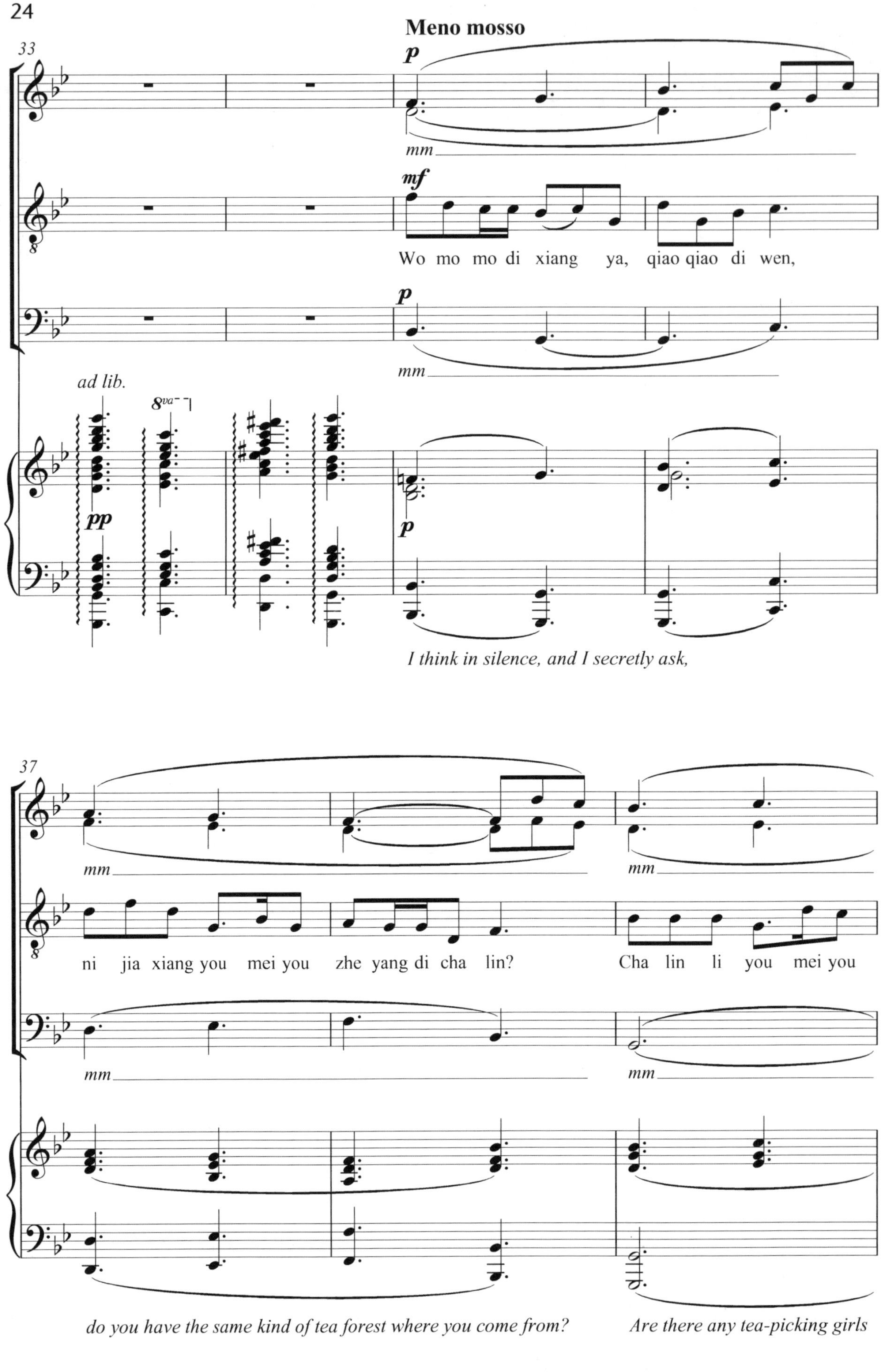

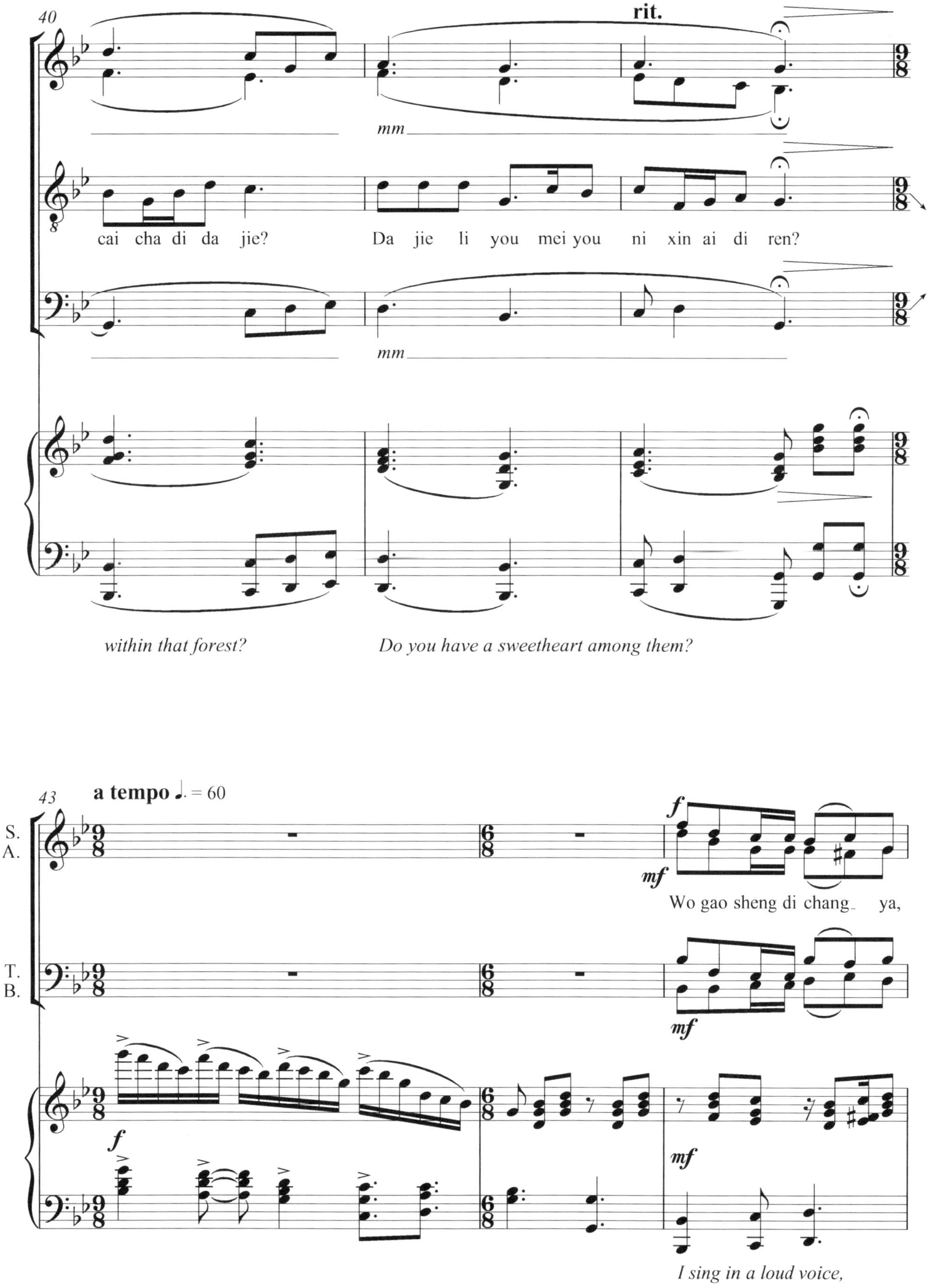

Oh, the tea is so fresh and the water so clear!

I made tea with fresh water to give to my sweetheart,

my dear, please take a rest when you go down the mountain,

have a fresh cup of tea as a token of my love.

Diu Diu Dang Ah | Old Train Song

Diu Diu Dang Ah is an arrangement of a folksong from Yilan County in northeast Taiwan. It describes the sounds of water droplets falling on a train as it passes through a tunnel.
Language: Taiwanese.

Arranger

Chien Shan-hua is a professor in the Music Department and Graduate Institute of Ethnomusicology at National Taiwan Normal University in Taipei. He has long been a researcher of Taiwan's indigenous music and has simultaneously pursued composition and choral conducting. Chien received a Master of Fine Arts from the University of California at Irvine and a Diploma in Composition from the Hochschule für Musik und darstellende Kunst in Vienna. As a composer, he was the recipient of the Alban Berg Foundation Award and has received noteworthy commissions. He has also been active as a choral director of various university and civic choirs in Taiwan, as well as serving in chief administrative positions at academic institutions and music associations.

Folksong

The tune of this folksong had predecessors before the twentieth century, but this particular version was most likely sung during the early twentieth century, which was a time of important social change from agricultural to industrial lifestyles. Previously called *Yilan Melody*, it is regarded by some as a children's song because of its simple, stepwise melody and lively rhythm. But its pentatonic structure is irregular, with six beats in the first phrase, centred on D, and eight beats on the second phrase, centred on A. It is very famous on the island, existing in many different arrangements.

Yilan has traditionally been a farming area, where local residents are proud of their fresh air and clean environment. Previously, when there was no road connecting Yilan and Taipei, trains were the easiest way to travel between the two. There were many tunnels on the way, where condensation resulted in falling droplets. When the train passed through the tunnels, the drops falling on the roof of the train made a sound imitated in the local dialect as '*diu diu dang*'. The song was sung as the train went through the tunnel, but these words may have originally come from a coin used in a gambling game from that area. The vocables '*a mo i do diu*' are thought to have been used by the workers who built the train tunnels, perhaps to describe the young farm girls they saw working in the fields.

This setting

This unaccompanied choral setting was premiered by the Yin Qi Choir in 1990. It represents the sound of the train starting up very slowly, getting faster, and finally reaching its destination. The folksong text mixes with the '*wu*' sound of the train whistle and the unvoiced '*chi*' sound of the released air, as well as other vocables in various voices to depict the chugging train. The folksong appears in its entirety four times throughout: first in the sopranos alone over ostinato patterns in the other voices (b. 12); then beginning f with sopranos and altos singing in octaves (b. 22), interrupted by a build-up of '*ho ho*' rhythms before continuing harmonized in all voices; then twice in three-part canon on D and G, with contrasting p–f dynamics, before the slowing '*ho ho*' rhythms bring the train to a halt.

Performance notes

Good preparatory work will help achieve the essential effects of the piece. Choose a soloist who can aptly mimic the train whistle, and practise the unvoiced 'chi' at the different pitch levels to imitate the steam locomotive starting and stopping. *Staccato* notes on 'hei ya' and 'ho' should be given more length when starting very slow and during the final *rallentando*; also practise these with staggered breathing at full speed on prolonged, repeated patterns. To help prepare for the passage at bars 26–30, use warm-up exercises on *staccato* 'ho' syllables at different rhythms and speeds (start slowly and gradually get faster through the weeks), pulsing the abdomen on accented beats while maintaining open vowel space in the vocal mechanism. Also refer closely to the online Pronunciation Guide and practise speaking the Taiwanese text thoroughly at fast tempos.

The folksong melody needs a light, carefree innocence. The Taiwanese diphthongs should be very connected and invite a natural, nasalized sound, while monophthongs can be separately articulated. The 'n' and 'ng' endings are not fully intoned, but slightly stopped, while the word 'gia' has an implied, stopped 'ng' at the end, as in 'gia(ng)'. All pitches at bar 25 can be accented, but fully intone the final 'do' before releasing. Work toward an even *poco a poco accelerando* at bars 4–11, and match with an equally even *ritardando* at 15–16 and *rallentando* effect at 46–9. The tempos at 17–21 and 42–5 can be slightly relaxed, while moving 'a mo i do diu' pitches in those passages should be sung very *legato*. Staggered breathing in the sustained pitches of those passages is important, as it is in ostinato patterns throughout. The 'diu' of beat 3 in bar 30 should be the climax of the *crescendo* starting in 28. Keep the tone focused on the soft canon at 33–6, while *f* entries from bar 37 should not be too heavy; save breath to achieve a resonant pause chord at 41. Don't slow down too early from 48, and slightly bring out the pitch changes at bar 49. The final 'chi' should be articulate and long.

Literal translation

Hue chia	gin	gia.					
Train	faster	to go.					

Hue chia	gia	gao	*i do a mo i do diu a yo*	bon kang	lai,		
Train	to go	to	(onamatopeic sounds)	tunnel	inside,		

bon kang	e	dsui	do	*diu diu dang ah i do a mo i do diu ah i do*	di	lo	lai.
tunnel	of	water	all	(onamatopeic sounds . . .)	droplets	to fall	to come.

Diu Diu Dang Ah
丢丢銅仔
Old Train Song

Taiwan Yilan folksong
arr. Chien Shan-hua

The train goes faster and faster.

© 2000 by Chien Shan-hua. Published and distributed solely by Earthsongs. Reproduced by permission.

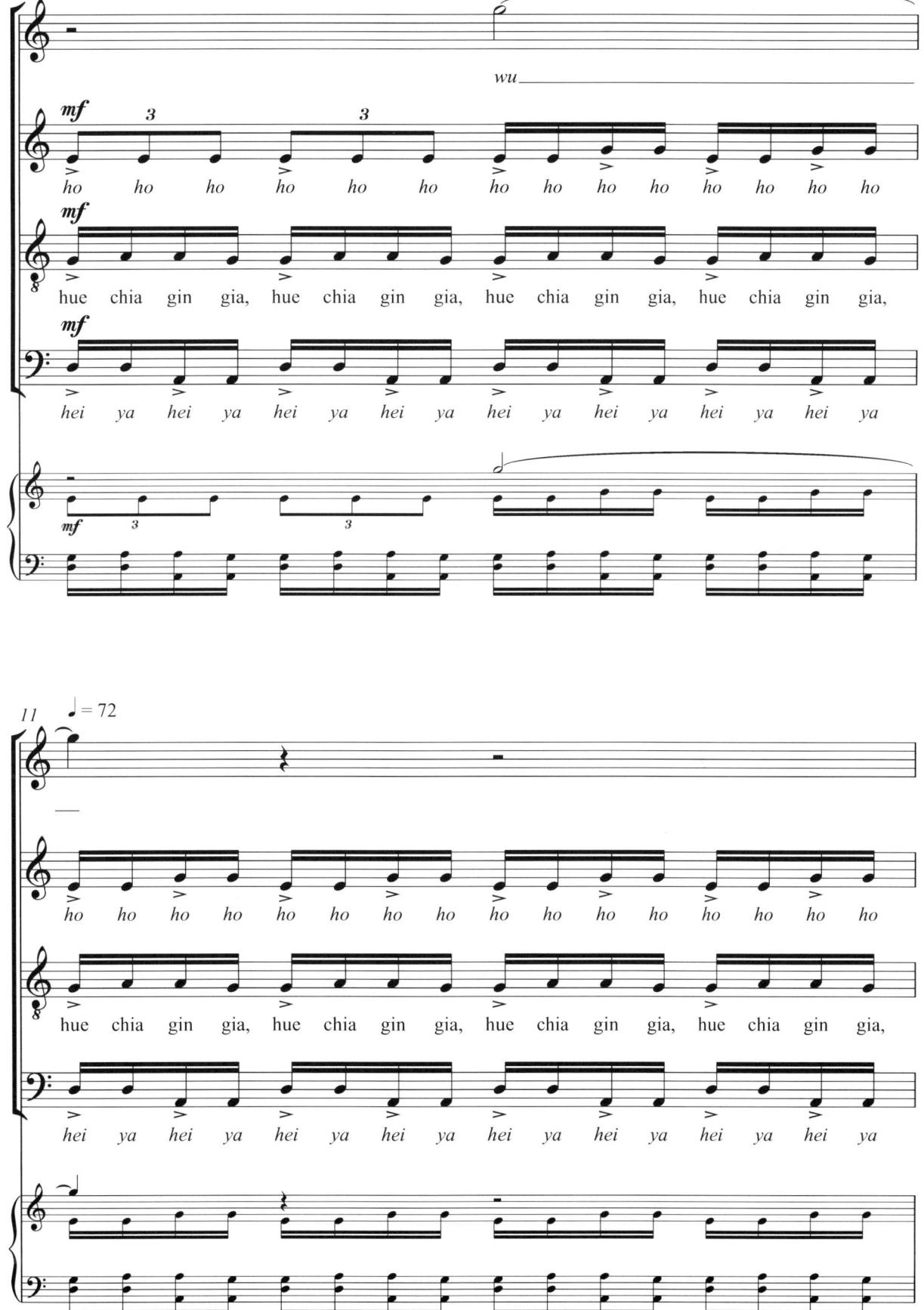

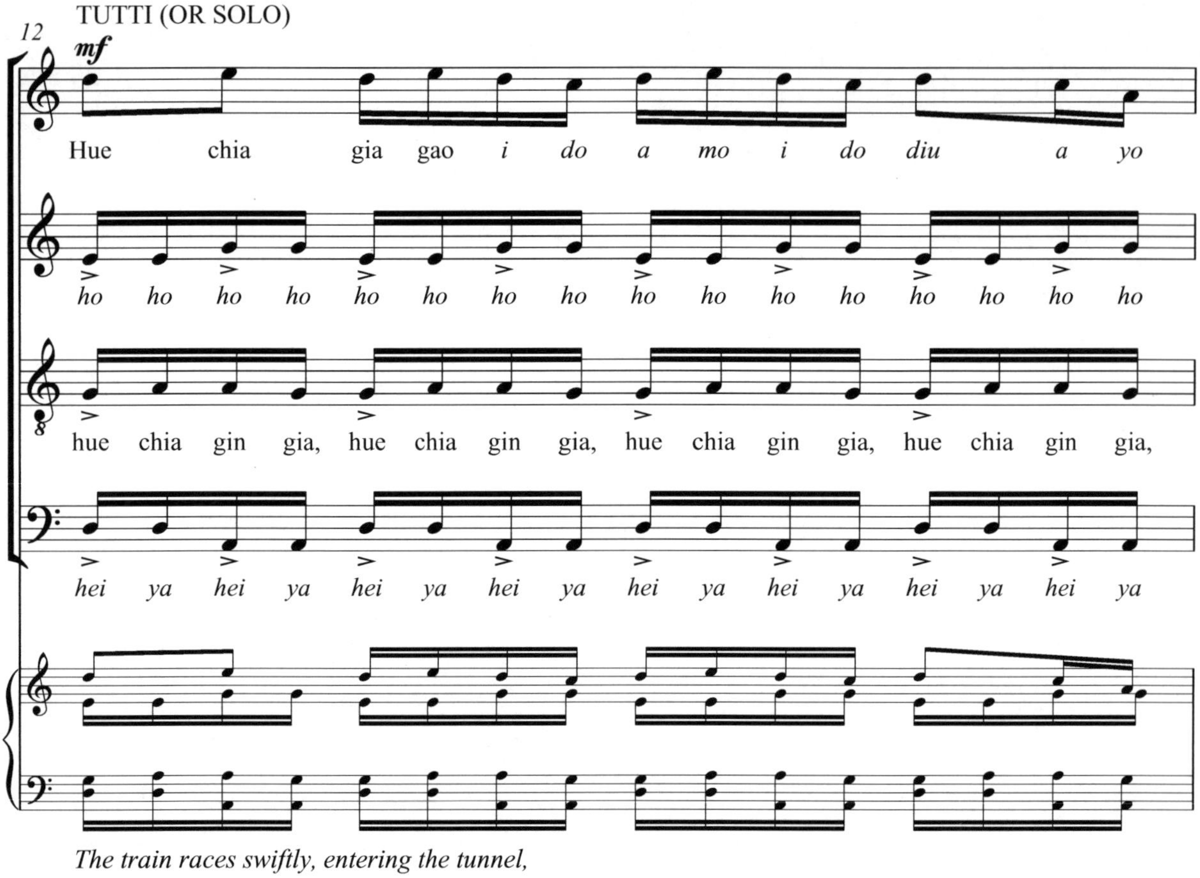

TUTTI (OR SOLO)

12
mf

Hue chia gia gao *i do a mo i do diu a yo*

ho ho ho ho ho ho ho ho ho ho ho ho ho ho ho ho

hue chia gin gia, hue chia gin gia, hue chia gin gia, hue chia gin gia,

hei ya hei ya hei ya hei ya hei ya hei ya hei ya hei ya

The train races swiftly, entering the tunnel,

13

bon kang lai, bon kang

ho ho ho ho ho ho ho ho ho ho ho ho ho ho ho ho

hue chia gin gia, hue chia gin gia, hue chia gin gia, hue chia gin gia,

hei ya hei ya hei ya hei ya hei ya hei ya hei ya hei ya

inside the tunnel,

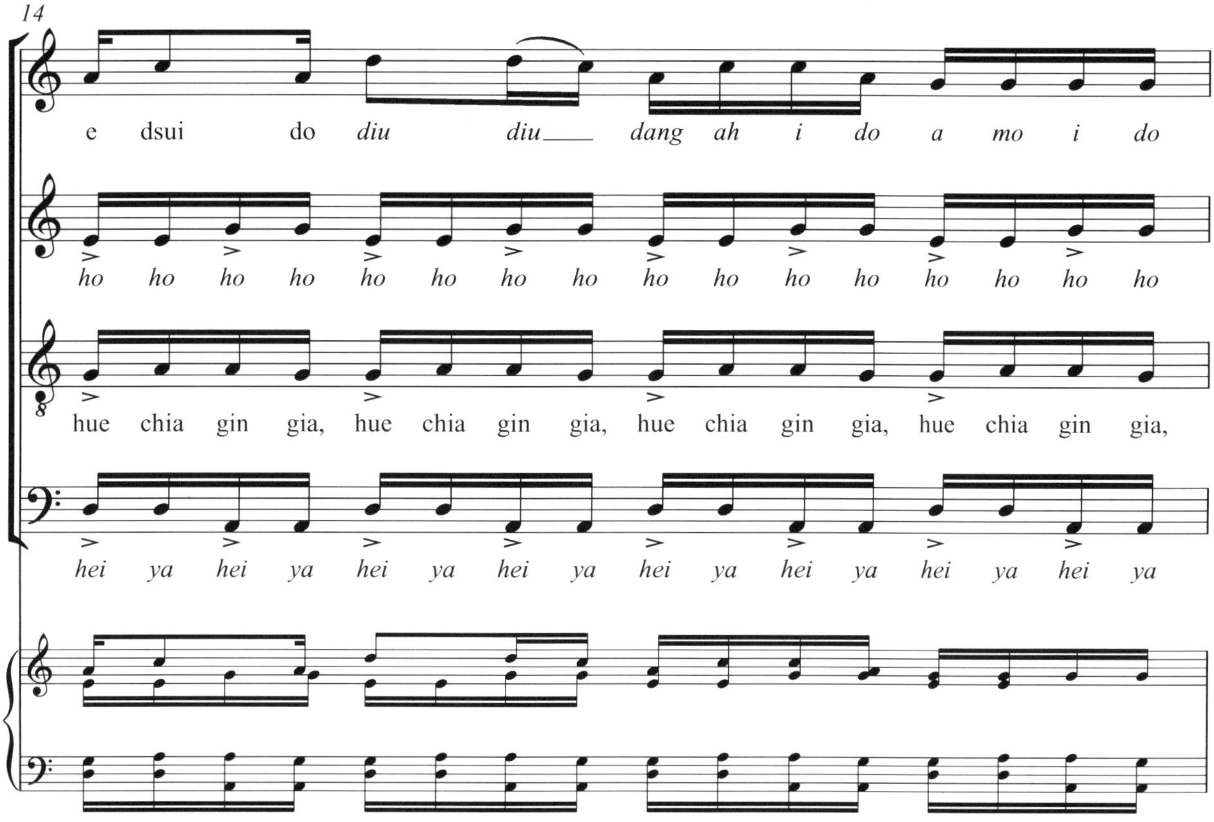

The train races swiftly, entering the tunnel,

(The train goes faster and faster.)

inside the tunnel, water droplets fall on the train.

and make the sound 'diu diu dang';

31 TUTTI

a mo i do diu ah i do di lo lai. *la la la la la la la la la la la la hei!*

a mo i do diu ah i do di lo lai. *la la la la la la la la la la la la hei!*

a mo i do diu ah i do di lo lai. *la la la la la la la la la la la la hei!*

a mo i do diu ah i do di lo lai. *la la la la la la la la la la la la hei!*

as the train moves on, the sound of its whistles mixes with the 'diu diu dang' tune.

33 *p*

Hue chia gia gao *i do a mo i do diu a yo* bon kang lai, bon kang

Hue chia gia gao *i do a mo i do diu a yo* bon kang lai,

Hue chia gia gao *i do a mo i do diu a yo*

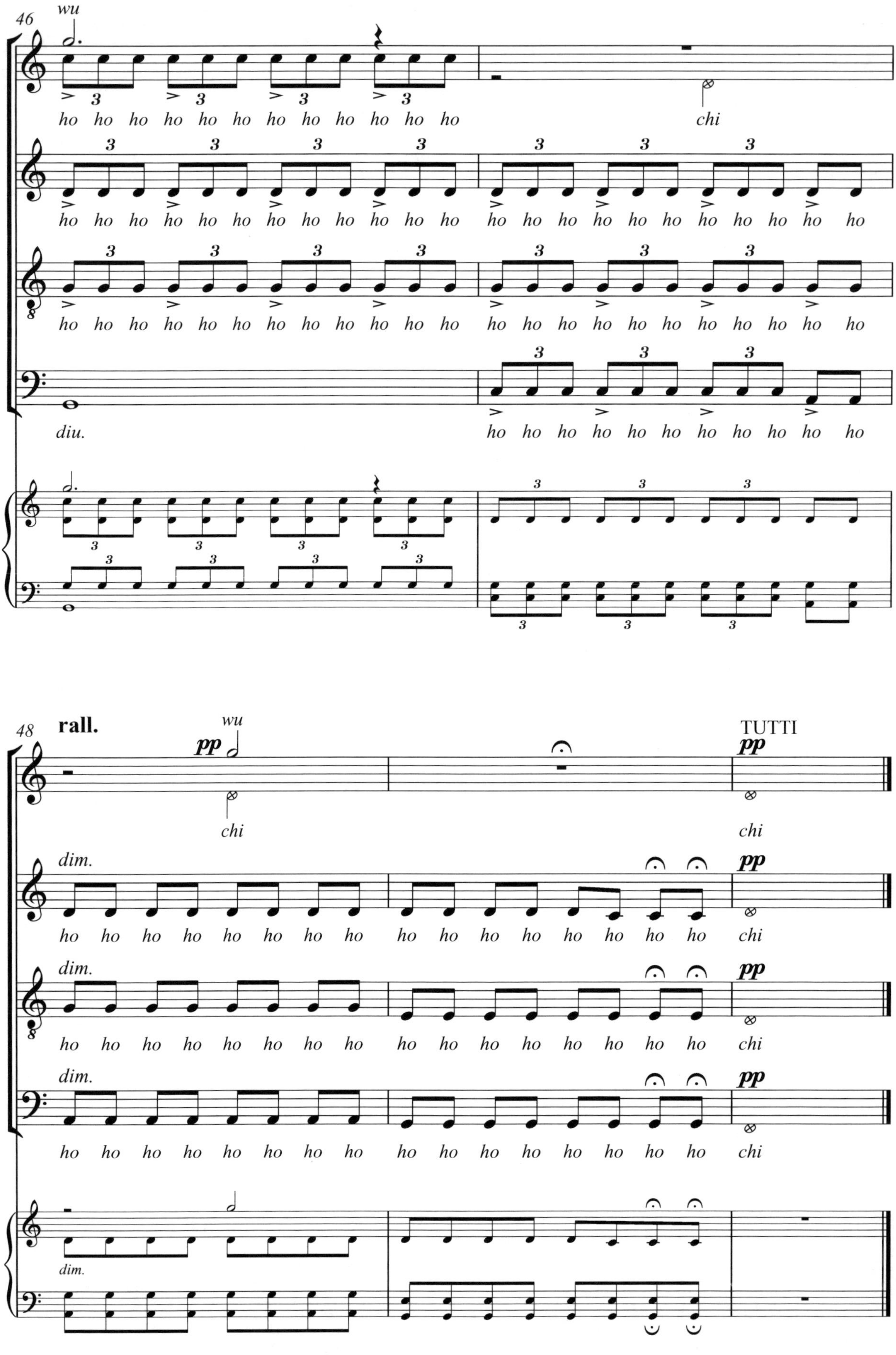

Dui Hua | Antiphonal Flower Song

Dui Hua is an arrangement of a folksong from Anhui province in east-central China. Set for piano and SATB chorus, the lively, call-and-response tune depicts the spirit of love as a blooming flower in different seasons of the year. **Language**: Mandarin.

Arranger

Shi Jin Bo (1932–97; also known as Shi Kum Por) grew up in Guangdong province and studied composition at the Shanghai Conservatory in the 1950s. He moved to Hong Kong in 1963 and made a major contribution to Hong Kong's musical development as composer and educator on the faculty of Tsing Hua College. His prolific output includes orchestral, chamber and piano works, as well as numerous vocal and choral pieces. Shi was highly regarded for his style of blending Chinese musical forms with Western compositional techniques.

Folksong

Dui Hua draws its lively flavour from the folk music of Anhui province. *Dui Hua* means 'conversation' in everyday Chinese, but *Dui Hua* is also a common type of folksong, where the '*Dui*' refers to 'question-and-answer' and a different character for '*Hua*' means 'flower'. While *Dui Hua* melodies and styles can be highly distinct in different regions, they are often sung antiphonally between males and females in the form of a flower-guessing game.

This folksong has images of flowers from different seasons of the year presented in each verse with call-and-response dialogue at different layers. The simple D minor pentatonic melody appears in lively rhythms and in four-bar, antiphonal phrases over 16 bars. The first two four-bar phrases repeat musically: their first two-bar sub-phrases ending upwards like a question, and the following sub-phrases ending downwards like an answer. The third four-bar phrase intensifies with call-and-response in each bar. The final four bars of each verse insert vocables '*de er nong dong lai dong lai*' before repeating an earlier sub-phrase.

This setting

Shi Jin Bo arranged this work in 1970. It highlights the theme of innocent love via the playful call-and-response between the female and male chorus. It typifies mid-twentieth-century compositions that heighten Chinese folk elements with little Romanticism or modernism. The arrangement has four verses framed by a piano introduction and two interludes. The lively rhythms and folksong dialogue are enhanced by extreme dynamic contrast and then all voices singing together at verse endings. Verse 3 at bar 45 is suddenly slow and expressive in G minor with the tenor and alto soloists in dialogue. Verse 4 at bar 63 starts *tutti* to represent all seasons and flowers. The final section from bar 71 is extended with intricate interaction between the voices, ending in seven-voice *divisi*.

Performance notes

The piano introduction and interludes should be dance-like without too much weight. On- and offbeat accents in verses 1, 2 and 4 are jocular, so play them with upward spring rather than downward force. Rolled chords from bar 46 should have a plucked-instrument effect with enough upward speed. Stylistically, grace-notes (e.g. bar 9) start on the beats as quavers followed by crotchets. The first two four-bar phrases of verses 1, 2 and 4 should be *legato* and lively, contrasting with lighter, separated 'Qi bu nong' phrases. The downward leap from F to A (e.g. at the downbeat of bar 7) may include a *portamento*. The third verse may be sung by soloists, solo groups or entire sections. Layer the dynamics carefully in the final verse. The choir may add a dramatic breath break before the final 'lai!' at the end of bar 83.

Literal translation

1.
Chun ji li lai shen me hua er kai?
Spring season in to come what flower to blossom?

Chun ji li kai di ying chun hua.
Spring season in to blossom of winter jasmine.

Ying chun hua kai shen me ren er dai?
Winter jasmine to blossom what people to wear?

Mei li di gu niang dai qi lai.
Beautiful of girl to wear on.

Refrain:
Qi bu nong *dong* lai *dong* lai, dai qi lai!
Seven not to do (vocable) to come (vocable) to come, to wear on!

Ba bu nong *dong* lai *dong* lai, dai qi lai!
Eight not to do (vocable) to come (vocable) to come, to wear on!

De er dong, de er dong, de er nong dong lai dong lai,
(vocables)

mei li di gu niang dai qi lai!
beautiful of girl to wear on!

(Verse 2 and 4 refrains finish similarly with their respective final verse lines.)

2.
Xia ji li lai shen me hua er kai?
Summer season in to come what flower to blossom?

Xia ji li kai di shi liu hua.
Summer season in to blossom of pomegranate flower.

Shi liu hua kai shen me ren er dai?
Pomegranate flower to blossom what people to wear?

Piao liang di xiao huo zi dai qi lai.
Handsome of guy to wear on.

3.
Hei! Qiu ji li lai shen me hua er kai?
Hey! Autumn season in to come what flower to blossom?

Qiu ji li kai di huang ju hua!
Autumn season in to blossom of yellow chrysanthemum!

Dong ji li shen me hua er kai?
Winter season in what flower to blossom?

Dong ji li kai di hong mei hua!
Winter season in blossom of red plum!

4.
Yi nian si ji bai hua kai,
One year four season hundred flowers to blossom,

bai hua ya kai fang ren ren ai,
hundred flower ah to blossom everyone to love,

ren ren ai lai ren ren dai.
everyone to love to come everyone to wear.

Gu niang ya xiao huo zi dai qi lai!
Girl ah guy to wear on!

Dui Hua
對 花
Antiphonal Flower Song

Anhui folksong
arr. Shi Jin Bo

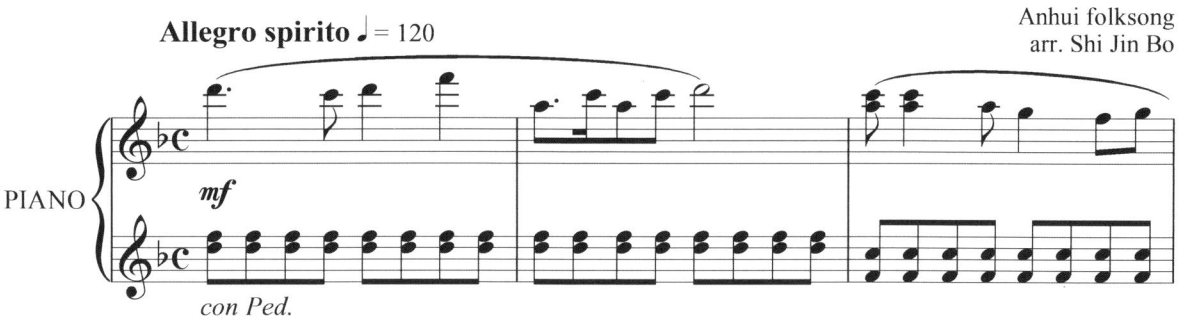

© Shi Jin Bo. Reproduced by permission of the Composers and Authors Society of Hong Kong (CASH).

46

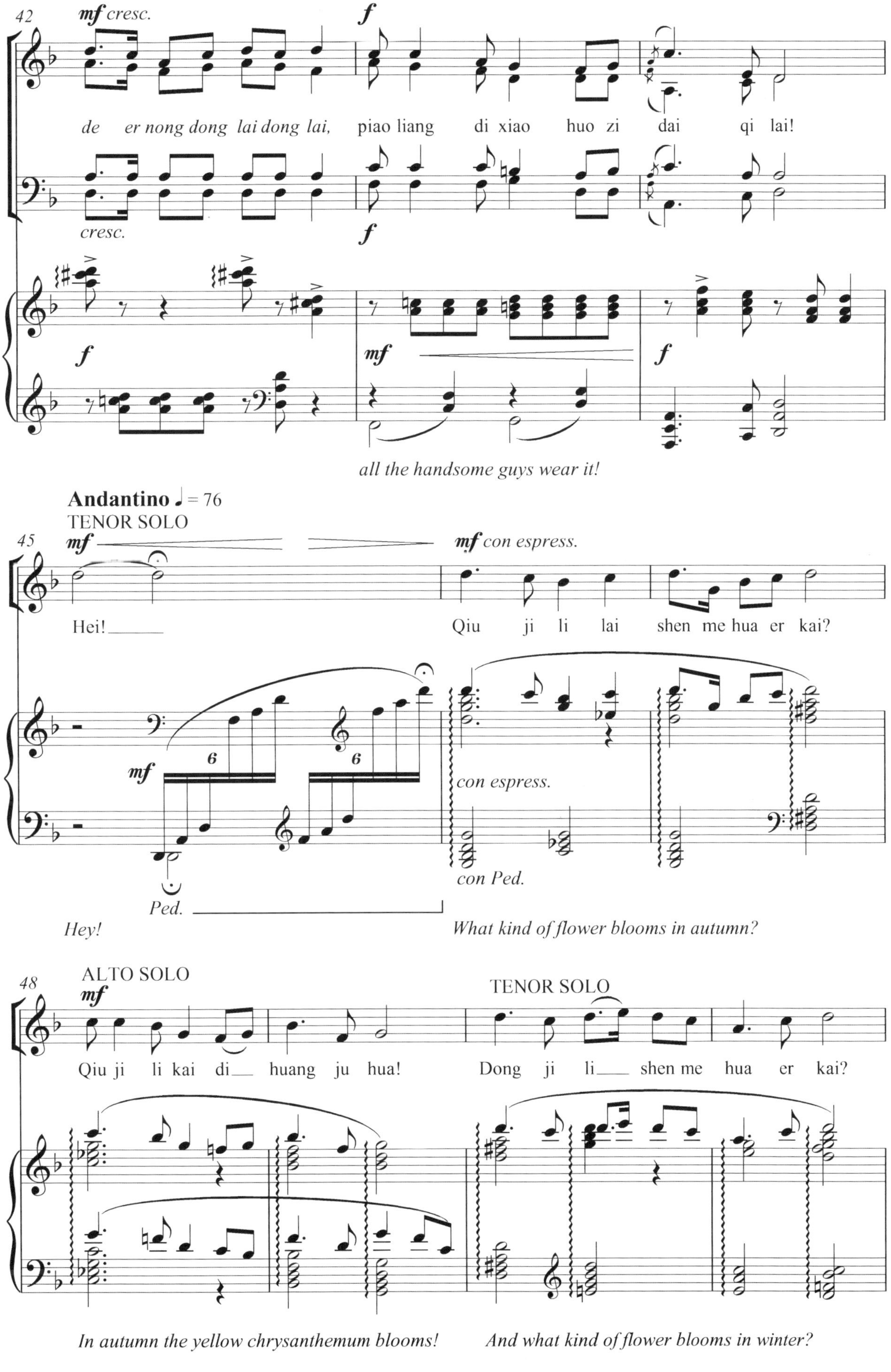

So girls and guys all put them on!

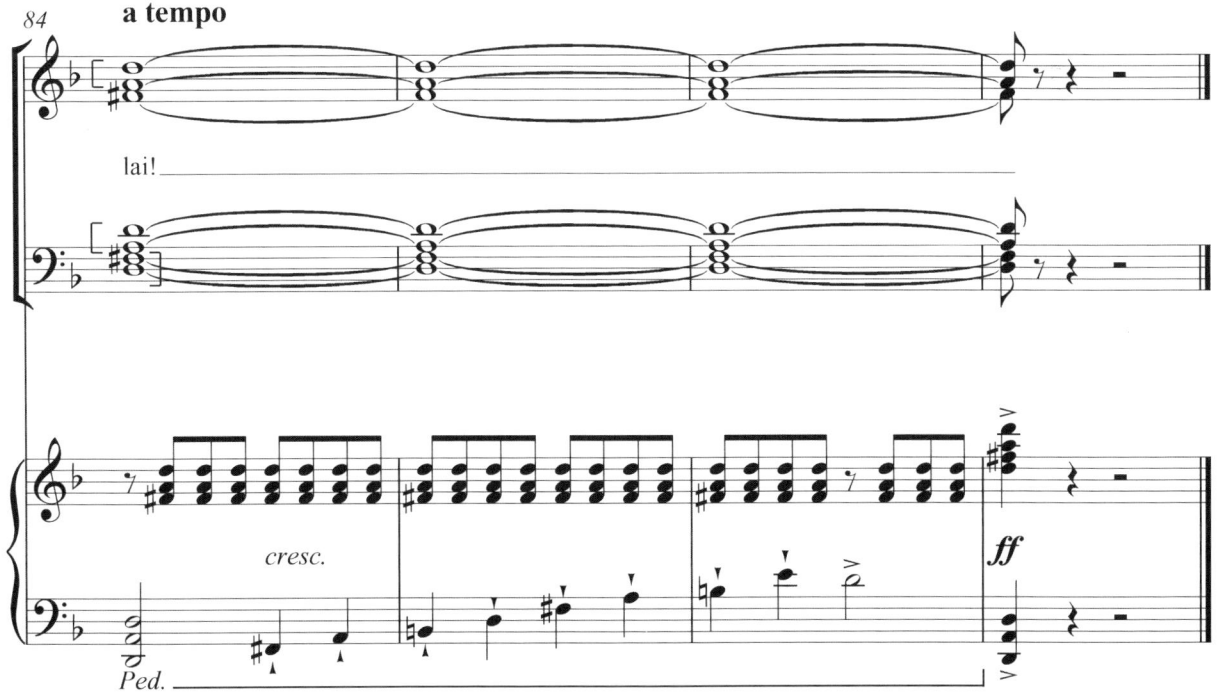

Gai Tau Hong Mei | Street Calls

Gai Tau Hong Mei is a late twentieth-century composition depicting the calls of food vendors advertising their Chinese delicacies on the street. More commonly referred to by its English title *Street Calls*, it uses modern Western musical language to reminisce about daily life in mid-twentieth-century Singapore. **Language**: Cantonese.

Composer

Leong Yoon Pin (1931–2011) has often been exalted as a pioneer in Singaporean composition. Leong studied at the Guildhall School of Music and Drama in London in the 1950s and received a scholarship to study in Paris for a year with Nadia Boulanger in 1966. He later earned a Master's degree in music from the University of Newcastle. Most of Leong's career was spent in Singapore, working as a composer, conductor and educator. He served as head of the Music Department of Singapore's Institute of Education and mentored some of Singapore's most active contemporary musicians. His numerous instrumental and choral works portray Singapore's unique blend of Chinese, English, Malay and Indian culture.

Text

Singapore's population of just over 5 million is extraordinarily heterogenous in terms of ethnic groups and languages. Its four official languages are English, Mandarin, Malay and Tamil, but numerous other dialects are spoken. Cantonese is one of the main Chinese languages used, and the corresponding language of food inevitably exists alongside it. This unique piece has no grammar or text phrases. It simply calls out different food specialities that were once common in street markets and are still part of restaurant life in Singapore, Hong Kong and Guangdong. While this anthology uses the standard pinyin for transliterating Mandarin works, Cantonese does not have such a standardized system, and many different methods are used by different people in different places. The two Cantonese pieces in *Half Moon Rising* — *Gai Tau Hong Mei* and *Seui Diu Go Tau* — use different systems for transliterating the Cantonese in order to reflect the different Singaporean and Hong Kong backgrounds of their composers.

This setting

Leong Yoon Pin wrote this work for the 1997 Singapore Youth Festival competition. It recreates the microcosm of roaming street food vendors that existed in Singapore until the mid-twentieth century. Today, hawker centres are consolidated areas where customers can go to choose from a great variety of edibles, but in the past many street hawkers would roam the streets and alleyways, calling out their best dishes. This piece dramatizes the growing calls of hawkers in three sections (ABA'). In bars 1–39 we hear first just a few lone hawkers from the distance, paired as TB and SA voices, selling chicken and fish congee. This is followed by more vendors selling noodles, represented by basses and sopranos, before a full *tutti* section at 27. At bar 40 a deluge of hawkers suddenly arrives selling rice, dumplings and noodle rolls, shown musically in a fugal section with three main melodies. All voices come together in a climactic frenzy, before the coda at 72–82 brings back the solitary vendors from the opening section. The irony of the lost past is captured in the heavily dissonant harmony, sometimes over veiled pentatonic melodies in the middle section.

Performance notes

If you have a dim sum restaurant in your area, go and try out the dishes in this work to inspire deeper musical association! All dynamic levels and articulations need to reflect the context of a busy street market, where calls overlap near and far. Softer dynamics represent distance, not lack of vitality. Articulate all entries with energy, regardless of dynamic level, including the preparatory breath. The 'modern' sounding dissonance of this piece becomes one of its most appealing features after the first rehearsals. Prepare the chorus for more challenging sonorities separately during warm ups, for example, have tenors and sopranos sing the whole-tone scale for their first entries. Re-spell the bass line at bars 5–7 to create an F♯ minor chord.

The vendors at bars 1–19 appear in isolation. Sopranos and altos at 10 should imagine they are the very first vendor to appear, so that their *pp* is as soft as that in the tenors at bar 1. Only in the soprano-bass build-up at 19–27 do the numbers of vendors grow, so make that *crescendo* convincingly *poco a poco*. Speak the text in rhythm repeatedly at 34–6 so that all entries and releases are accurate, and prepare for the *pp* entry at 37. Show steady but restrained *crescendos* for each delicacy being promoted in this opening section. The middle section at 40 is very *legato*. The minims on 'Ho fen, sui gao', and 'fen' of 'Ju qiung fen', can be approached from underneath with connected grace-notes starting before the beats to reflect the Cantonese text. Maintain a sense of growth from 67 to 71.

Consult the online Pronunciation Guide carefully to learn a few of the special Cantonese syllables. Note that certain consonants lie in between those commonly used in Western choral pieces, while the 'k' of 'chuk' is stopped. All diphthongs need full articulation of both vowels. Unlike *bel canto* diction, however, in which the first diphthong vowel is usually sustained, there is more flexibility of Cantonese interpretation according to the context and contrasting sections of this piece. One 'street call' effect may be better gained by going immediately to the second diphthong of certain words like 'geui' (sustaining the final 'i'). A contrasting effect could be attained in bars 40–59 by sustaining the first diphthong vowels.

Literal translation

Geui chuk, yu sang chuk!
Chicken congee, fish raw congee!

Kon lou min, wen ten min!
Lo mein, wonton noodles!

Ho fen, sui gao!
Rice noodles, boiled dumplings!

Ca xiu fan, no meui geui!
Roast pork rice, sticky rice chicken!

Xiu mai, ha gao!
Steamed dumplings, shrimp dumplings!

Ju qiung fen!
Pork rice noodle rolls!

Gai Tau Hong Mei
街頭巷尾
Street Calls

Leong Yoon Pin

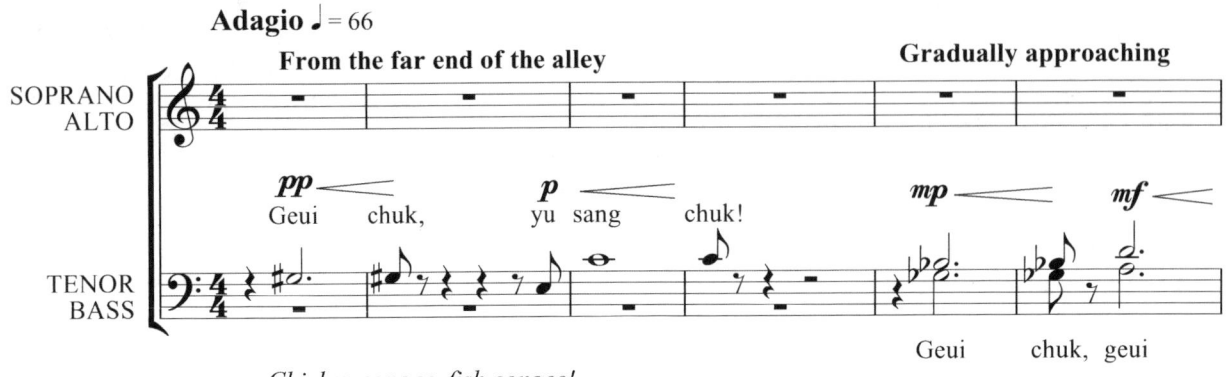

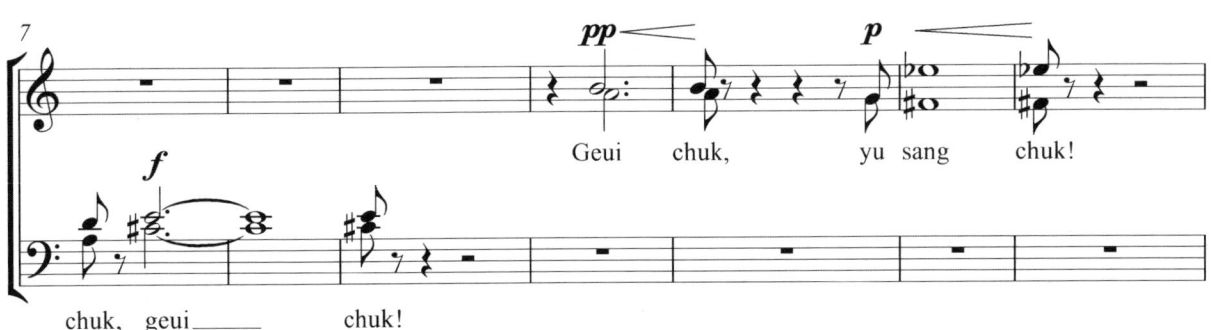

© 1997 by Leong Yoon Pin. Reproduced by permission of the Composers and Authors Society of Singapore (COMPASS).

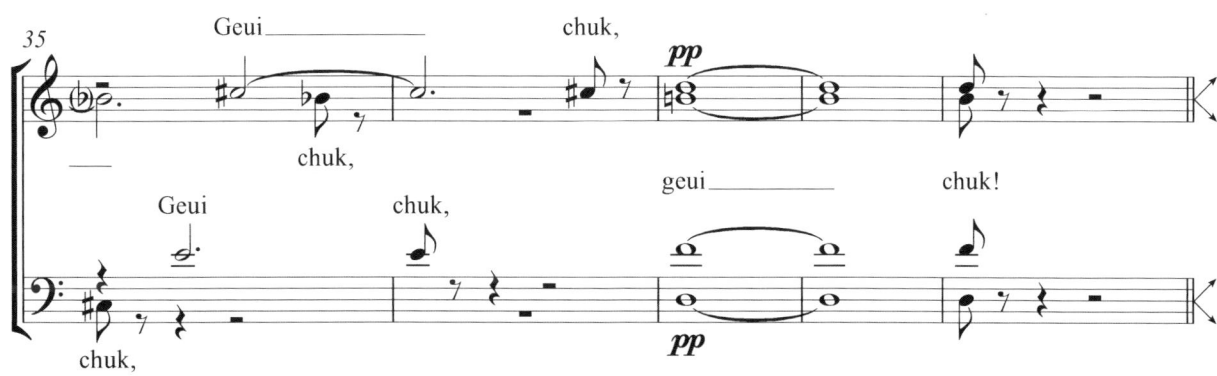

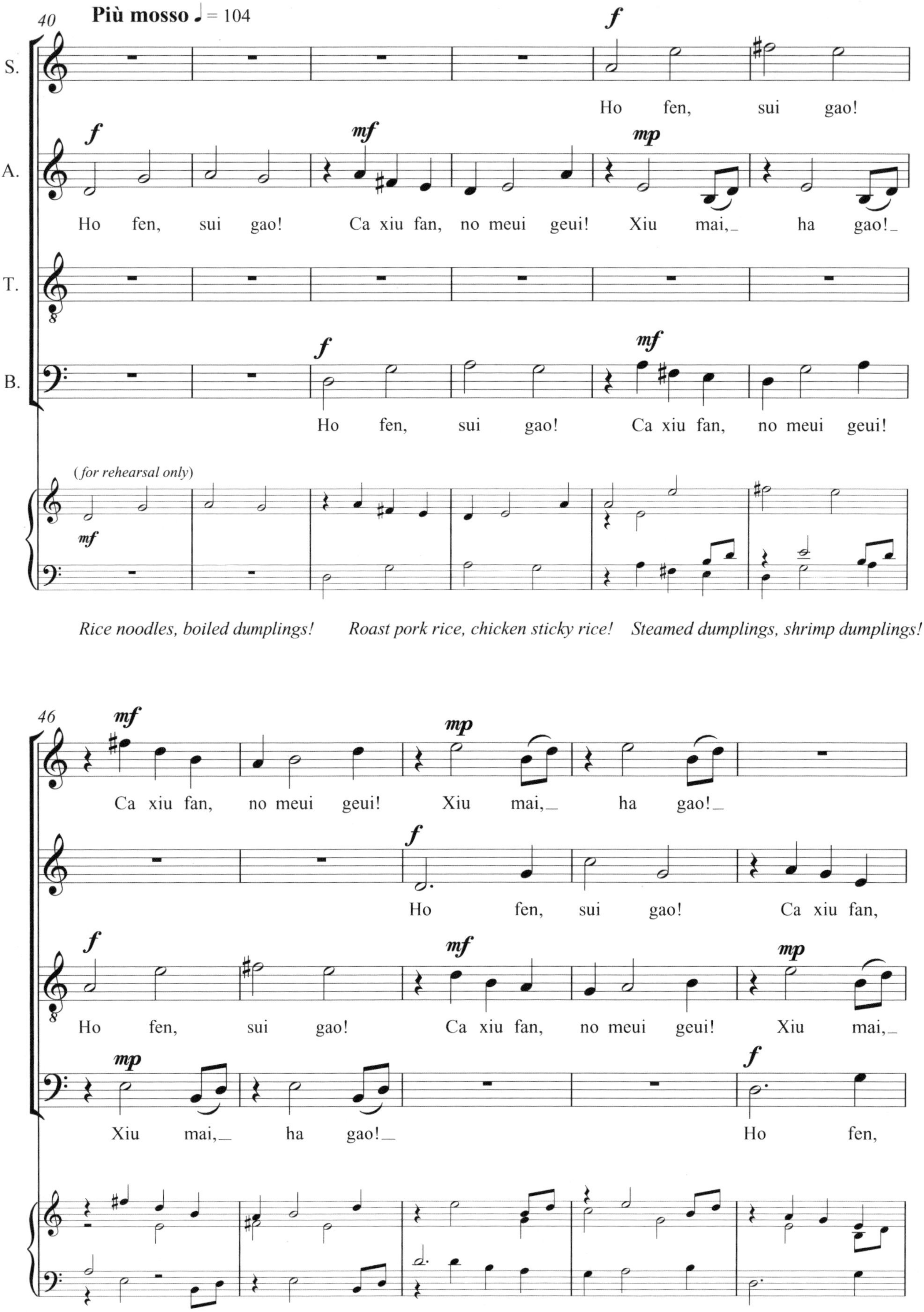

Rice noodles, boiled dumplings!   Roast pork rice, chicken sticky rice!   Steamed dumplings, shrimp dumplings!

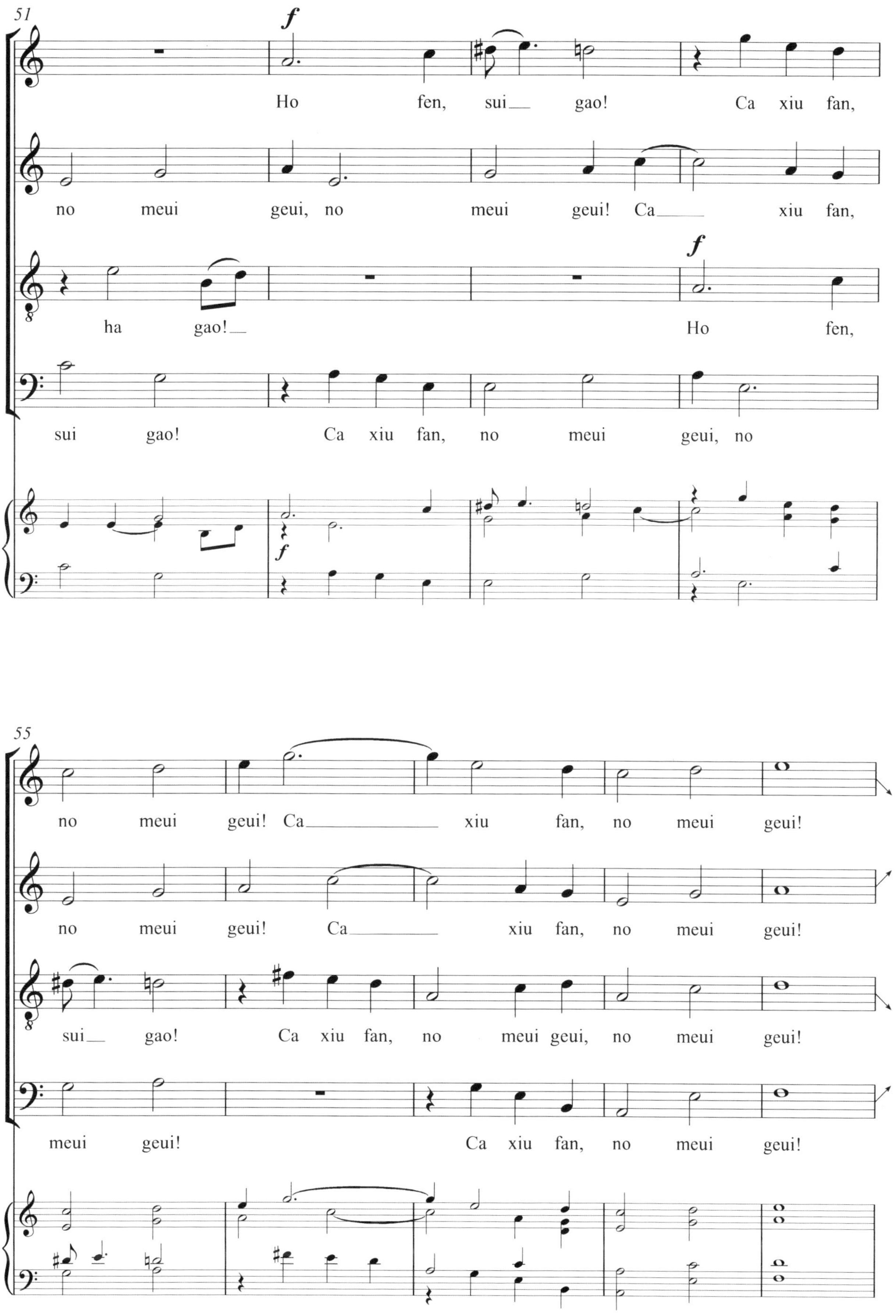

Ho fen, sui gao! Ca xiu fan,
no meui geui, no meui geui! Ca xiu fan,
ha gao! Ho fen,
sui gao! Ca xiu fan, no meui geui, no

no meui geui! Ca xiu fan, no meui geui!
no meui geui! Ca xiu fan, no meui geui!
sui gao! Ca xiu fan, no meui geui, no meui geui!
meui geui! Ca xiu fan, no meui geui!

Chicken congee!

Pork rice noodle rolls!

Ge Lao Huan Ge | Happy Song of the Gelao

Ge Lao Huan Ge is an arrangement of combined folksongs from the Gelao minority of southwestern China. The rewritten texts highlight ideological themes promoting unity and economic reform. **Language**: Mandarin.

Arranger

Zhou Zhengsong was born in Jiangxi province in 1952. After graduating from Beijing Normal University, Zhou went on to do his Master's work in conducting at the Central Conservatory of Music in Beijing, and he has served on the faculty at South China Normal University in Guangzhou. In addition to his vocal and instrumental compositions, Zhou authored or edited numerous publications, including the 2003 publication *The Collection of Chinese Folk Choruses* representing music of China's fifty-six ethnic groups.

Folksong

The Gelao minority group numbers less than a million and resides in Guizhou and other provinces of southwestern China. Gelao means 'bamboo', as an indication of the natural surroundings of that area. Among the many Gelao festivals are two celebrated during the first month of the lunar year, which include singing, dancing and playing a special *lusheng* reed-pipe instrument. The Gelao also have a rich variety of folksongs, extending from mountain songs, work songs and drinking songs to those of courtship, marriage and rituals. Many of these are sung in groups or pairs, and Gelao forms include call-and-response singing and triple-metre patterns not usually found in Han Chinese music.

Ge Lao Huan Ge actually incorporates two separate pentatonic melodies centring on four main pitches with frequent upward and downward leaps of a perfect fourth or a fifth. The fast melody of the outer sections starts like a regular four-bar phrase, but adds an extra bar at the end, making it five bars. It has the style of Gelao festival songs and certain stone-moving work songs. Its rhythms are characterized by six fast-moving notes followed by a long note at the end of each bar. The slower middle melody is in the style of a love song with less active rhythms and fewer leaps in its four-bar, triple-metre phrases.

This setting

This is a type of musical arrangement that serves both musical and ideological goals: it promotes the umbrella of national unity over China's Han majority and ethnic minority groups and praises the policy of economic reform in recent decades. The two Gelao songs are arranged in three sections (ABA) but with new words written by the arranger under a common theme. The first section (bars 1–23) creates images of a rural utopia. Bars 15–21 demonstrate text painting, where the slower and faster tempos represent contrasting paces of development in the past and present. The middle section at 24–46 extols the finer attributes of the Gelao people and the economic reform policy. The final section from bar 47 partly repeats the first section and concludes in a Presto tempo with all voices singing in harmony. Much of the work alternates between male and female voices singing the unison or harmonized melody while the others sing added vocables. It is framed by four points (bars 1, 22, 46 and 56) where all voices sing or shout vocables together.

Performance notes

This work is best performed with nimble dance vigour in the outer sections and sincere affection in the middle Andantino. Practise speaking the Allegro text so that you can effortlessly sing two-bar phrases without being restrained by the successive 'ng' endings and triphthongs like 'liao' and 'xiao'. Sing all 'du' rhythms with lively articulation in these outer sections. Keep the flow of a triple-metre dance in the middle section, and let the 'ng' of 'beng' vocables ring with an open vocal position. Hummed slurs should be both warm and bright, with each one leading toward the following 'beng'. Make the 'wu' and 'hei' shouts innocent and optimistic. Vocal colour can be nasalized, especially in female voices, with projection as if singing outdoors. Bars 15–18 should still maintain a forward flow, while the Allegro tempo should be carefree so to leave room for the sudden Presto at 52. Maintain chordal resonance from 52 even as the atmosphere becomes more festive.

Literal translation

1.
Mu   ye   sheng sheng ba   ge chang, ge   sheng liao liang ru   yun   duan,
Wood leaf sounds   to make to sing,   singing sound clear bright to enter cloud ends,

chang chang Ge lao   xin sheng huo, yi   tian yi   tian ben   xiao kang   luo.
to sing about the Gelao new life,   one day one day to rush toward moderate prosperity oh.

Jin   guang da   dao ping you kuan, kai xin   ri zi guo de   huan,
Bright light big road level and wide, delightful days to be passed happy,

(v.1) zhi ma kai hua   jie jie   gao, xing fu ri zi nian nian   chang luo.
(v.1) sesame to blossom little by little high, joyous days year by year long oh.

(v.3) zhi ma kai hua   jie jie   gao, huan le ge er chang bu wan.
(v.3) sesame to blossom little by little high, happy   song to sing no end.

Guo   qu   Ge lao   fa zhan   man, ri zi guo de   ting jian nan,
In the past the Ge lao to develop slow, days to be passed very difficult,

zi cong gai ge   kai fang liao, ri zi yi   tian yi   ge yang   luo!
since   reform   to open has, days one day one of appearance oh!

2.
Ge lao   xiao huo qin lao   yong gan, Ge lao   gu niang qing   shen yi   chang,
The Gelao lad   hardworking brave,   the Gelao girls   feeling deep meaning long,

gai ge kai fang, zheng ce hao ei!
reform to open, policy   good hey!

Ge lao   ren min xin   huan chang luo,
The Gelao people heart happy,   oh,

Ge lao   ren min xin   huan chang luo!
the Gelao people heart happy   oh!

Ge Lao Huan Ge
仡佬欢歌
Happy Song of the Gelao

Words by Zhou Zhengsong

Gelao folksong
arr. Zhou Zhengsong

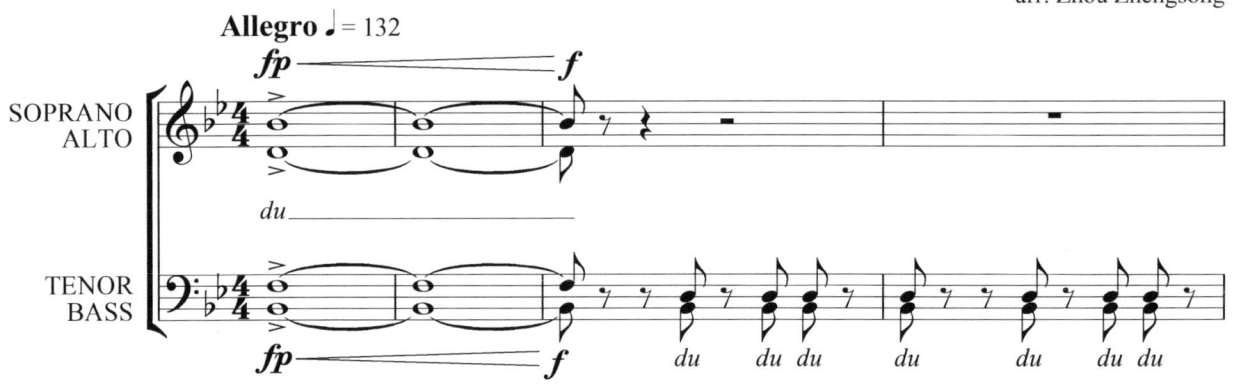

The sounds of wood and leaves turn into singing, the voices resonate bright and clear to the farthest clouds,

singing about the new life of the Gelao, with each day moving towards a better life.

© Zhou Zhengsong. Reproduced by permission of the Music Copyright Society of China (MCSC).

The Gelao guys are hardworking and brave,  the Gelao girls are thoughtful and deep in feeling, in the time

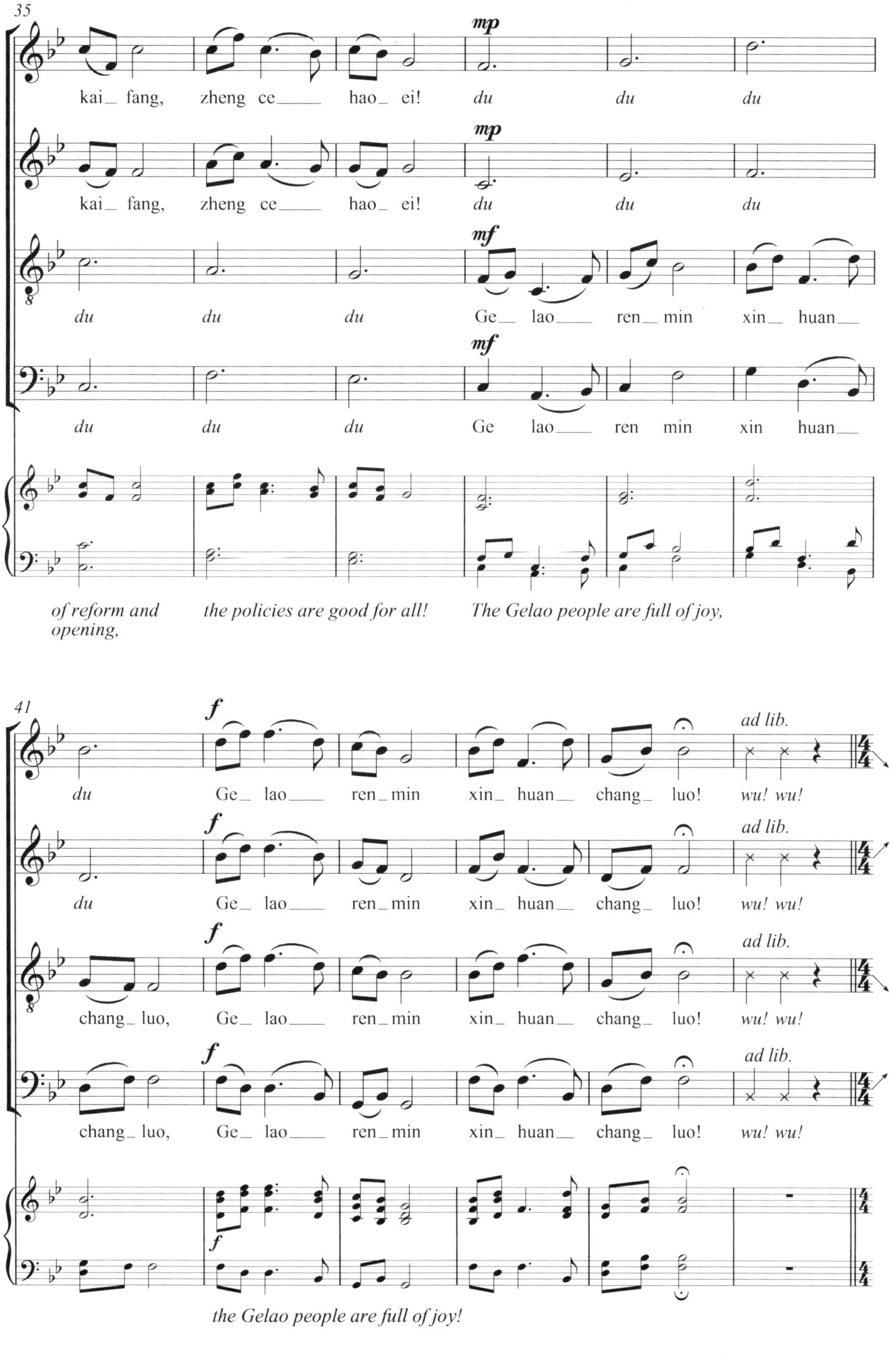
35
mp
kai_ fang, zheng ce___ hao_ ei! du du du
mp
kai_ fang, zheng ce___ hao_ ei! du du du
mf
du du du Ge_ lao___ ren_ min xin_ huan_
mf
du du du Ge lao___ ren min xin huan_
of reform and opening,
the policies are good for all!
The Gelao people are full of joy,
41
f
ad lib.
du Ge_ lao___ ren_ min xin_ huan_ chang_ luo! wu! wu!
f
ad lib.
du Ge_ lao___ ren_ min xin_ huan_ chang_ luo! wu! wu!
f
ad lib.
chang_ luo, Ge_ lao___ ren_ min xin_ huan_ chang_ luo! wu! wu!
f
ad lib.
chang_ luo, Ge_ lao___ ren_ min xin_ huan_ chang_ luo! wu! wu!
f
the Gelao people are full of joy!

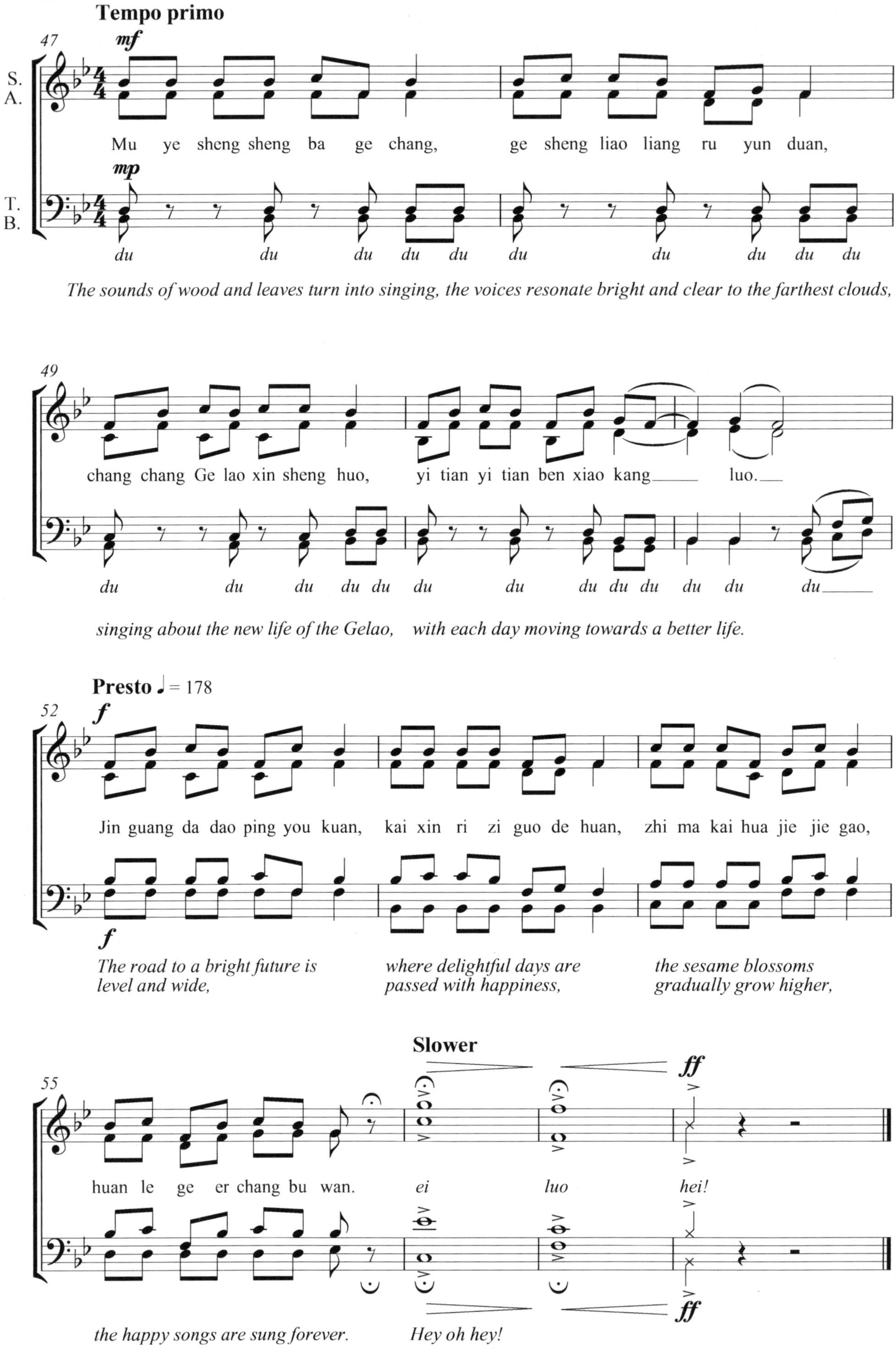

The sounds of wood and leaves turn into singing, the voices resonate bright and clear to the farthest clouds,

singing about the new life of the Gelao, with each day moving towards a better life.

The road to a bright future is level and wide, where delightful days are passed with happiness, the sesame blossoms gradually grow higher,

the happy songs are sung forever. Hey oh hey!

Hong Dou Ci | Red Bean Poem

Hong Dou Ci is a choral arrangement of an art song written by Liu Xue'an in 1943. The text is from one of China's Four Great Classical Novels, adapted for use in a modern Chinese stage drama. **Language**: Mandarin.

Composer and arranger

Liu Xue'an (1905–85) was from Sichuan province in southwestern China. He studied music in Shanghai in the 1930s and wrote a number of patriotic songs, children's songs and music textbooks during those years. He started writing film scores after graduating from the National Institute of Music (today's Shanghai Conservatory) in 1936 and became further involved in music for the war effort, moving to Chongqing in 1938. After 1949, Liu worked for various educational institutions as he continued to compose. He endured hardship at various times due to the fluctuating political climate of the 1950s and 1960s, but was later recognized for his contribution to modern Chinese music. (For a biography of Hwang Yau-tai, see p. 217.)

Art song

During the Second World War China's capital temporarily moved to the southwest city of Chongqing, and it was there that Liu Xue'an composed *Hong Dou Ci* for solo voice and piano. It became famous after it was recorded by soprano Zhou Xiaoyan in Shanghai in 1947. The melody, largely pentatonic (D-F-G-A-C) in D minor, has features of a traditional Chinese folksong, but it unfolds over a long chain of smaller phrases, covering a wide range of emotions with its numerous unpredictable leaps. The repeated 'Ya!' lament follows a more agitated passage, adding to the heavy sentiment of the work. Contemporary vocalists often interpret the piece with extreme emotional weight, but Zhou's 1947 recording, presumably in collaboration with Liu, shows a lighter, if not helpless, restraint.

Text

The text originally comes from the eighteenth-century Chinese novel the *Dream of the Red Chamber*, also known as the *Story of the Stone*, written by Cao Xueqin and regarded as one of China's Four Great Classical Novels. It is about an aristocratic family and two cousins Daiyu and Baoyu who grow up together. Their hopes to marry are dashed by elder family members who trick Baoyu into marrying someone else. Daiyu dies heartbroken and Baoyu eventually turns to the religious life of a monk. The 'Red Bean Poem' is sung by Baoyu while at a small party in Chapter 28, well before the tragic events play out.

Liu Xue'an's art song was composed for the 1943 stage drama *Yu Lei (Suppressed Thunder)* by Zhu Tong. Written and published in Chongqing, the play was republished and performed in Shanghai in 1946, with a 'cross-dresser' actress Sun Jinglu playing the part of the young male Baoyu. Based on the *Dream of the Red Chamber*, *Yu Lei* was meant as a political statement focusing on the oppressive nature of China's feudalistic society. Unlike the party setting of Cao Xueqin's novel, in the play *Hong Dou Ci* appears late in the climactic Act 3, sung by Baoyu in a state of deep melancholy immediately after he discovers that his bride is not his beloved Daiyu. But it retains its original eighteenth-century text, which is noteworthy for the appearance of 'bu' — meaning 'no' or 'not' — ten times throughout the song text to highlight helplessness. It is also characterized by its rhyming scheme centred on the syllable 'ou'.

This setting

Hwang Yau-tai's choral setting from 1974 closely follows the original art song melody and harmony, but he varies the choir textures to enhance the dramatic mood of the piece. For example, tenors and basses hum the opening line, with sopranos and altos singing a duet texture, but the restlessness of 'shui bu wen' ('uneasy sleep') is increased by all four parts singing in harmony, with added rests mid-sentence to break up the phrase. Each voice part alternates in call-and-response entries at varying dynamic levels from 'zhan bu kai mei tou', before all voices come together again, as if wailing collectively on 'Ya!' The soprano-alto restatement of 'liu bu duan di lü shui you you' in the final three bars reflects the shape of the light, flowing text.

Performance notes

Clearly articulate the second vowels of diphthongs, like the 'u' of the 'ou' syllables and the 'i' of 'shui'. Diphthongs and triphthongs that begin with 'i', such as 'liu' and 'liao', should unfold slowly and smoothly from the initial 'i' consonant. Clear dynamic contrast is needed in bars 17–20, especially in the alto and soprano entries. In bars 22 and 28 'Qia si' is sometimes pronounced as 'Qia shi' when singing. The repeat at the end of bar 26 may be omitted. In the coda, a *poco ritardando* and breath break could be added at the end of bar 31 before a relaxed *a tempo* in 32–3 and more definitive *ritard.* at 33–4. Take care to maintain the p dynamic in the ascending soprano line on 'liu bu duan' in bar 32.

Literal translation

Di   bu jin   xiang si   xue   lei   pao   hong dou,
To drop countless to yearn blood tears to toss red   bean,

kai   bu wan chun liu   chun hua   man hua lou.
to bloom endless spring willow spring flower full pavilion.

Shui   bu wen sha   chuang feng yu huang hun hou,
To sleep restless screen window wind rain twilight   after,

wang   bu liao   xin chou   yu   jiu chou.
to forget unable to new to worry and old to worry.

Yan   bu xia   yu li jin bo   ye   man hou,
To swallow not down fine food and wine to choke full throat,

qiao   bu jin   jing   li hua rong   shou.
to look at endless mirror in complexion thin.

Zhan bu kai   mei tou, ai   bu ming geng lou.
To be unable to open eyebrow, to endure not bright water clock (*to mark night watch*).

Ya! Ya! Qia si   zhe   bu zhu   di qing   shan   yin yin,
Ah! Ah! Just like to cover constantly of blue-green mountain faint,

liu   bu duan   di lü   shui   you you.
to flow unceasing of green water lasting for ages.

Hong Dou Ci
紅豆詞
Red Bean Poem

Words by Cao Xueqin
(Qing Dynasty)

Liu Xue'an
arr. Hwang Yau-tai

Countless drops of lovesick tears are shed like red beans being tossed about, the pavilion is filled with endlessly blooming willows and flowers in spring.

In the twilight after a sleepless night

Copyright © 1943 EMI Music Publishing Hong Kong. Copyright Renewed.
This arrangement Copyright © 1974 EMI Music Publishing Hong Kong.
All Rights Administered by Sony/ATV Music Publishing LLC, 424 Church Street, Suite 1200, Nashville, TN 37219.
International Copyright Secured. All Rights Reserved. Reprinted by Permission of Hal Leonard Corporation.

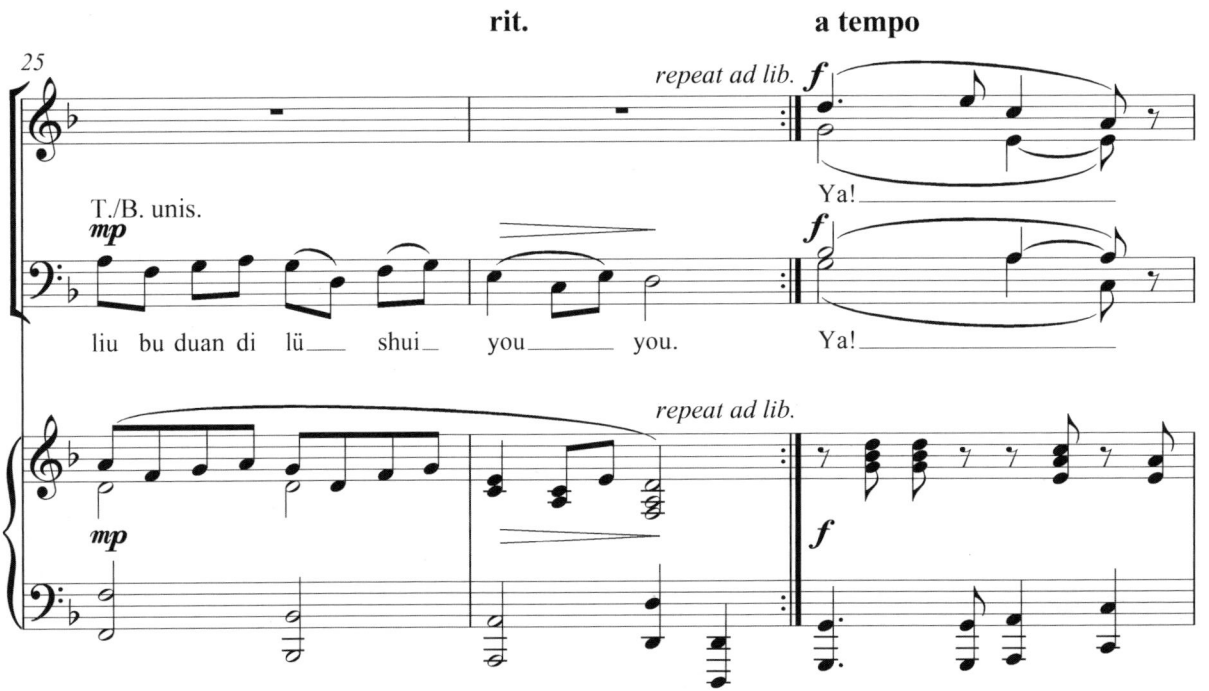

Just like the blue mountains forever covered in mist,

like the green waters that flow unceasing throughout the ages.

Ken Chun Ni | Cultivating Spring Soil

Ken Chun Ni was written as incidental music for the 1940 film *March of Victory*, directed by Shi Dongshan. One of China's earlier unaccompanied choral works, it adapts the style of a Chinese work song for the purpose of rousing national pride. **Language**: Mandarin.

Composer

He Lüting (1903–99) was an important composer, educator, administrator and writer in China's twentieth-century musical development. A native of Hunan province, he later studied in Shanghai and spent several years writing film music there before moving to Chongqing during the early war years of the late 1930s. He spent most of the 1940s at communist bases doing music, administrative and propaganda work. He was a prolific composer of theme songs and incidental music for films, vocal genres, including patriotic songs for the masses, choral works, and solo pieces, as well as instrumental works that combined Chinese styles with Western musical language.

Text

The text of *Ken Chun Ni* was written by Tian Han, screenwriter of the original film and an important literary figure in modern China. In the late 1930s, as the Sino-Japanese War progressed and the Second World War began, artists and writers drew upon agrarian themes that would help rouse China's population into battle. The planting metaphor ('zhong chu') appears five times in bars 3–7, first drawing images of the spring soil that produces peaches, cotton, trees and grain, then likening this work to the ultimate fight for freedom. The key word 'bu' (not) appears five times in the second section of the piece as an affirmation of courage, sacrifice and unified determination in the face of the enemy. Throughout the piece, the syllable 'yo' continuously punctuates text lines as a means of exhorting countrymen into action, and chants of 'hei ya yo' are murmured underneath to signify forward marching motion.

This setting

The film *March of Victory* is set in wartime Changsha around the time of a famous battle in 1939 that helped stop the advance of invading troops further into the Chinese interior. The film itself has not endured, but *Ken Chun Ni*, which was written as one of two choruses for the film, was well known during the war due to its publication and recording in 1942, and is still regularly performed in China today.

Ken Chun Ni presents four-part *a cappella* choral music in the style of a traditional Chinese *haozi* work song. Work songs are characterized by heavy, steady beats that workers use to coordinate their collective body movements when digging, farming, rowing or marching into battle. Here, the heavy beat keeps the choir together in the first section, where the melody is sung in different voices from phrase to phrase; in the second section all voices join together in unity. He Lüting also employs folk music styles of his native Hunan, where the film takes place. *Ken Chun Ni* is an early example of Chinese folk music mixing with the Western choral style for the political aim of strengthening national feeling.

Performance notes

Give an exaggerated emphasis on beats 1 and 3 throughout to suggest digging and marching into battle (in rehearsal, mimic digging or hammering gestures with one hand on these beats to gain the work song feel). Sopranos should carefully phonate the unique 'Ri' vowel as they prepare for their entry in bar 1 by adding some of the high placement of the second 'chu' syllable in advance. The soprano-alto C♯-G♯ in bar 2 should not be given undue weight. All voices should maintain a slightly open 'e' vowel in 'hei' so that it retains a sturdy sound. Recurring 'yo' syllables should also have open vowels that reflect a deep, *pesante* resonance.

All of the fast-moving four-note groups that begin each bar should be loose, open-vowelled, and moving toward beats 2 and 3. Practise the different words that follow 'zhong chu' each time so that they can be effortless and resonant. Give weight to the 'bu' (not) syllables in bars 8 and 9, and add accents with growing intensity beginning on beat 2 of bar 12. Sopranos and altos in bar 13 should be *legato* but resolute. Add a *ritardando* at the end of bar 14, and fully coordinate the breath for a hushed yet accented attack in bar 15. This is a short piece and may be easily repeated by returning from bar 14 back to the beginning.

Literal translation

Ri chu dong lai   you dao xi yo,
Sunrise east to come and again to fall to west oh,

jun min he zuo ken chun ni yo,
soldiers and civilians to cooperate to cultivate spring soil oh,

zhong chu tao hua hong man di ya,
to plant out peach flower red filled ground ah,

zhong chu mian hua bai man qi yo,
to plant out cotton flower white filled field oh,

zhong chu yang liu hao zhe yin na,
to plant out willow tree so as to shade cover ah,

zhong chu gu zi hao fang ji.
to plant out grain so as to prevent hunger.

Zhong chu zi you wu jia bao ya,
To plant out freedom priceless treasure ah,

bu fen gao lai bu fen di yo,
not to regard high to come not to regard low oh,

bu chou shi lai bu chou yi,
not to worry about food to come not to worry about clothing,

na pa di ren bo lang yong ya,
not to be afraid of enemy wave to surge ah,

wo men jie cheng yi dao tie chang di,
we to form into a path of iron long embankment,

huan huan xi xi bu fen li. Hei ya ha! Hei!
happy joyful not to separate. Hey ah ha! Hey!

Ken Chun Ni
垦 春 泥
Cultivating Spring Soil

Words by Tian Han

He Lüting

zhong chu mian hua bai man qi yo,

zhong chu tao hua hong man di ya, zhong chu mian hua bai man qi yo, hei ya

hei yo! Hei ya hei yo!

ho, hei ya ho, hei yo!

planting peaches to make red-covered earth,   *planting cotton to make white-covered fields,*

hei ya hei yo! Hei ya hei yo!

hei ya hei yo! Hei ya hei yo!

zhong chu yang liu hao zhe yin na, zhong chu gu zi hao fang ji.

zhong chu yang liu hao zhe yin na, zhong chu gu zi hao fang ji. Hei ya!

planting willows to make a cover for shade,   *planting grain to protect us from hunger.*

Zhong chu zi you wu jia bao ya, bu fen gao lai bu fen di yo,

Zhong chu zi you wu jia bao ya, bu fen gao lai bu fen di yo,

Zhong chu zi you wu jia bao ya, bu fen gao lai bu fen di yo,

Zhong chu zi you wu jia bao ya, bu fen gao lai bu fen di, hei ya

Planting seeds of freedom as our priceless treasure,   *without distinguishing between high and low,*

bu chou shi lai bu chou yi,

bu chou shi lai bu chou yi,

hei ya hei yo! Hei ya hei yo!

hei yo! Hei ya hei ya hei yo!

without worrying about food and clothing,

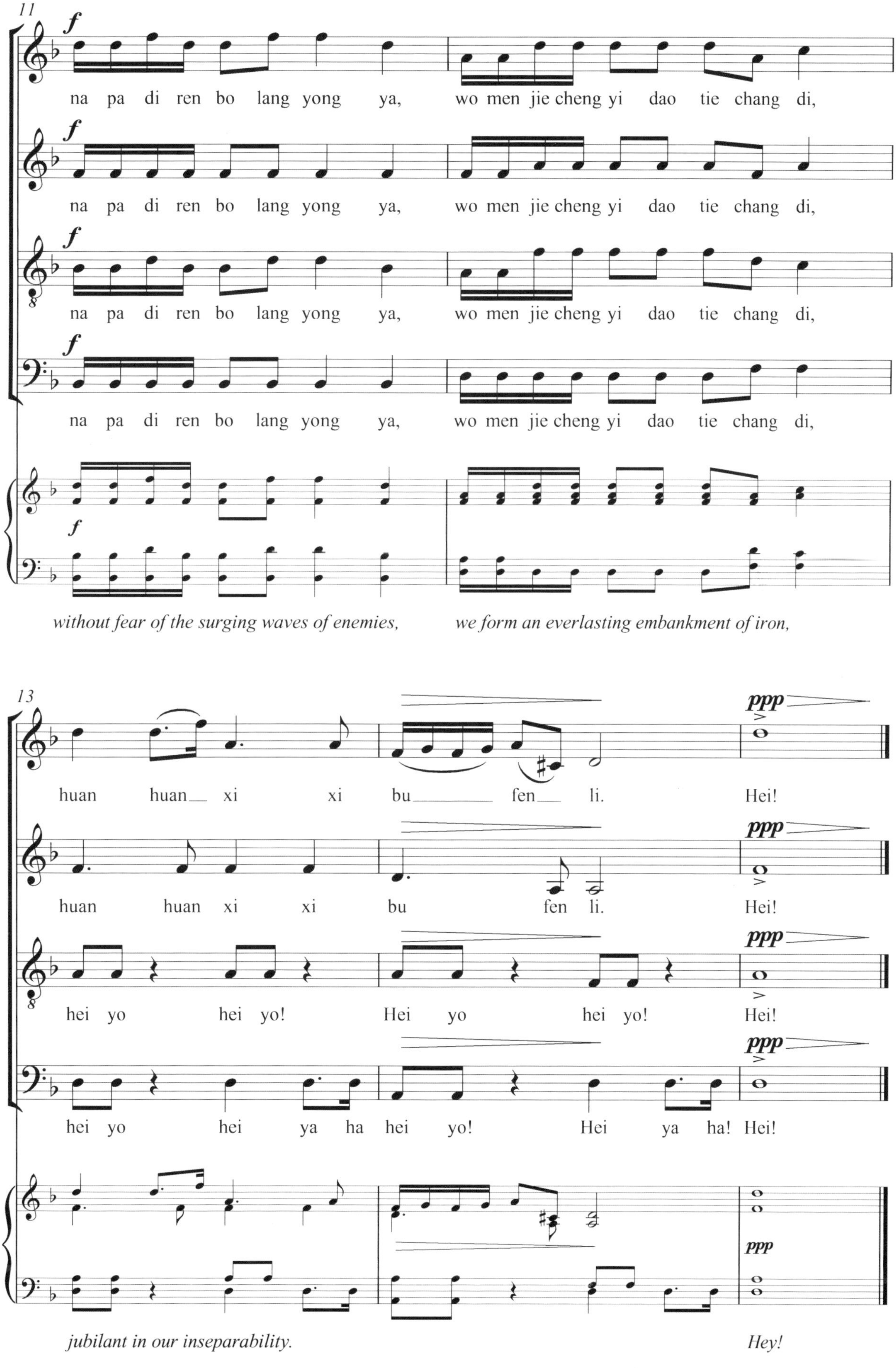
11
f
na pa di ren bo lang yong ya, wo men jie cheng yi dao tie chang di,
na pa di ren bo lang yong ya, wo men jie cheng yi dao tie chang di,
na pa di ren bo lang yong ya, wo men jie cheng yi dao tie chang di,
na pa di ren bo lang yong ya, wo men jie cheng yi dao tie chang di,
without fear of the surging waves of enemies, we form an everlasting embankment of iron,
13
ppp
huan huan xi xi bu fen li. Hei!
huan huan xi xi bu fen li. Hei!
hei yo hei yo! Hei yo hei yo! Hei!
hei yo hei ya ha hei yo! Hei ya ha! Hei!
jubilant in our inseparability. Hey!

Kuai Le De Ju Hui | Happy Reunion

Kuai Le De Ju Hui is a choral arrangement of an ancient song from the Ita Thao people of Sun Moon Lake in south-central Taiwan. **Language**: Thao (Taiwan).

Arranger

Chuan-Sheng Lu (1916–2008) grew up in the central Taiwan city of Taichung during the period under Japanese rule from 1895–1945. He studied music in Japan in the 1930s and worked there as a vocalist for several years as he continued his composition studies, before returning to Taiwan in 1943. Lu began conducting choirs and arranging local folksongs in the late 1940s. He established the Rong Shing Chorus in 1957 and developed it into one of Taiwan's premiere ensembles in the following decades. During this period he also served on the faculty of Shih Chien College and continued to write vocal music. Lu spent his final years in the US, but maintained close ties to Taiwan during that time.

Folksong

Kuai Le De Ju Hui is the Mandarin title of an ancient song by the indigenous Thao people of south-central Taiwan's Sun Moon Lake Region. The Thao form one of Taiwan's smallest indigenous groups. Traditionally, the group engaged in hunting, fishing and agriculture because of its promiximity to the forests, lakes and mountains in that area. Thao music is closely related to these activities, including its famous pestle music, where villagers strike different sizes of rice-husking tools on large stones in interlocking rhythms and sing polyphonically. The Thao also perform dances and songs for ceremonies, including ancestral worship and return from hunting expeditions.

The *Kuai Le De Ju Hui* tune was first transcribed using the Japanese alphabet by Zhang Fuxing in 1922 (it was later transliterated both in Romanized and Chinese script in the choral score); it is pentatonic in five phrases. The melody is characterized by what looks like very simple stepwise motion on just three pitches in the first two, repeating phrases, but this is followed by a wide upward leap and slurred syllables in the third phrase. The fourth phrase 'a yi ya no' is very short, and the final phrase has the same ending as the third phrase. The 1922 transcription offers a rough meaning of the song text in Japanese: 'We strong and brave heroes drink and celebrate our close bonds together'.

This setting

Chuan-Sheng Lu wrote *Kuai Le De Ju Hui* in 1948 as Taiwan came under the authority of the Kuomintang and Republic of China following the Second World War. Its aboriginal, Japanese and Chinese links together represent Taiwan's unique history and cultural blend. Lu's arrangement has become one of the better-known choral works on the island.

The work follows the style of the Thao people of Sun Moon Lake. Here, the chorus recreates in the Thao language a celebration dance after a group returns from hunting and fishing. As with a number of arrangements in this collection, it contains repeating folksong verses flanked by an introduction and coda. The pentatonic melody forms the basis for the choral harmony, including dissonant D-E pitches in the repeating 'pin pin pon pon' tenor-bass gestures. Many vocables not found in the original tune have been added in the choral version to create interlocking *ostinatos* for the march-like dance. The regional vocal style is also enhanced by the added shouts of 'hei', 'hei ya', 'hei yi ya' and 'ha ha ha' throughout. The song was originally transcribed at the gentle Allegretto tempo from bar 9. In this arrangement, the two other tempos — the slow outer sections and the Allegro dance section from 22 — form a dramatic contrast.

Performance notes

Choirs adopt different ways of handling the introduction and coda sections at bars 1 and 45: some carefully pursue the nuanced dynamics of the arrangement, while others attack all phrases fervently. A more nuanced approach to the successive 'hei ya' entries will leave more space for layering dynamics at bars 6-8 and 49-52. The Allegretto tempo from bar 9 should be moderate with a welcoming flow. Sopranos and altos can add a mild *crescendo* toward 'si yo la ma sen' on each 'ka wu ka wu pin do' phrase, and altos can do the same on sustained 'wu' syllables in 34 and 36. Carefully rehearse the tenor and bass transition from bar 20 of the first ending back to bar 9, so that the 'yo', 'wu' and 'ha' gestures can be effected seamlessly. (Some choirs shout 'hei!' instead of 'wu' at the end of bar 20.) Do the same when moving from bar 19 to the second ending bar 21, where tenors and basses suddenly adopt the *legato* articulation of the soprano-alto line.

The *staccato* 'pin pon' figures, while separated, need adequate resonance in order to hear the dissonance and chords. Second sopranos should add some length and open vowel space for a hearty *sf* 'hei' from bar 24, and first sopranos should closely coordinate their rhythms with them up to bar 31. Begin the section at 42 with a sturdy *mf* dynamic and very gradually *decrescendo* so that the chords remain focused all the way to the pause at 44. The start of the final phrase (bar 49 to the third beat of bar 50) may be sung as written or with all voices in unison (octaves) on the soprano melody, before breaking back into harmony.

Kuai Le De Ju Hui
快 樂 的 聚 會
Happy Reunion

ancient tune of Sun Moon Lake
arr. Chuan-Sheng Lu

© Chuan-Sheng Lu. Reproduced by permission of Summery Music Publishing Ltd.

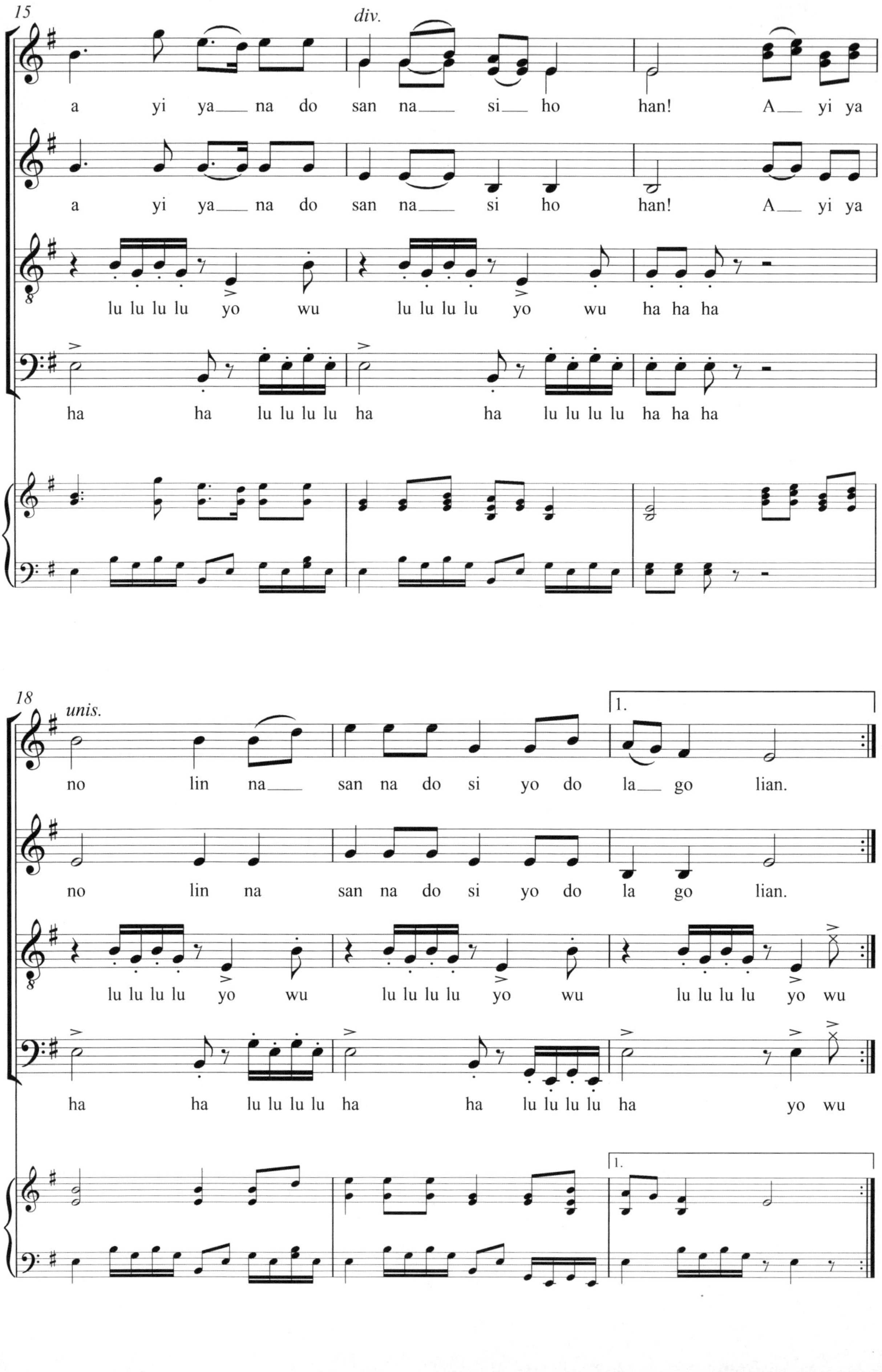

Lok Sui Tien | Rainy Days

Lok Sui Tien is an arrangement of a Hakka folksong from southern China. Hakka is one of the main dialects spoken by Chinese immigrants and their descendants in Southeast Asia.
Language: Hakka.

Arranger

Toh Ban Sheng was born in Malaysia of Chinese descent and now lives in Singapore. Toh obtained a Bachelor of Science degree in Physics and a Post-graduate Diploma in Education before pursuing his formal studies in music. He eventually received Master of Music degrees in Choral Conducting and Voice from the University of South Carolina. He has since become recognized in Singapore for his outstanding contribution to choral music there as both a conductor and educator, and was conferred with the national Young Artists Award in 2006. Toh has received equal distinction internationally, and is now sought after as adjudicator, clinician, coach and conductor throughout the world. Toh has a growing list of sacred compositions and folk choral arrangements that reflect the special mixture of Chinese, Malay and other cultures of Malaysia and Singapore.

Folksong

Lok Sui Tien is a traditional Hakka folksong originally popular in Guangdong province of southern China. Hakka people are ethnically part of the Han Chinese majority, but due to ongoing mass migrations over the centuries and their distinctive dialect, they became known as the 'guest people' in Chinese. While many Hakka still live in southern Chinese provinces, numerous others emigrated to Taiwan and parts of Southeast Asia. This folksong, a mountain song sung in the Hakka dialect, originated in northern Guangdong province and became well known in places like Malaysia and Singapore. Chinese mountain songs are not necessarily sung in the mountains. Rather, they describe songs sung in open, outdoor spaces with great resonance and expressing deep emotion. In the past, *Lok Sui Tien* described — possibly with some irony — the resilient condition of people so poor they could still continue their work on the land even with nothing to protect them from the rain. Nowadays, it also sings of the pitiful situation of children during rainy days — how even the rain encroaches upon their personal space, drenches them, and leaves them no place for shelter.

The folksong melody appears simplistic, using only four main pitches from the pentatonic scale. It nonetheless communicates deep emotion in two main ways. First, the text is organized into four main phrases (of six, eight, eight and seven syllables respectively), but each sub-phrase (made of three or four syllables) has its own distinct combination of pitches, contour and rising-falling motion toward the final pitches, resulting in four rising and four falling finals. Second, the recurring rhythmic pattern based on medium-medium-short-long is unique and challenging in its own right.

This setting

This choral arrangement brings out the wistful sentiment of a rainy day. The repeating folksong verses are framed by an introduction and coda on varying motives, with the different voices repeating 'zin ko lien' ('how pitiful'). The focus on the text's pathos and descending minor motive of the last verse phrase adds a blues flavour to the arrangement. The folksong is sung twice in full, primarily in the sopranos. The lower voices both support the melody and form their own often chromatic countermelodies, phrase by phrase. The repeated verse from bar 26 is extended by the repetition of the second half when each voice enters successively from bar 36. The otherwise simple tune is enhanced by meticulous attention given to harmonic and dynamic variations, as well as accent and *tenuto* articulations. The arrangement was written for the 2011 Catholic Junior College Choir (Singapore) European Tour and premiered in Germany that year.

Performance notes

Despite the numerous *divisi* in this arrangement, it is suitable for large and small groups alike, as long as staggered breathing can be achieved convincingly. Have the entire choir learn the main melody and text together so that the individual parts can better interact. Individual pitches of the first soprano chord clusters in the introduction and coda should be focused enough to lean against each other, at a restrained dynamic level, so that the dissonant sonority forms a lustre for the 'zin ko lien' motives in the other voices. But those other voices also need adequate shape and interaction to bring out the blue emotion.

Pay careful attention to the varied articulations throughout. Each accent and *tenuto* should be tastefully expressed within the context of the piece. Sing *staccato* notes with enough length to maintain the forward vocal line. First sopranos should balance the f dynamic level with the other voices when reaching the upper register at bars 31–2. In the Agitato section from bar 36, carefully tune the downbeat and entry chords, and instruct lower voices to take staggered breaths in 40–1 to bring the section to a conclusive cadence at 43. The *diminuendo 'al niente'* of the final bars still needs adequate resonance for the final G minor chord. The Hakka dialect is quite distinct from Mandarin, so refer to the online Pronunciation Guides for thorough reference.

Literal translation

Ah, zin ko lien.
Ah, truly pitiful.

Lok sui tien, lok sui tien, lok sui lok do ngai ge sin bien.
To fall water day, to fall water day, to fall water to fall to my body side.

Sib le yi son you mao za goi, gong ze tel loi, zin ko lien.
To be wet clothes yet without to cover, bare head to become, truly pitiful.

Lok Sui Tien
落 水 天
Rainy Days

Hakka folksong
arr. Toh Ban Sheng

Ah, how pitiful.

© 2012 by Toh Ban Sheng. Published and distributed solely by Earthsongs. Reproduced by permission.

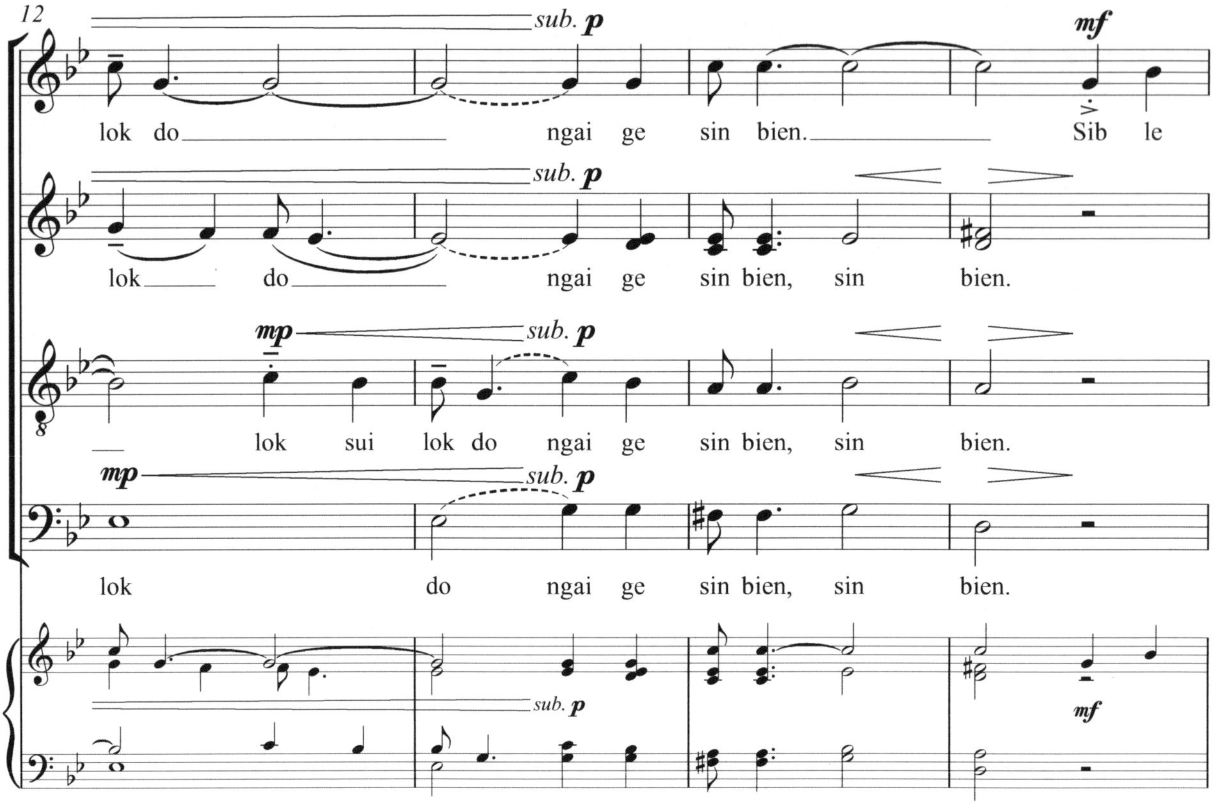
12
sub. p
mf
lok do ngai ge sin bien. Sib le
sub. p
lok do ngai ge sin bien, sin bien.
mp
sub. p
lok sui lok do ngai ge sin bien, sin bien.
mp
sub. p
lok do ngai ge sin bien, sin bien.
sub. p
mf

next to my body.

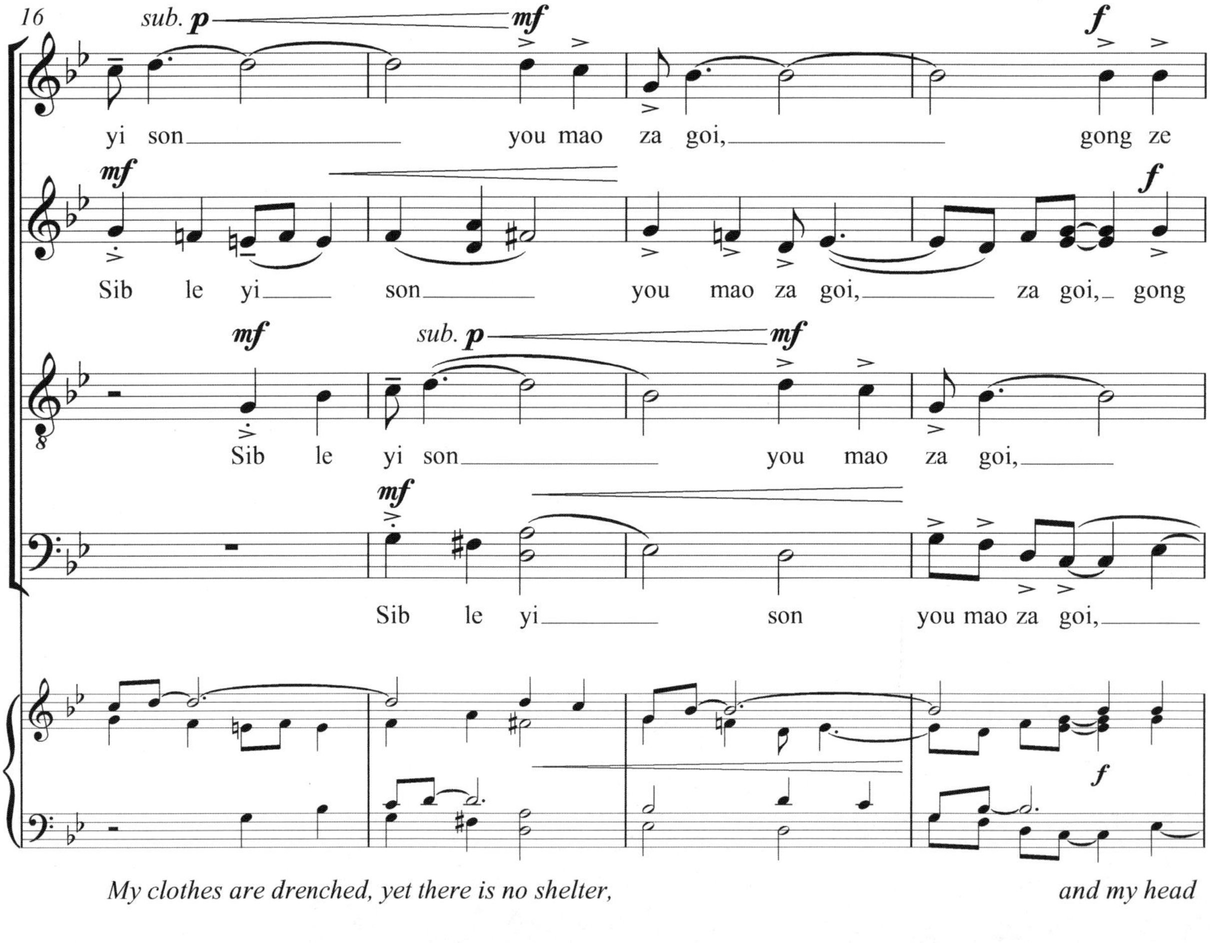
16
sub. p
mf
f
yi son you mao za goi, gong ze
mf
f
Sib le yi son you mao za goi, za goi, gong
mf
sub. p
mf
Sib le yi son you mao za goi,
mf
Sib le yi son you mao za goi,
f

My clothes are drenched, yet there is no shelter, *and my head*

Mo Li Hua | Jasmine Flower

Mo Li Hua is one of the best-known Chinese folksongs both inside and outside China. It has become a significant national symbol and used at important ceremonies and in famous musical works. **Language**: Jiangsu dialect.

Arranger

Chen Yi was born in the southern Chinese province of Guangdong (near Hong Kong) and was an adolescent during China's tumultuous 'Cultural Revolution' years of the late 1960s and early 1970s. She was in the famous first group of composition students admitted to the reopened Central Conservatory of Music in Beijing in 1978. This group became known as the 'New Wave' composers because they experimented with mixing contemporary Western compositional techniques and traditional Chinese forms. Chen eventually became the first woman composer to receive a Master's degree in composition in China, and she later earned her Doctor of Musical Arts degree from Columbia University. She is now a professor of composition at the University of Missouri, Kansas City.

Folksong

The folksongs *Mo Li Hua* and *Shui Xian Hua* (also found in this volume) are based on variations of the same melody (the tune itself has roots that go back hundreds of years). Chinese folksongs are generally divided into three types — work songs, mountain songs and ballads — depending on their singing contexts, social functions and musical features. *Mo Li Hua* is of the ballad type. Chinese ballads, sung in numerous settings by people of all backgrounds, are considered more 'artistic', because of the design of their phrasing and the flow of their melody, often reaching wide ranges. The melody for Chen Yi's arrangement spans nearly two octaves and is highly fluid, as can be seen by additional moving notes and embellishments.

While *Mo Li Hua* has many variations in different Chinese provinces, Chen Yi adapts the most famous version from Jiangsu province near Nanjing. This version became highly popularized from the late 1950s after being transcribed by the young He Fang during a field visit to the Jinniushan Reservoir of Nanjing's Liuhe District in the early 1940s, where he heard it sung and played on a Chinese fiddle by a local musician. The version of the text he encountered referred to a different flower in each verse (jasmine, honeysuckle and rose), and the second line of each verse began with 'the servant (slave) wants to pluck it'. He made the jasmine flower the sole focus, and did away with feudalistic references by changing the subject to 'I'. However, the romantic metaphor of unfulfilled desire remains.

This setting

This song is from the majority Han ethnic group, which constitutes over ninety per cent of the Chinese population. The tune has such a symbolic effect that it has been used to represent China on ceremonial occasions, and has even been adapted by Western composers such as Puccini. Chen Yi arranged it as part of a set of Chinese pieces commissioned for Chanticleer when she was Composer-in-Residence with the group during the 1990s. The SATB arrangement is set in the Jiangsu dialect, with Romanized text below the corresponding pitches. The syllables slightly deviate from the standard Mandarin pronunciation, which is the national dialect used in China. The Jiangsu dialect includes stopped 't' final consonants (where air is stopped before it is fully articulated) on syllables like 'yit' and 'but'. It also has a special 'ng' initial consonant on the word 'ngo' ('I').

The melody uses the anhemitonic pentatonic scale (five-note scale with no semitones) that is typical of Han Chinese folk music. Segments of the three verses are sung in unison or perfect fifths, but some underlying chords also group pentatonic pitches. The arranger includes various ornaments from the Chinese instrumental tradition, such as rising and falling acciaccaturas, downward *portamentos*, and folk style mordents. All of these enhance the melodious flow and folk flavour.

Performance notes

The unison melody requires a gentle, flowing motion. When it briefly divides, add a slight *tenuto* at the first point of departure (e.g. the third note of bar 2). Tune the shifting melodic fourths and unison pitches as you maintain the *legato* phrase, avoiding accents on higher phrase pitches. Embellishments, notated primarily for visual reference, require special stylistic attention. Grace-notes, which can fall just before the following sub-beat, should not be stressed, with tonal focus gradually weighted toward the primary notes. Sounding the upper-neighbouring mordents somewhere between a semitone and whole tone above the primary pitch will add to the folk flavour. Falling *portamentos* can be connected almost as *glissandi* but without too weighty a tonal focus. In bars 15–22 sopranos and altos should form their '*ha*' vowels during the preceding quaver rests and sing these unaccented. Take care that upper voices don't go sharp in bars 23–8, and in the penultimate bar get sopranos to add *tenutos* to the slowing '*ya*' pitches.

Literal translation

Hao yit duo mo li hua,   hao yit duo mo li   hua,
Good a   Jasmine flower, good a   Jasmine flower,

mun yun   hua kie   xiang ye xiang   but go   ta.
to fill garden flower to bloom scent so fragrant not more than it.

Ngo you   xin   cie   yit duo die,   you pa   ken   hua   di jen er   ma.
I   to have in mind to pick one   to wear, yet   to fear to watch flowers of person to curse.

Hao yit duo mo li   hua,   hao yit duo mo li   hua,
Good a   Jasmine flower, good a   Jasmine flower,

mo li   hua kie   xue ye bat but go   ta.
Jasmine flower to bloom snow so white not more than it.

Ngo you   xin   cie   yit duo die,   you pa   pang jen   xiu wa.
I   to have in mind to pick one   to wear, yet to fear other people to mock.

Hao yit duo mo li   hua,   hao yit duo mo li   hua,
Good a   Jasmine flower, good a   Jasmine flower,

mun yun   hua kie   bi   ye bi   but go   ta.
to fill garden flower to bloom contrast so comparable not more than it.

Ngo you   xin   cie   yit duo die,   you pa   lie   nin but fa ya.
I   to have in mind to pick one   to wear, yet to fear next year not to bud.

Mo Li Hua
茉 莉 花
Jasmine Flower

Jiangsu folksong
arr. Chen Yi

Jasmine flower, such a beautiful flower,

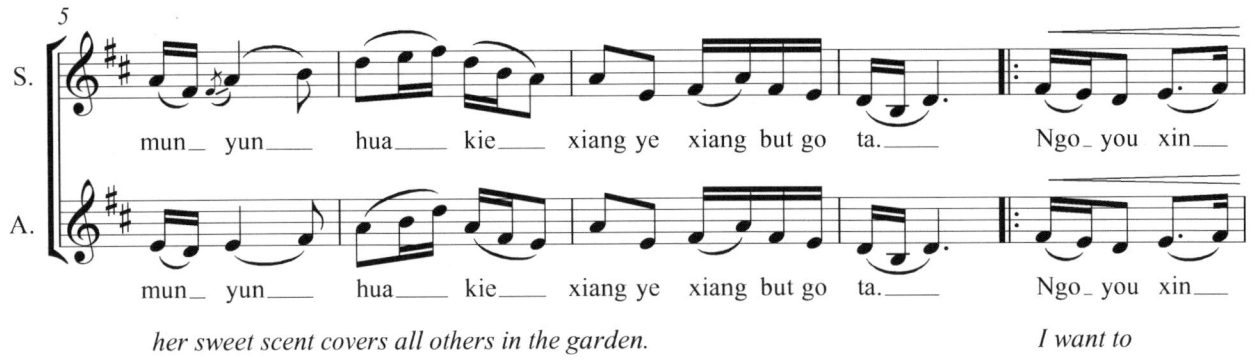

her sweet scent covers all others in the garden.   *I want to*

pluck her for myself,   *but I'm afraid of the garden's keeper.*

Copyright © 1995 by Theodore Presser Company. All rights reserved. Used with permission.

Jasmine flower, such a beautiful flower,

she is as white as snow when she is blooming.

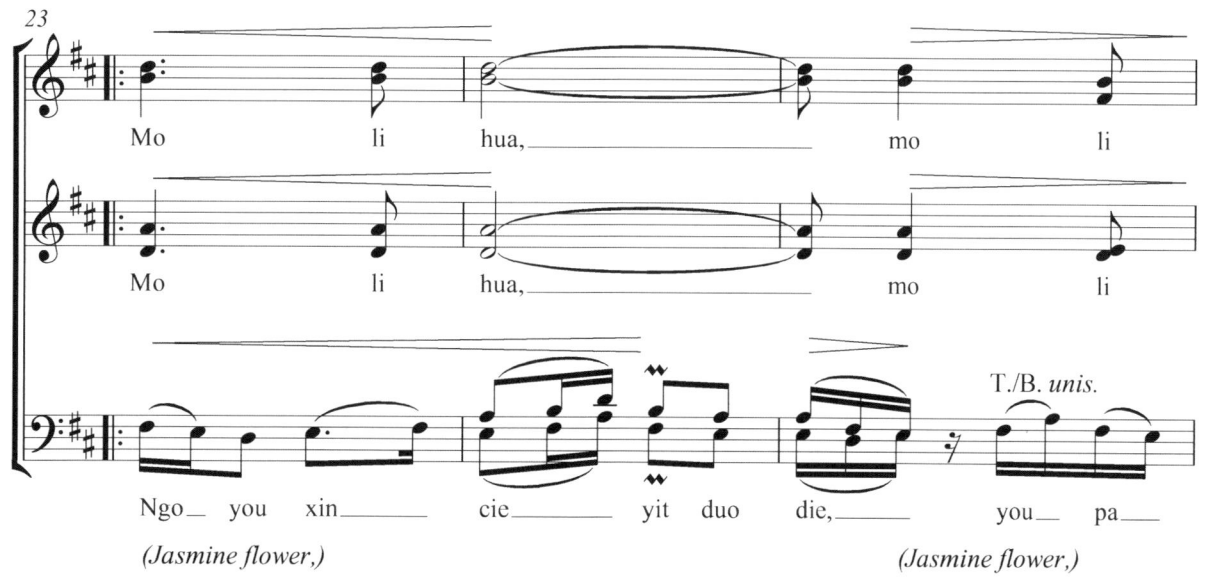

(Jasmine flower,)   (Jasmine flower,)

I want to pluck her for myself,   but I'm afraid of

* Sing lower note if possible.

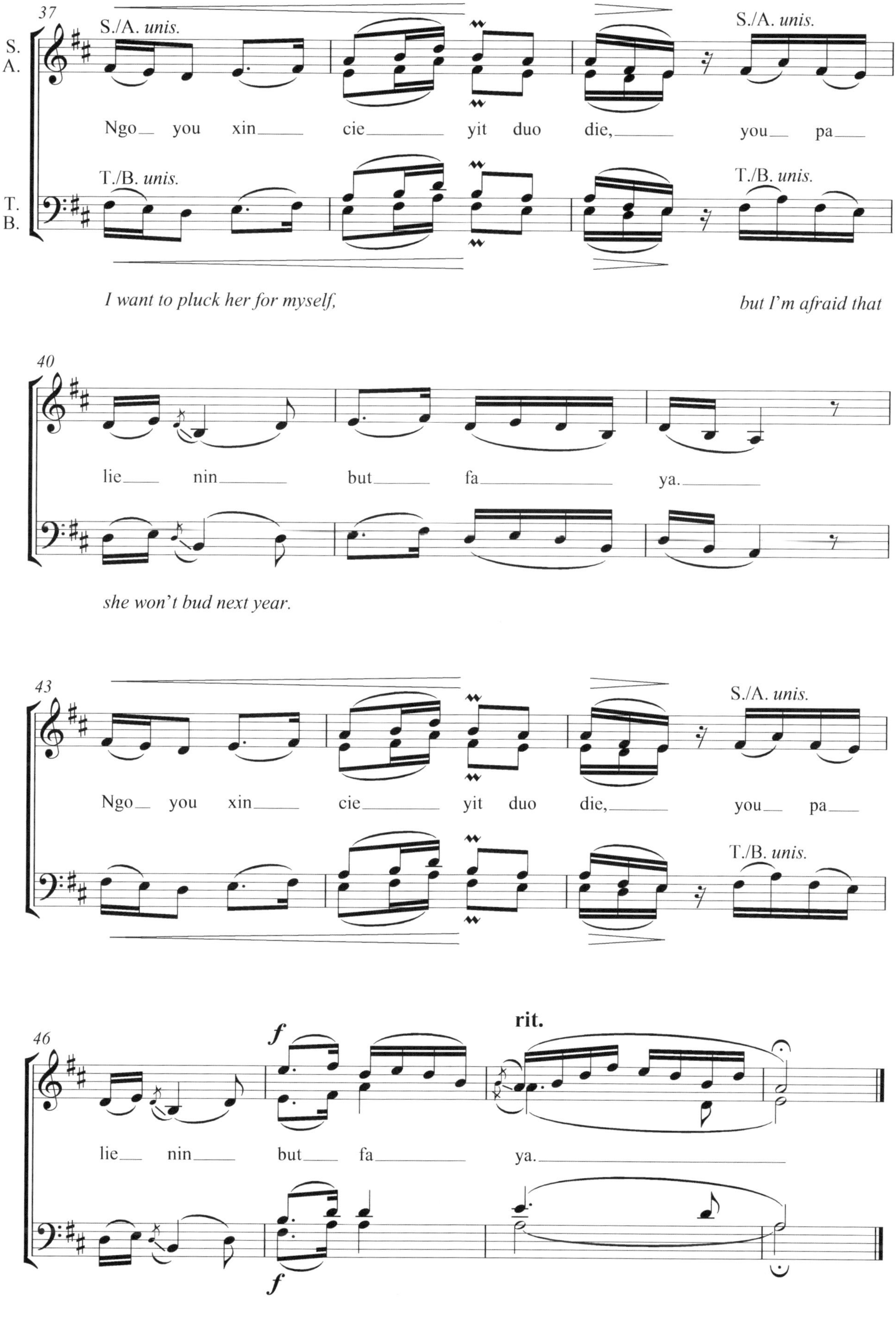

Mu Ge | Shepherd's Song

Mu Ge is an arrangement of a folk tune from eastern Mongolia in northern China.
Language: Mandarin.

Arranger

Qu Xixian (1919–2008) was a leading composer of Chinese choral music after the establishment of the PRC in 1949. Born in Shanghai, she received her degree in composition from the Shanghai National Training School of Music (now the Shanghai Conservatory of Music) in 1948. She then moved to Beijing, where her main work was with the Central Philharmonic Orchestra organization, alongside important posts in official PRC musical associations. Her arrangements and original compositions have been performed widely around China and internationally.

Folksong

Inner Mongolia is known for its rolling grasslands and tent-like yurt dwellings. Though vast in area, its population is relatively small for China. It includes the Han Chinese majority and nearly fifty different ethnic minority groups. Mongolians form the largest of these minority groups, and their nomadic, pastoral lifestyle is still widely practised today. Their unique traditional music is perhaps most famous for 'throat singing' (in which singers maintain a low-pitched drone and simultaneously produce higher melodic notes of the overtone series), along with tunes played on the horse-head fiddle. *Mu Ge* comes from another type called 'urtiin duu', or 'long song', so-called because many of the text syllables are sung over long durations. Long songs are important for many kinds of celebrations and festivities. They are highly ornamented, with the poetry usually praising the region's scenic beauty and expressing emotion for loved ones. The flowing melodies have extremely wide vocal ranges and are heavily embellished with scoops, trills, yodelling and sudden rhythmic changes.

This setting

Shortly after 1949, great attention was given to the national traditions of various groups and regions around China. Choral music was still relatively new to the country and there were few unaccompanied Chinese works. Qu Xixian arranged *Mu Ge* and two other Mongolian pieces for chorus from 1954 as part of this effort to create works based on China's own traditions. Her main inspiration came from hearing folksongs sung by the Mongolian musician Sherasi and the Chinese ethnomusicologist An Bo. She did not visit Mongolia herself, so she arranged the works based on her image of its landscape and lifestyle and from the advice they gave her.

The musical approach to *Mu Ge* combines Mongolian, Chinese and Western features, and the work is set in three verses plus a short introduction and closing section. Qu's overall idea was to create a scenic portrait using different approaches in each verse. The introduction sets the panoramic scenery in the background. Verse 1 paints the first layer of colours and shapes on the canvas. Verse 2 adds a deeper image of serenity, with tenors projecting above the other voices and sopranos lightly imitating the melody. Verse 3 is expansive and unrestrained, combining ideas from the first two verses. The ascending lines and sustained seventh chord of the closing section create an open-ended vision of the future. The original Mongolian song had two verses; Qu added the final lines in the style of Mongolian verse to show fresh optimism for the new People's Republic.

Other general features capture the spirit of the Mongolian song. The introduction starts in the lower alto range before leaping to the upper octave at the soprano entry in verse 1;

long, slow-moving notes are followed by sudden, rhythmic bursts; and the melody flows with ascending and descending lines. The subtle folk flavour is set within the framework of Western harmony and interaction among the different voice parts.

Performance notes

Mu Ge has gone through a number of revisions since its publication in the 1950s, so slight variations exist between different scores in print. In this edition some hairpin *decrescendos*, such as in bars 11–12 and 15–16, have been added for clarity of phrasing and dynamics. The flowing lines should not be interrupted by breaths, so maintain a plentiful supply of breath beyond the marks indicated. The *portamento* on the soprano 'ei' at the end of bar 12 indicates a general style: give enough length and weight to the F♮ before a light *portamento* to the lower pitch. The tenor 'shi' in bar 28 can be handled the same way or with a trill for contrast, as existed in an early version. In bar 65 sopranos can lightly rearticulate the high F on the second beat.

Literal translation

Cui lü di cao di shang ei pao zhe bai yang,
Emerald green of grass on hey are running white sheep,

yang qun xiang zhen zhu sa zai lü rong shang.
flocks of sheep like pearls to scatter at green velvet on.

Wu bian di cao yuan shi wo men di gu xiang,
Without boundary of grassland to be our homeland,

bai yun he qing tian shi wo men di peng zhang.
white clouds and blue sky to be our tent.

Zao xia ying jie wo zi you di ge chang,
Early red glow to greet me freely to sing,

sheng huo shi zhe yang xing fu huan chang!
life to be this way joyous happy!

Mu Ge
牧 歌
Shepherd's Song

Eastern Mongolian folksong
arr. Qu Xixian

White sheep run across the emerald green grasses,

© Qu Xixian. Reproduced by permission of the Music Copyright Society of China (MCSC).

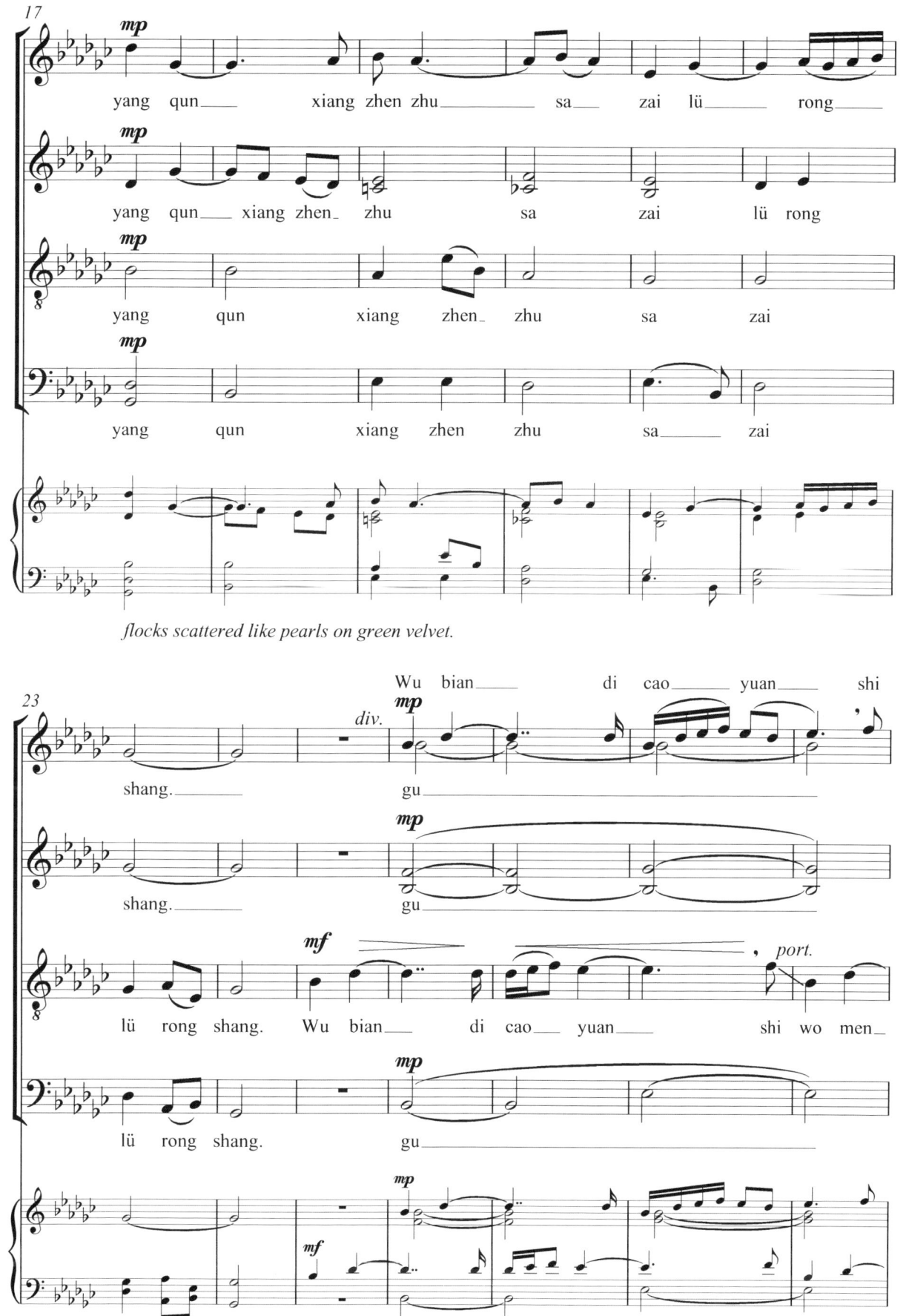

flocks scattered like pearls on green velvet.

The boundless grassland is our home,

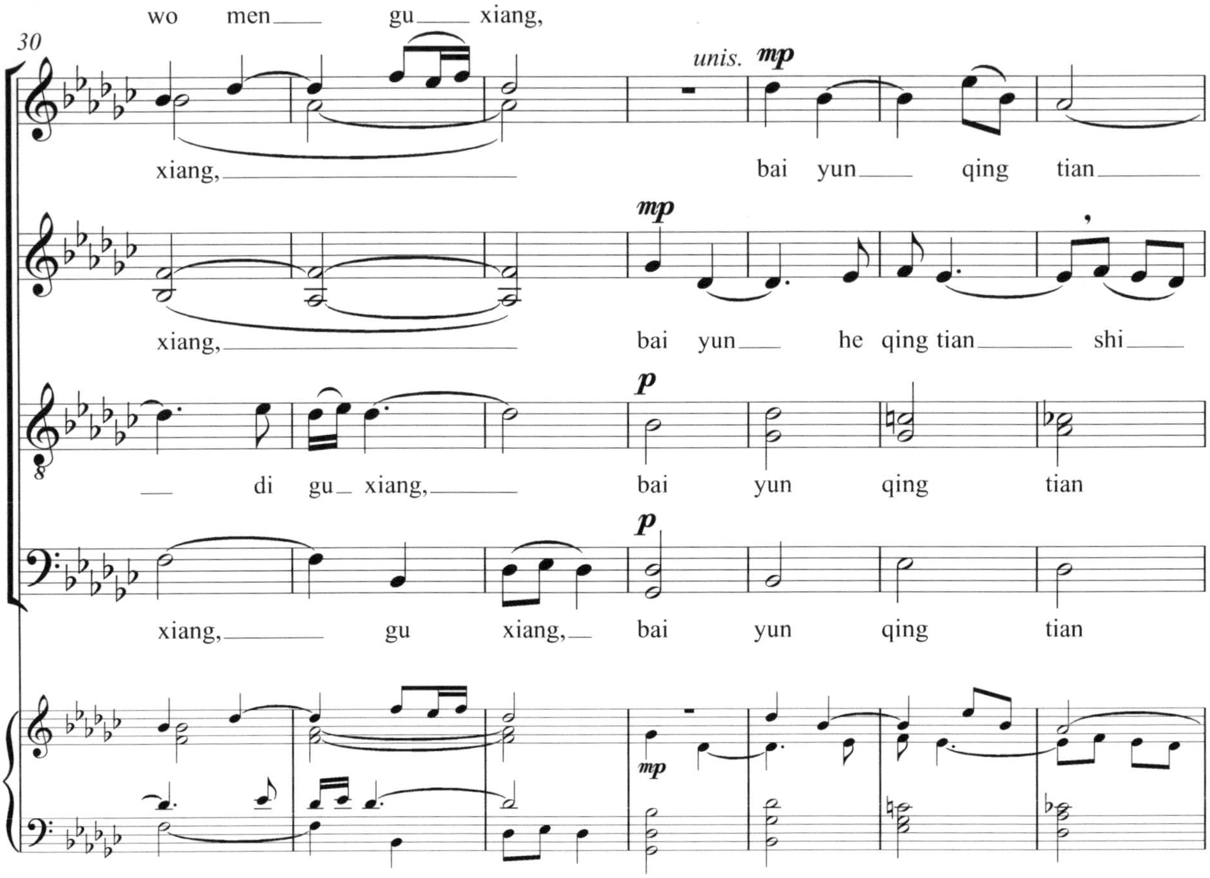
wo men gu xiang,
30
unis. mp
xiang, bai yun qing tian
mp
xiang, bai yun he qing tian shi
p
di gu xiang, bai yun qing tian
p
xiang, gu xiang, bai yun qing tian
mp

where white clouds and blue skies are our tents.

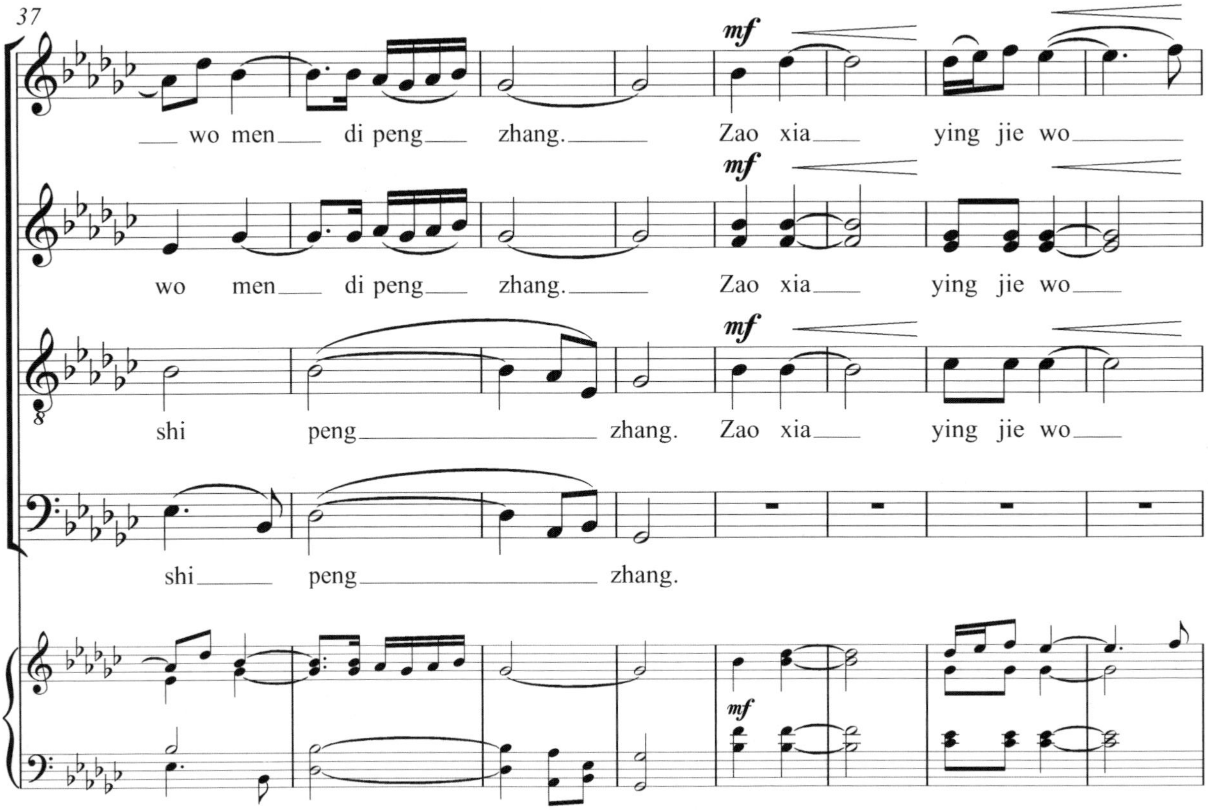
37
mf
wo men di peng zhang. Zao xia ying jie wo
mf
wo men di peng zhang. Zao xia ying jie wo
mf
shi peng zhang. Zao xia ying jie wo
shi peng zhang.
mf

The morning glow welcomes my carefree song,

such a life is so joyous and happy!

* This line may also be sung by altos.

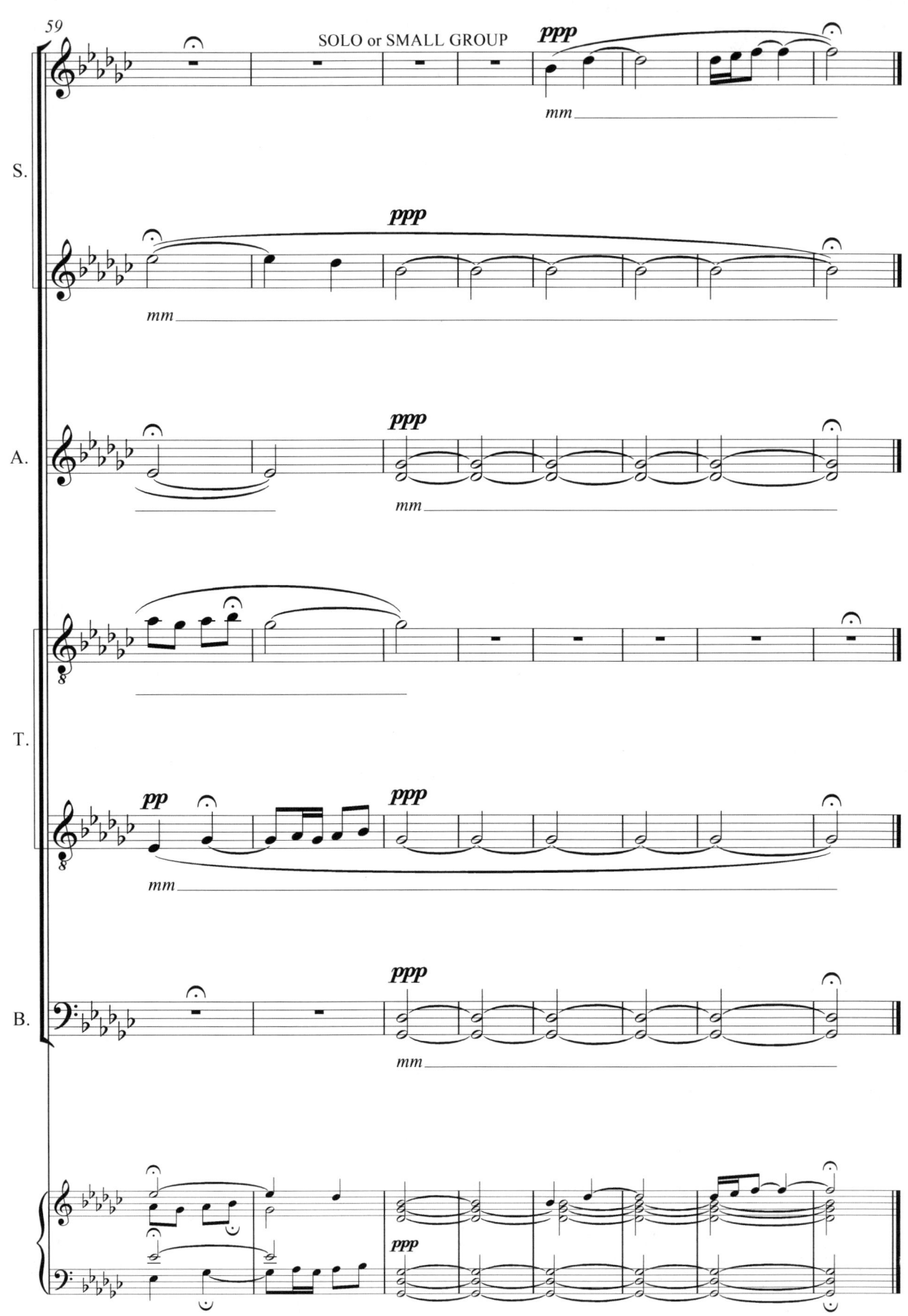

Pao Ma Liu Liu Di Shan Shang | Horses Run on the Mountain

Pao Ma Liu Liu Di Shan Shang is a popular song throughout China. Known also as the *Kangding Love Song*, it celebrates the mountainous Kangding area of western Sichuan province, which lies close to the southwestern edge of China, bordering Tibet. **Language**: Mandarin.

Folksong

Sichuan folk music reflects its different ethnic traditions, and its mountain songs are rich in melodic variety. Songs often reflect people's livelihoods, tied to the land, rivers and animals. The love songs of Kangding possess more subtle melodic contours, even as they describe the passionate emotions between females and males.

This 'Xikang' (western Kangding) folksong is believed to have originated in Kangding's Yala township around the 1930s, and was probably sung while doing daily work on the mountain, such as gathering firewood and herding. Originally called *Liu Liu Diao* (*Liu Liu Melody*), it was 'discovered' and set to accompaniment in the 1940s in nearby Chongqing, from where it quickly gained popularity throughout the country. The song itself is representative of music by Tibetans and other ethnic groups that inhabit that region. It is characterized by its mimicry of galloping horses, as well as its resounding tone and warm, gentle melodies. The melody uses the minor pentatonic, based on D in this arrangement and moving up a step at bar 55.

Text

The text is very characteristic of Western Sichuan. Each main text phrase contains seven Chinese characters, with the exception of the 'Yue liang wan wan' refrain, which has four. The text 'liu liu' is central to the work, appearing in each of the seven-syllable lines. The character 'liu' by itself means 'to flow'. However, it carries multiple meanings, and when the same character appears twice in a row ('liu liu'), it can take on various descriptive nuances that vary according to context, as seen in the different verses. In this way, the song becomes a play on words.

The themes of the four verses also reflect the Kangding region. The first verse creates the evening scene of the local landscape; the remainder treat the theme of rustic love. For example, verse 2 does not specifically refer to a daughter and son from actual Li and Zhang families; rather, these names are used more generally as part of local Chinese custom to refer to male and female youth. The use of 'ren cai' (talent) in verse 3 also carries a special usage in this particular region, meaning both 'beautiful' in Tibetan and 'pretty' in Chinese. And interjections like 'yo' that punctuate the text lines are commonly found in folksongs from this part of Sichuan.

This setting

In this choral arrangement the song verses are framed by an introduction and coda where the chorus sustains chords under the cry-like line of the soprano soloist. The fast folksong section is in contrast to this. The rapid '*la la la*' figures of the men's voices reflect the galloping horses and prepare for the opening text lines, which set the general scene of the piece, focusing on the mountain, clouds, moon and the city. The choral texture varies from verse to verse. After a brief hesitation at bars 52–4, there is a sudden outburst of new '*la la la*' figures in the chorus, marked by a new key centre and return to the fast tempo.

Performance notes

Balance is a key aspect of this arrangement, between the soloist and choir in the opening and closing sections, and between the melody and accompaniment in the verses. The *staccato* articulations for the *'la la la'* accompaniment should not be too clipped, but rather could be lengthened to reflect both forward momentum and the resonant, open mountain range. Melodic lines should be more fluid, with extra *legato* on 'Yue liang wan wan'.

In the verses, choirs should aim for a speed that suggests a forward galloping motion, but without undue haste. Tenor and bass parts in bars 5–22 may be reassigned to achieve a better balance. Altos should blend carefully with sopranos in the higher pitches at bar 57, or opt out seamlessly. Treat the tempo variations at bars 69–79 flexibly, to achieve a 'winding down' to the closing bars.

Within the text, triphthongs and diphthongs require adequate articulation of all vowels (including finals), but with a degree of evenness and connectedness (some even becoming glides). When 'wan' occurs on the descending minor third interval, it can be done with a tasteful *portamento*.

Literal translation

1.
Pao ma liu liu di shan shang, yi duo liu liu di yun yo.
To run horse gliding of mountain on, one gliding of cloud oh.

Duan duan liu liu di zhao zai, Kang ding liu liu di cheng yo.
The moon glistening of to lighten on Kangding neighbouring of city oh.

Yue liang wan wan, Kang ding liu liu di cheng yo.
The moon crescent, Kangding neighbouring of city oh.

2.
Li jia liu liu di da jie, ren cai liu liu di hao yo.
Li family stunning of elder daughter, pretty girl stunning of good oh.

Zhang jia liu liu di da ge, kan shang liu liu di ta yo.
Zhang family dazzling of elder son, to fall in love with swiftly of her oh.

Yue liang wan wan, kan shang liu liu di ta yo.
The moon crescent, to fall in love with swiftly of her oh.

3.
Yi lai liu liu di kan shang, ren cai liu liu di hao yo.
The first reason line of to fall in love, pretty girl stunning of good oh.

Er lai liu liu di kan shang, hui dang liu liu di jia yo.
The second reason line of to fall in love, can take care of proper of family oh.

Yue liang wan wan, hui dang liu liu di jia yo.
The moon crescent, can take care of proper of family oh.

4.
Shi jian liu liu di nü zi, ren wo liu liu di ai yo.
The world surrounding of girls, let me flowing of to love oh.

Shi shang liu liu di nan zi, ren ni liu liu di qiu yo.
The world surrounding of boys, let you selective of to choose oh.

Yue liang wan wan, ren ni liu liu di qiu yo.
The moon crescent, let you selective of to choose oh.

Pao Ma Liu Liu Di Shan Shang
跑 马 溜 溜 的 山 上
Horses Run on the Mountain

Xikang folksong
arr. Zhao Yushu

Horses run on the mountain,

© Zhao Yushu. Reproduced by permission.

wan, Kang ding liu liu di cheng yo.

wan, Kang ding liu liu di cheng yo.

la la la la la la la la   la la la la la la la la

la la la la la la la la   la la la la la la la la

and nearby Kangding city.

mf
Li jia liu liu di da jie, ren cai liu liu di hao yo.

p *stacc.*
la la la la la la la la   la la la la la la la la

p
la la la la la la la la   la la la la la la la la

mp *non stacc.*
Li jia liu liu di da jie, ren cai liu liu di

The stunning elder daughter of the Li family is a pretty girl.

The dazzling eldest son of the Zhang family swiftly falls in love with her.

The moon, the crescent moon, and he swiftly falls in love with her.

First he loves her because he knows she is pretty.

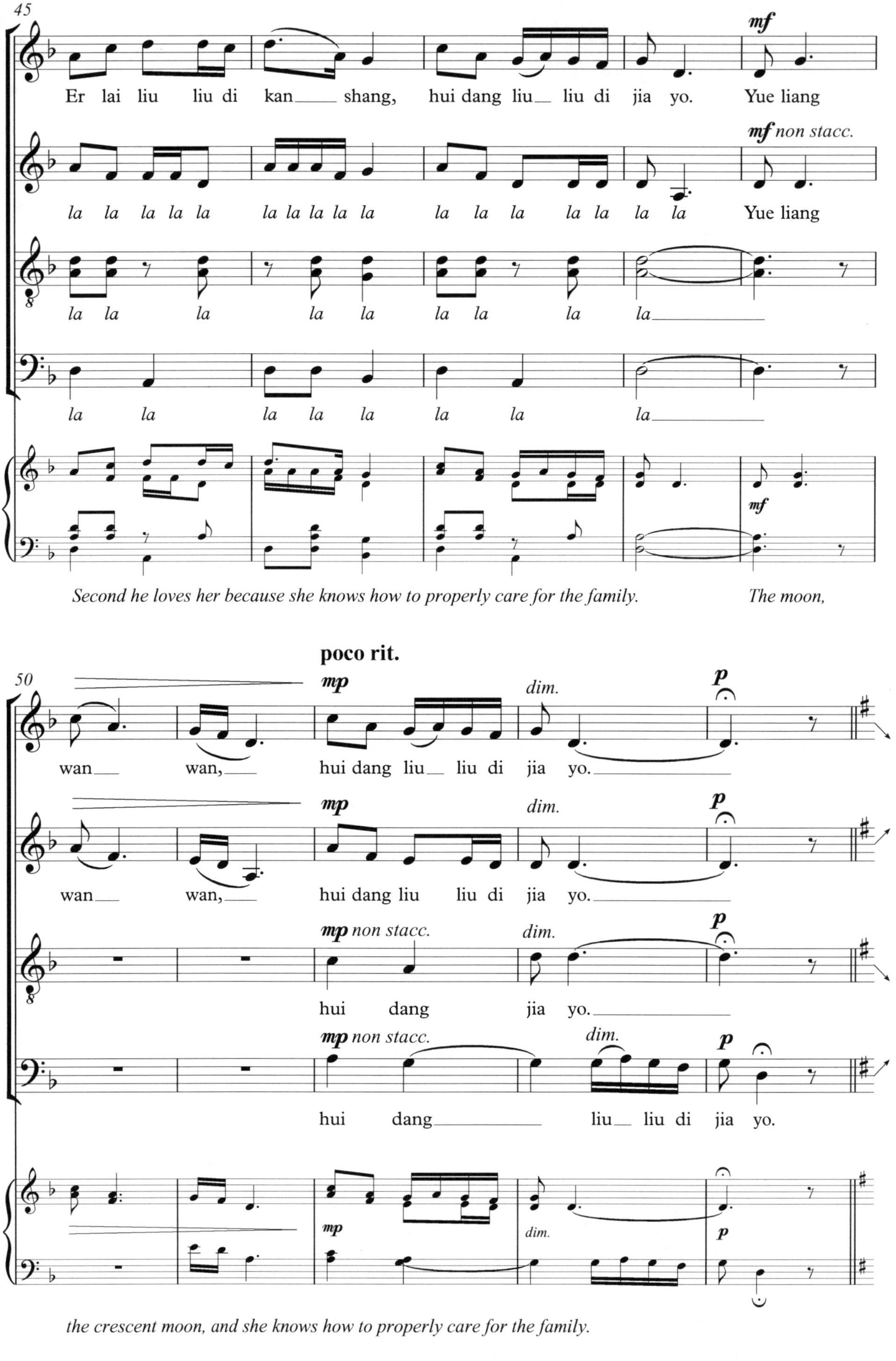
45
mf
Er lai liu liu di kan shang, hui dang liu liu di jia yo. Yue liang
mf non stacc.
la la la la la la la la la la la la la la la la la Yue liang
la la la la la la la la la
la la la la la la la la
mf
Second he loves her because she knows how to properly care for the family. The moon,
poco rit.
50
mp
dim.
p
wan wan, hui dang liu liu di jia yo.
wan wan, hui dang liu liu di jia yo.
mp non stacc.
hui dang jia yo.
hui dang liu liu di jia yo.
mp
dim.
p
the crescent moon, and she knows how to properly care for the family.

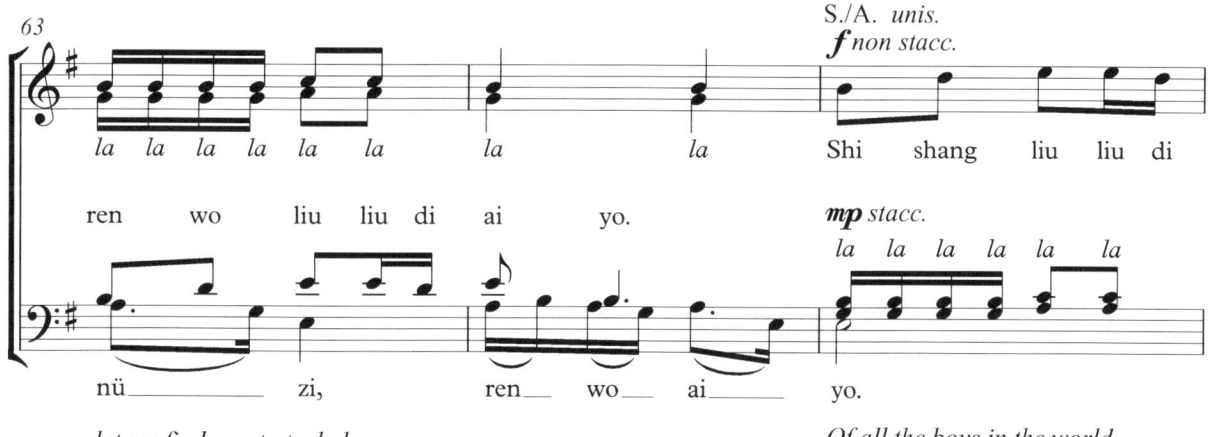

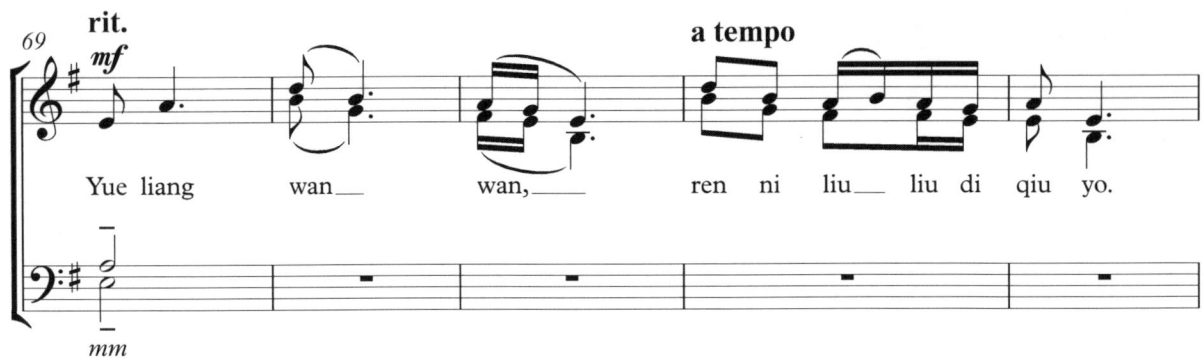

The moon, the crescent moon, and let you choose the right one.

Of all the boys in the world, let you choose the right one.

* The lower cue-sized pitches are an alternative to the upper notes.

Qing Chun Wu Qu | Dance of Youth

Qing Chun Wu Qu is based on a Uyghur folksong from northwestern China. The Mandarin text and florid piano mix with the folk melody and rhythms to create a modern Chinese choral arrangement. **Language**: Mandarin.

Arrangers

Wang Luobin (1913–96) was an eccentric figure in modern Chinese music. He was born in Beijing and joined China's war effort in the late 1930s, after which he spent much of his life in northwestern China. Wang suffered many years in prison, first in the early 1940s because of his communist ties, and later in the 1960s and 1970s for his connection to a warlord and for his perceived 'decadent' music. Over the decades he arranged many popular songs in Mandarin based on melodies or musical styles of northwestern ethnic groups. Some of them have ignited controversy because of their 'exotic' portrayal and authorship, but Wang was a genuine lover of these tunes.

Choral arranger Wang Shiguang studied composition at the Central Conservatory of Music. Some of his best known orchestral and vocal works were written when he was a composer for China's Central Opera. He has also held important administrative posts with the Central Opera Institute and the Chinese Musicians Association.

Folksong

The Uyghur ethnic group of northwestern China has a small population — under 10 million — in relation to the country's nearly 1.4 billion people. As well as love songs, historical songs and narratives, Uyghur traditional music includes dance songs, which are often performed accompanied by folk instruments at special social occasions, such as wedding festivities, harvest celebrations and local festivals.

Qing Chun Wu Qu was collected by Wang Luobin in 1939 (see *Ban Ge Yue Liang Pa Shang Lai*), after he heard it sung by a Uyghur raisin vendor in Gansu province. He revised the original tune structure and set it to Mandarin Chinese. The song has become popularized in its Mandarin version as a celebration of youth and love, and it became especially popular when recorded by singer Zhu Fengbo in a stylized, Chinese-Middle Eastern pop version in the 1970s.

The fast tempo and boisterous atmosphere reflect its short, playful text, which refers to recurring daily and seasonal cycles as shown by the sun, flowers and birds. But unlike the morning dawn and springtime bloom, the birds — and metaphorically love — only have one chance at youth! In contrast to many pentatonic tunes in this anthology, *Qing Chun Wu Qu* is based mainly on the first five notes of the minor scale. The text phrases vary in length, with longer phrases on the first, second, fourth and sixth phrases, and shorter ones on the third and fifth. In each case, they begin with short, fast rhythms and end on longer-held notes.

This setting

Wang Shiguang arranged the song for accompanied chorus in the 1990s, since when it has gained popularity with Chinese choirs. While the main tune and text as notated by Wang Luobin had seven main phrases, this choral version eliminates one of these. The second, fourth and sixth phrases are similar, while the first, third and fifth ones vary. The work features a florid, fast-moving piano part and three repeating verses in different voice combinations and textures. The outer verses are in G minor, while the middle verse is in D minor. The dynamic level builds from one verse to the next, climaxing in the final bars.

Performance notes

This work requires a balancing of brisk yet manageable tempos for choir and pianist alike. Anything under ♩=148 could seem languid, while exceeding 162 could result in uncontrollable tone and incomprehensible text. Feeling the piece in two (at ♩=76) will help determine the flowing style and tempo. Pianists should be especially careful to feel the piece in a flowing two, so as to avoid sounding agitated on moving quavers, offbeat accents and rapid runs.

Each verse requires careful attention to contrasting dynamics between phrases and among voices within certain phrases. In the first two verses give dynamic priority to melodic voices. The *accelerando* at 16 suggests taking bars 14–15 very slowly (around half tempo), which is customary, but aim for a coordinated and even *accelerando* back to tempo at 18. Corresponding passages at 30 and 46 would usually be taken at full tempo. 'Bie de na yo yo' (bar 18) is playful and can have slight separation between 'yo yo', where the first 'yo' is shorter than the second. The repeating section at bar 50 can be sung in a hushed tone the second time to prepare for a grander ending. Feel free to add a breath before the final 'lai' in bar 56 for dramatic effect. Practise speaking the verse text, gradually getting faster each time, so that it becomes second nature when singing at Allegro tempo. Try breaking up text phrases and repeating groups of four syllables, keeping lips and jaw loose; then put them together in two-bar phrases.

Literal translation

Tai yang luo (xia)   shan   ming zhao   yi jiu pa   shang lai,
Sun   to set (go down) mountain next morning still to climb up   to come,

hua er xie   liao   ming nian hai shi yi yang di   kai,
flowers to wither to finish next year still the same manner to open,

mei li xiao niao fei   qu   wu   zong ying,
pretty little bird to fly away without trace,

zhi   you   qing chun xiao niao yi yang bu   hui   lai.
only to have youth   little bird the same not to return to come.

Bie   de   na yo yo, bie   de   na yo yo,
Do not to become that oh oh, do not to become that oh oh,

zhi   you   qing chun xiao niao yi yang   bu hui   lai.
only to have youth   little bird the same not to return to come.

Qing Chun Wu Qu
青 春 舞 曲
Dance of Youth

Uyghur folksong
arr. Wang Luobin
choral arr. Wang Shiguang

Allegro ♩ = c.154

Tai yang luo shan ming zhao yi jiu pa shang lai, hua er xie liao ming nian hai shi pa shang lai, ah

The sun sets over the mountain, but still rises the next day, the flower withers but still blossoms

A simplified piano accompaniment is available to download at www.editionpeters.com/halfmoonrising

© Wang Luobin and Wang Shiguang. Reproduced by permission.

128

anew the next year,   *the sun sets over the mountain*

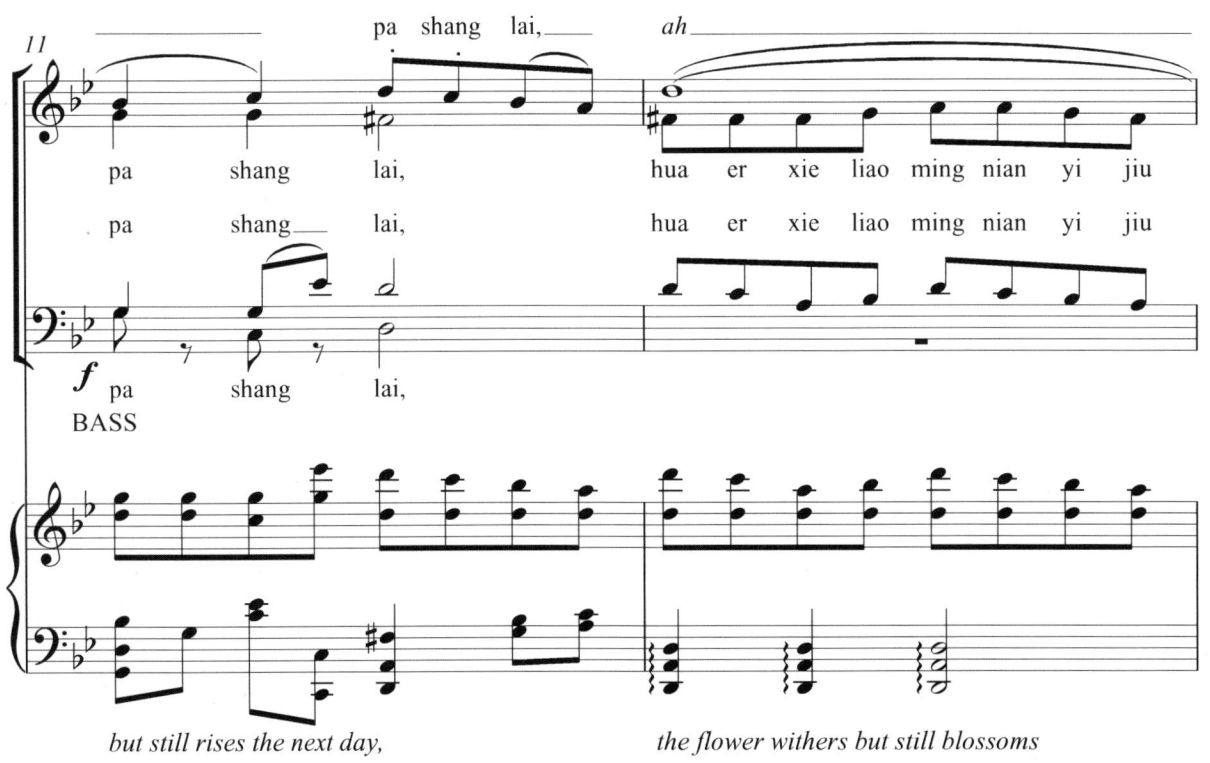

but still rises the next day,   *the flower withers but still blossoms*

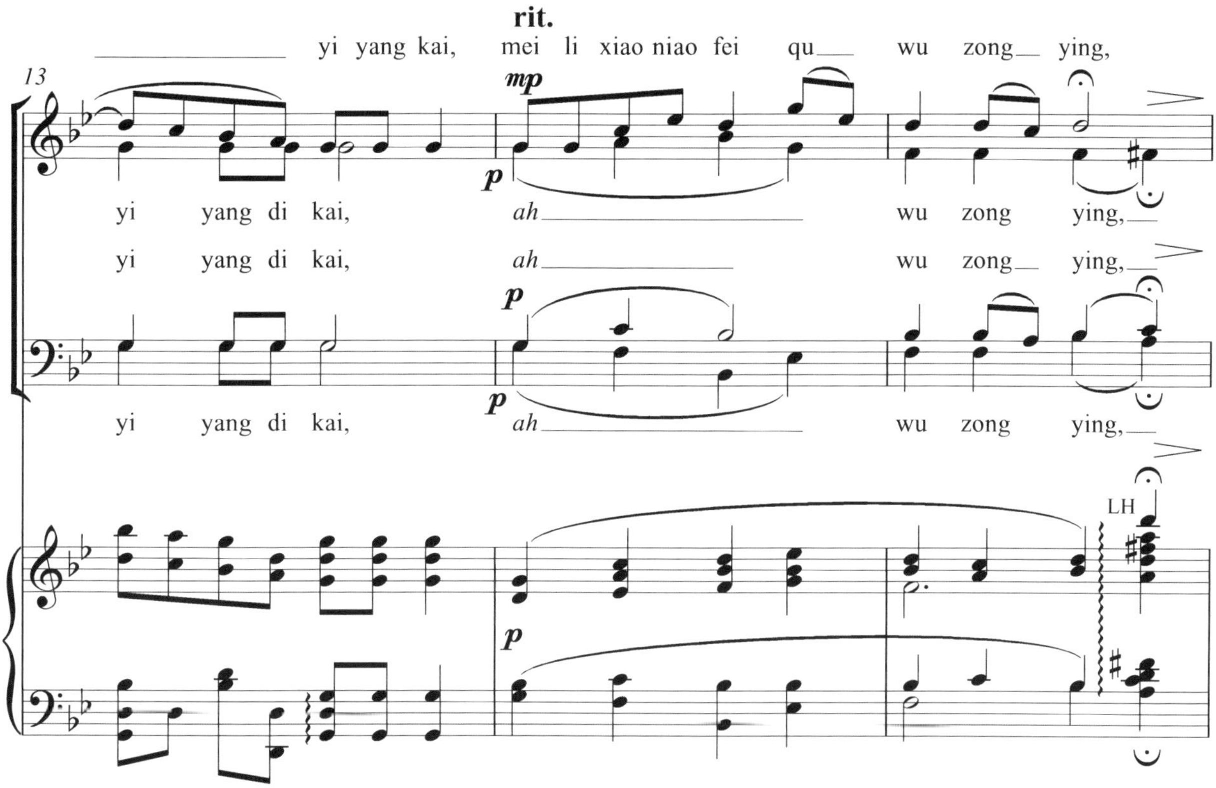

The sun goes down behind the mountain but still rises the next day,

the flower withers but still blossoms anew the next year,

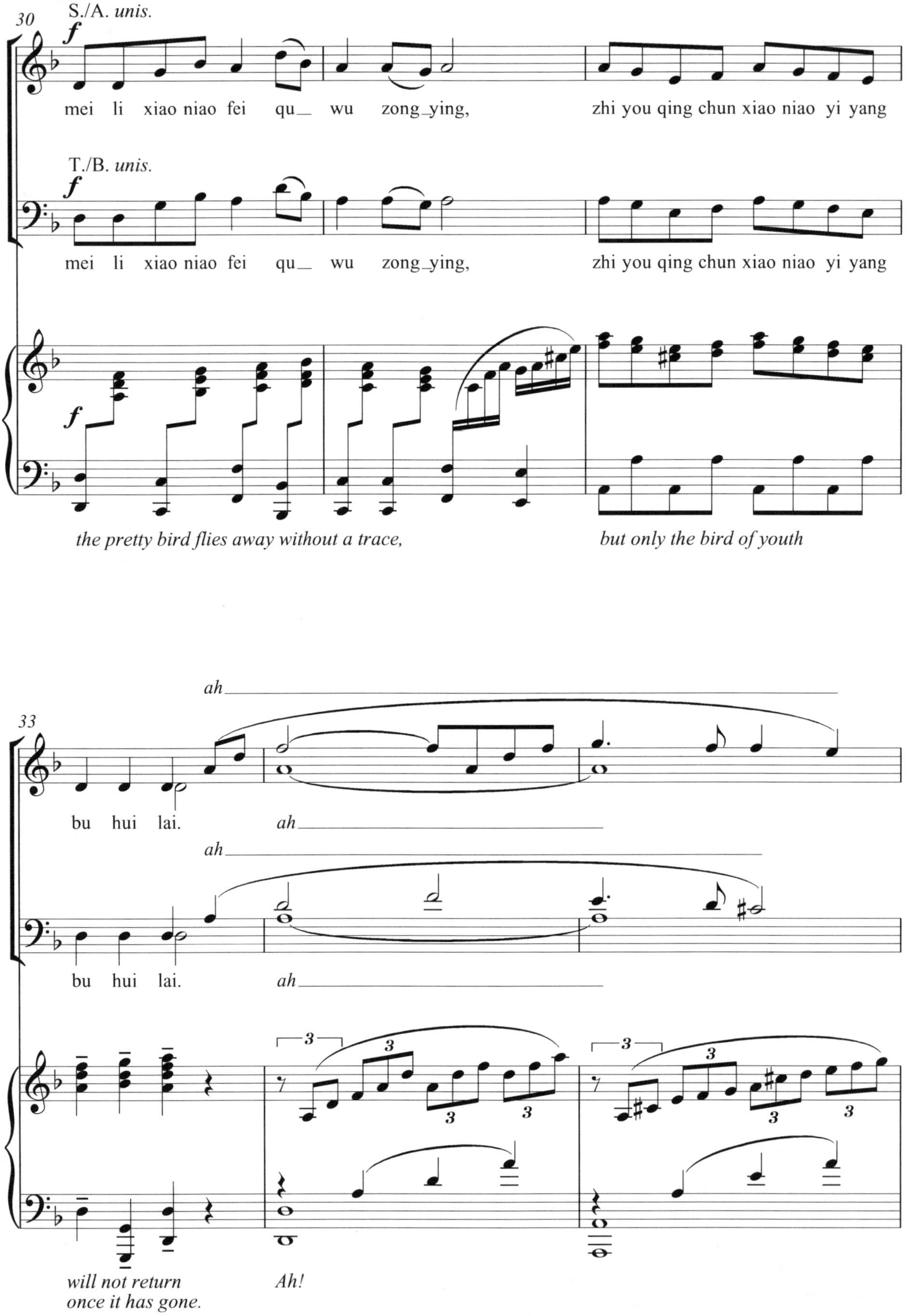

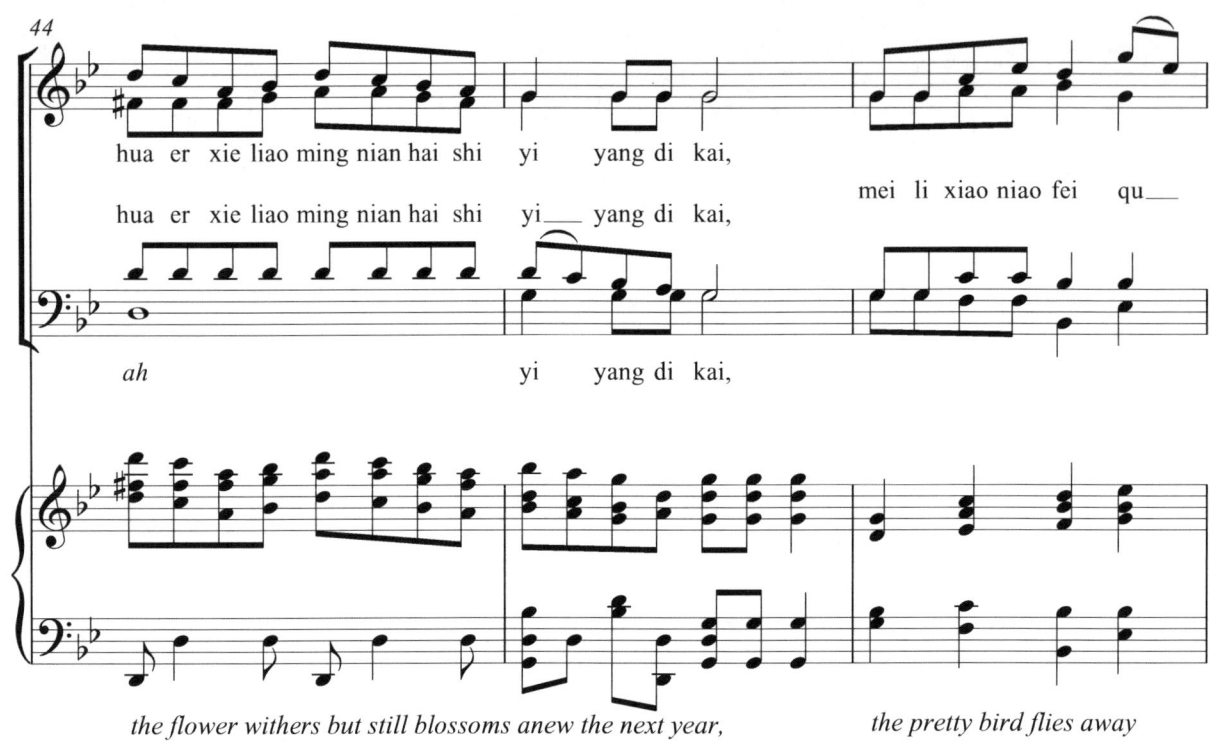

Ru Meng Ling | Like a Dream

Ru Meng Ling is a modern choral setting of two twelfth-century Chinese poems, originally written for an ancient tune of the same title. **Language**: Mandarin.

Composer

Richard Tsang has been a leading advocate of contemporary music composition in Hong Kong and internationally. Among his most noteworthy posts, Tsang has served as President of the International Society for Contemporary Music (ISCM) and Founding Chairman of the Hong Kong Composers' Guild. He was also Vice-Chairman of the Asian Composers League, and he founded a number of important international arts events in Hong Kong. As a composer, Tsang has received over sixty commissions and numerous performances from various local and international bodies. He was also a Founding Music Director of the Hong Kong Sinfonietta and has been active as guest conductor of performing groups in Hong Kong. Tsang received his Ph.D. in composition from the University of York, and he is currently a professor at the Hong Kong Institute of Education.

Text

This piece sets texts from two famous but different poems entitled *Ru Meng Ling* written by the Song Dynasty (960–1279) poet Li Qingzhao (1084–c.1155). The poems are similar in structure: both six lines long and based on a rhyming pattern of the ancient *Ru Meng Ling* tune, both full of symbolism, and both dealing with bitter reality and intoxication. Li Qingzhao was said to have experienced tremendous loneliness at the absence and then early death of her husband. The first poem, 'Zuo ye yu shu feng zhou', was written from the point of view of a lonely woman who recognizes the temporary nature of youthful beauty as represented by the colours of the begonias. The second, 'Chang ji xi ting ri mu', recalls the days of Li's youth spent at the Brookside Pavilion Spring in her hometown of Jinan, Shandong province. It also symbolizes the loss of carefree innocence.

This setting

Song Dynasty poets often wrote texts to well-known melodies of the time, and *Ru Meng Ling* was one such tune. Very few of these ancient tunes have been preserved, however. This new choral setting was commissioned by the Hong Kong Chorus in 1979 without any direct relation to the original melody. Instead, the composer's intention was to imagine the mood of Song Dynasty music within a modern framework. Both poems unfold in partially repeating verses, overlapping in the final two verses but with their own distinctive themes. The first poem is sung by the sopranos and altos, the second by tenors and basses. They are accompanied by a recurring, ascending bass line in the left hand and moving countermelody in the right hand of the piano that represents the restrained frustration of the poet. The dream-like state of the verses is framed by a piano introduction and postlude, in which the rapid sounding of pitches at different octaves portrays the imaginary bells of distant temples. The six-bar, chordal 'ah!' sung by all voices near the end is not from the original poems, but was added by the composer as a long, sighing gesture of grief and loneliness. It occurs 'misterioso' at the point of harmonic resolution in the F phrygian mode for a greater sense of completion to the work.

Performance notes

Give strong attention to the piano characterization and contrasting dynamic shades. The vocal quality should be ethereal in all voices, with emphasis on the floating melodic lines. SATB dynamic levels should never exceed *mf*. Sopranos should work toward achieving a free tone on the A flat 'Shi wen' by balancing adequate air pressure with high, forward focus on the 'wen' vowel. Sopranos and tenors should also prepare for the high F entry in bar 62 by phonating their respective vowels on the preparation breath. The subtle variations in *tenuto* articulations need attention from verse to verse, and the *staccato* vocal-piano chords in bars 50–1 should be distinctly chime-like with a slight rhythmic restraint. Form a 'w' glide in the lips before articulating the initial consonants on 'zuo' and 'juan'. The 'i' vowel on 'shi', 'zhi' and 'ri' is placed high and forward, sounding similarly to the first syllables of English 'Shirley' and 'jerky'.

Literal translation

Zuo ye   yu shu   feng zhou,   nong shui bu xiao   can   jiu.
Last night rain sparse wind abrupt, sound sleep not dispel residual wine.

Shi   wen   juan   lian   ren,   que dao   hai tang yi   jiu.
To try to ask to roll window shade person, but to speak begonia according to former.

Zhi   fou?   Zhi   fou?   Ying   shi   lü   fei   hong shou.
To know or not? To know or not? Should to be green fertile red thin.

Chang ji   xi   ting   ri mu, chen   zui   bu zhi   gui   lu.
Always to remember the stream pavilion sunset, to become intoxicated not to know to return route.

Xing   jin   wan hui   zhou, wu   ru   ou   hua   shen chu.
Interest exhausted late to return boat, mistakenly to enter lotus flower deep part.

Zheng   du,   zheng   du,   jing   qi   yi tan   ou lu.
To strive to pass through, to strive to pass through, in surprise to start a flock of herons.

Ru Meng Ling
如夢令
Like a Dream

Words by Li Qingzhao

Richard Tsang

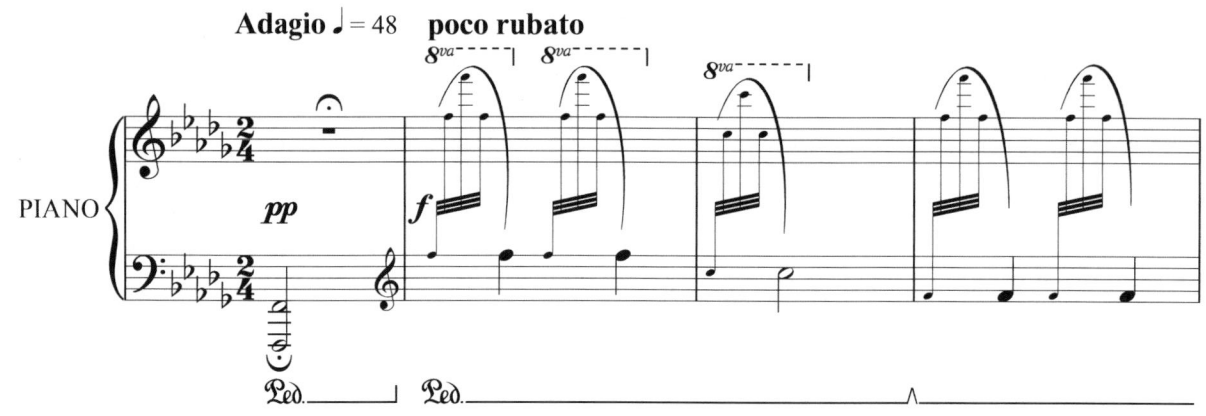
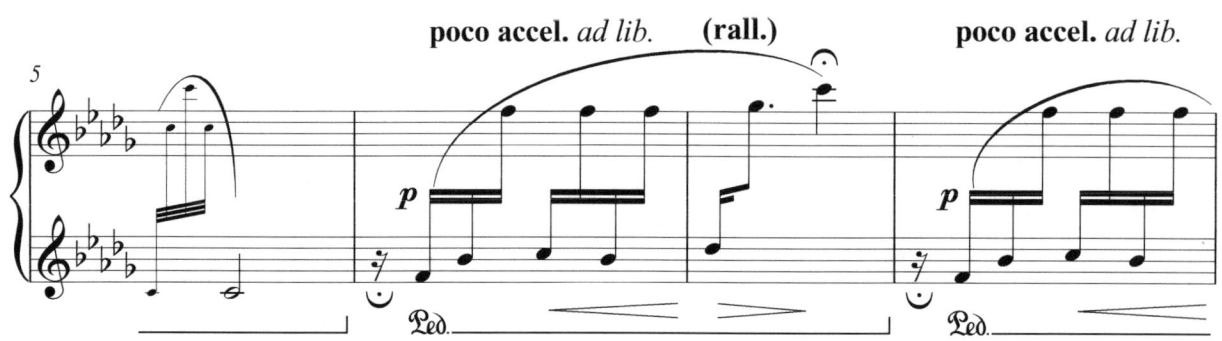
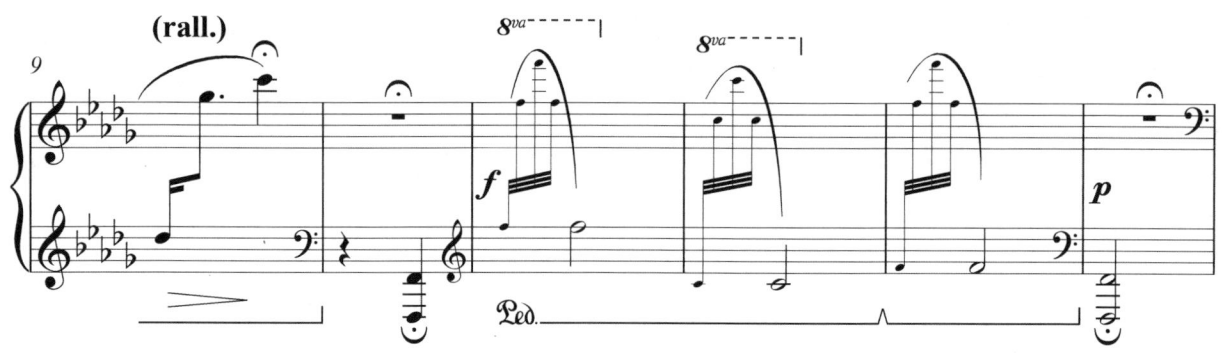

© 1982 by Richard Tsang. Reproduced by permission of the composer.

Wouldn't you know? Wouldn't you know?   The green leaves should grow

*fertile and the red
flowers should fade.*

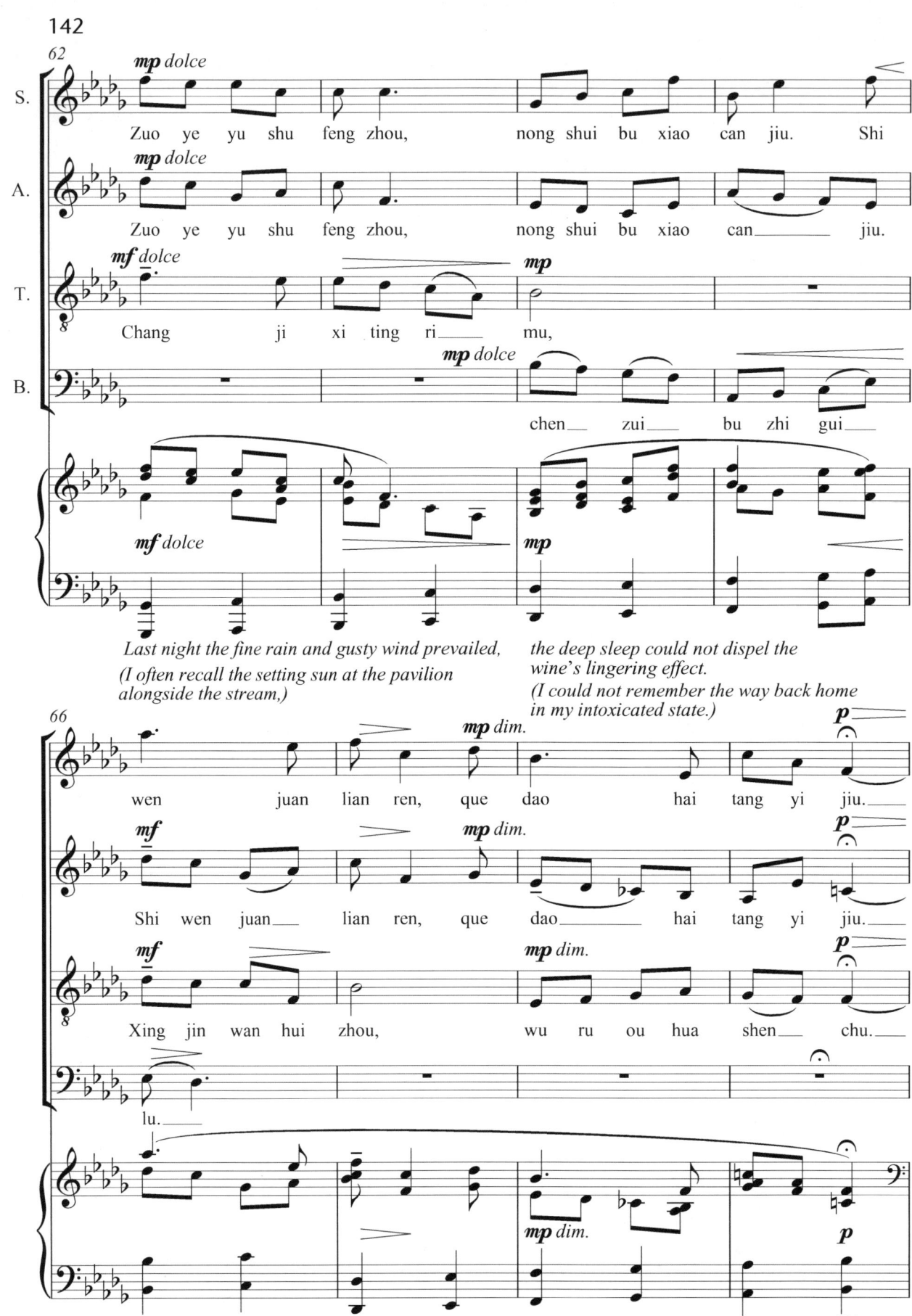

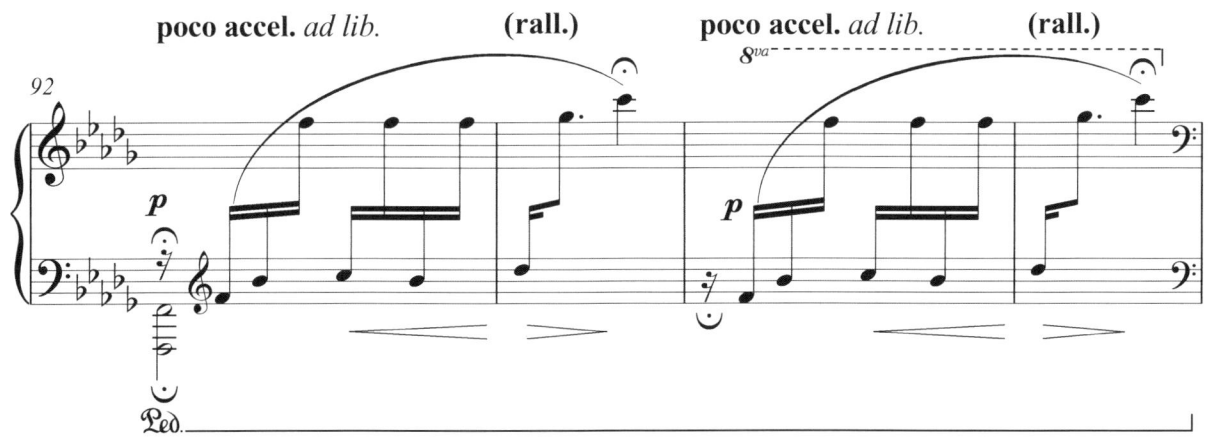

should grow fertile and
the red flowers should fade.

suddenly flew skyward
in surprise.)

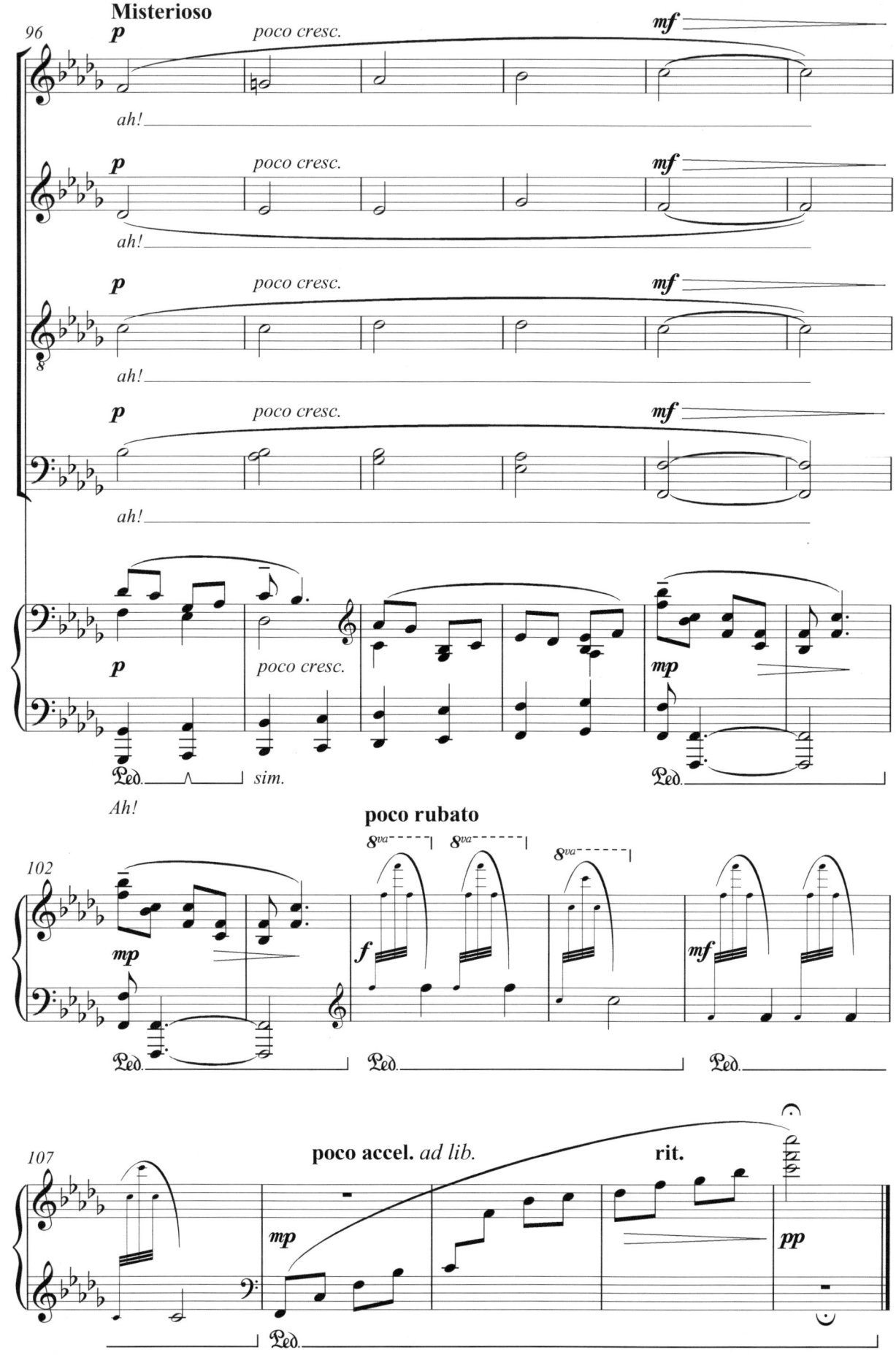

Seui Diu Go Tau | Under the Mid-Autumn Moon

Seui Diu Go Tau is a setting of an ancient poem about the Mid-Autumn Festival, traditionally one of the most important family occasions on the Chinese lunar calendar. **Language**: Cantonese.

Composer

Chan Kai-Young is a Benjamin Franklin Doctoral Fellow in composition at the University of Pennsylvania. Originally from Hong Kong, Chan received both his Bachelor and Master degrees from the Chinese University of Hong Kong Department of Music. His music has been performed by the Pittsburgh Symphony Orchestra, the Curtis Symphony Orchestra, the Daedalus Quartet, the International Ensemble Modern Academy, Ensemble XXI and the Hong Kong New Music Ensemble. Chan has also been featured in noteworthy international festivals, and he has won various composition competitions and scholarships in North America and Asia.

Text

'When will the moon be bright and clear?' is a famous work by Su Dongpo (also known as Su Shi, 1037–1101) from the Song Dynasty (960–1279). *Seui Diu Go Tau* (Water Melody Prelude) is the Cantonese title of the tune it would have been sung to. The poem praises the exquisite vision of the moon during the annual Chinese Mid-Autumn Festival and reminds the poet of his beloved brother Zi You, whom he has not seen for a long time. The poem's introduction (not included in the choral text) reveals the author's state while composing the work: 'During the Mid-Autumn Festival in the year *Bing Chen*, I drank happily until dawn and in a drunken state wrote this poem while thinking of *Zi You*'. The first two verses express resentment at the moon for reaching fullness only at moments of separation. But the final verse expresses the poet's hope for reunion with his family in spirit under the full moon of mid-autumn.

This setting

This piece was conceived in Philadelphia at the time of the Chinese Mid-Autumn Festival, which takes place every year on the fifteenth day of the eighth month of the lunar calendar. The full moon is a symbol of reunion and thoughts for families and friends in Chinese culture because 'full' and 'reunion' share the same written character. The custom of celebrating with family and friends dates back to at least a thousand years ago, and the moon has thus become a recurring theme in classical Chinese literature.

The tonal nature of spoken Cantonese creates a closer relationship between recitation and singing than exists in Western languages. Cantonese is the local dialect of Hong Kong and one of the oldest dialects in China. (Mandarin has been the official Chinese language for only several hundred years.) Whereas Mandarin has four main tones, Cantonese has nine tones at various registers. Hong Kong secular choral works have usually been written for performance in Mandarin, while Cantonese has generally been more limited to sacred works. Like most Hong Kong students, Chan Kai-Young learned to recite *Seui Diu Go Tau* in Cantonese during his school years, and in this choral setting he closely allies the melody of the different poem phrases with the Cantonese inflections as it might be recited.

Performance notes

This work calls for close attention to the piano part, as well as the Cantonese pronunciation and realization in the vocal lines. Pianists can help characterize the poem by the gestures scored in different sections. Bars 1–4 can be played somewhat freely, rather than in strict triplet rhythms. The four-note sequence of grace-notes that appear in the left hand throughout the work (bars 6, 9, 15 and later) are played before the downbeat in the style of a plucked Chinese *guzheng* zither (not too fast but directed toward the primary note, with each pitch getting distinct articulation). Maintain a light, forward motion in the moving right-hand part from bar 15, and place the grace-notes in bars 21–2 just before the left-hand notes. Bring out the three-beat grouping against the voices at 32 and 55. Play the section at bar 37 lightly as a texture variation. Bars 47–9 should be definitive without overshadowing the voices.

In the voice parts, thoroughly practise the spoken, *legato* Cantonese syllables before singing on pitches, and note that they are both related to yet quite distinct from Mandarin. (Refer to the online Pronunciation Guide and audio samples.) The grace-notes are more declamatory than musical as part of the natural Cantonese inflection. They should be connected to the primary notes and sung on the beat — sing them fast but not accented. In this piece Cantonese diphthongs should go quickly to the second vowel for sustaining (unlike *bel canto* singing). Give resonance to the many 'n' final consonants that appear throughout.

Literal translation

1.
Ming yut gei si yau?
Bright moon what time to have?

Baa jau man ching tin.
To hold wine to ask blue sky.

Bat ji tin seung gung kyut, gam jik si ho nin.
Not to know sky above palace, current season to be which year?

Ngo yuk sing fung gwai heui, yau hung king lau yuk yu,
I to want to ride wind to return to go, but to fear jade building jade room,

gou chyu bat sing hon.
lofty place not to overcome cold.

Hei mou nung ching ying, ho chi joi yan gaan?
To rise to dance to play moonlit shadow, how to appear at humans among?

2.
Jyun jyu gok, dai yi wu, jiu mou min.
To turn red pavilion, to hang silk window, to illuminate no sleep.

Bat ying yau han, ho si cheung heung bit si yun?
Not should to have to hate, why happening always toward parting moment full?

3.
Yan yau bei fun lei hap, yut yau yam ching yun kyut,
Humans to have sorrow joy parting reunion, moon to have dim bright full scarce,

chi si gu nan chyun.
this happening ancient difficult to be perfect.

Daan yun yan cheung gau, chin lei gung sim gyun.
May to bless humans long life, thousand miles to share beautiful moon.

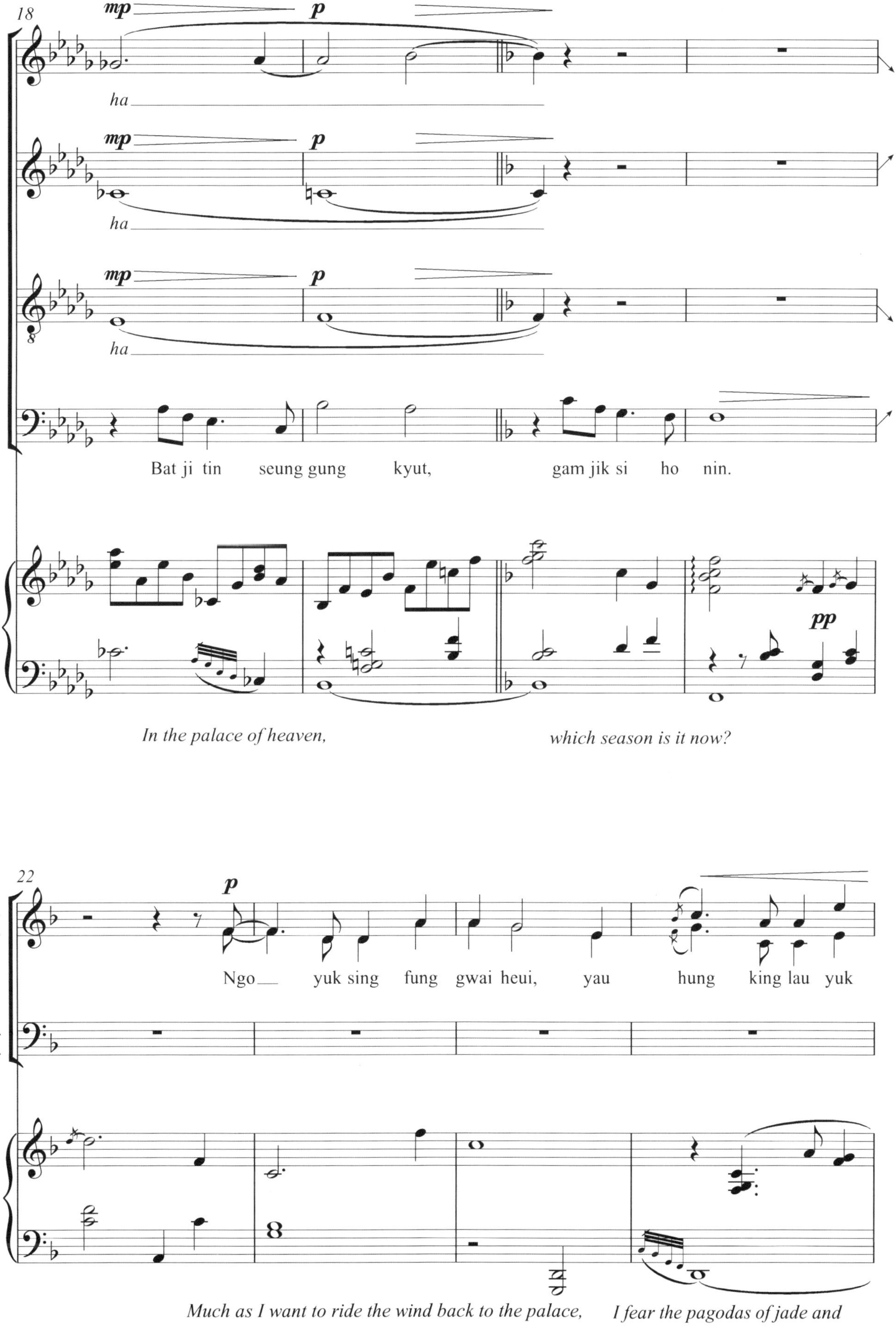

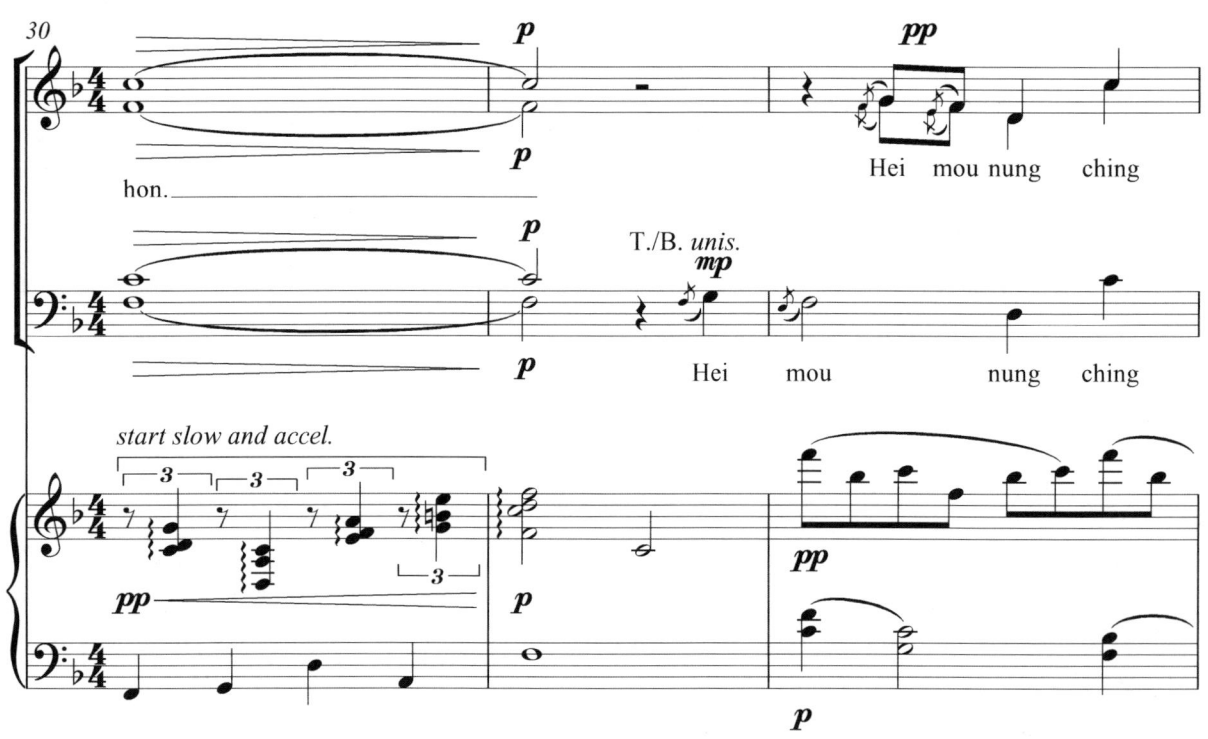

how can I remain part of the mundane world?

The turning moonbeam is shed on the rouge mansion, hanging upon the silk-padded window,

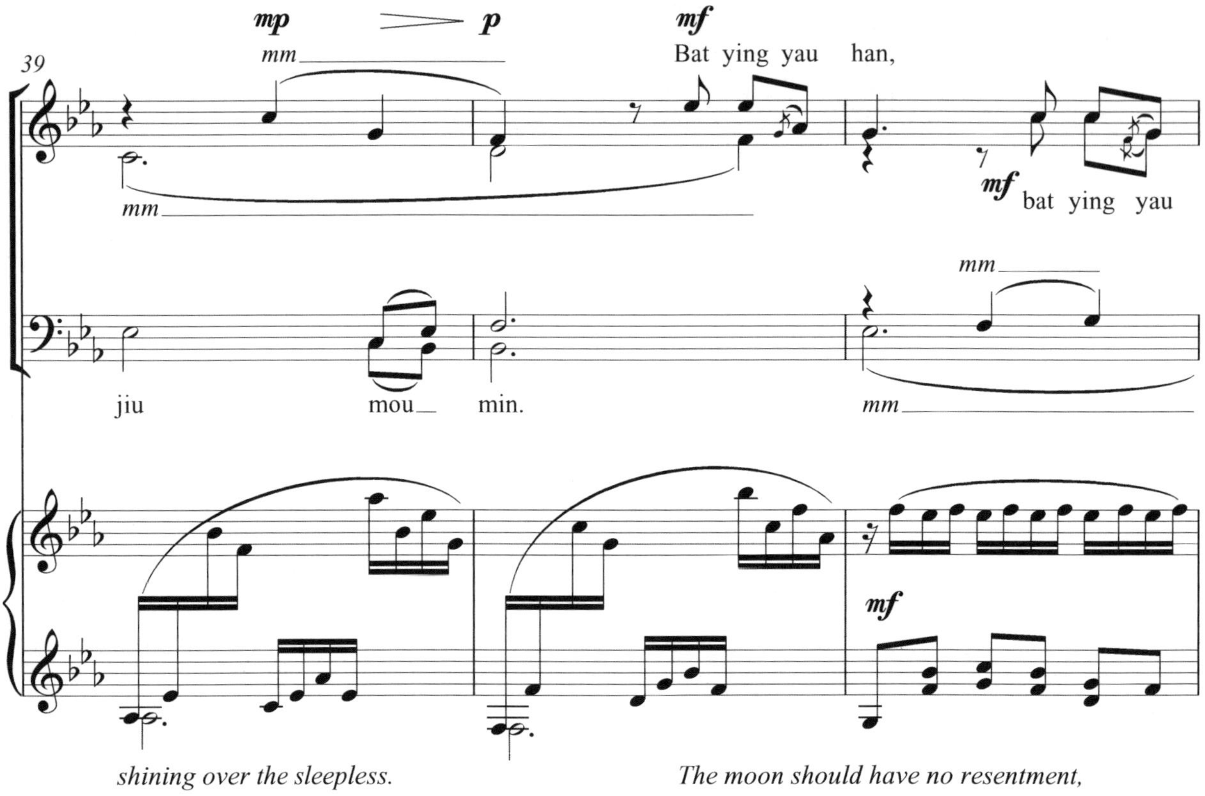

The moon should have no resentment,

but why is it always full in parting moments?

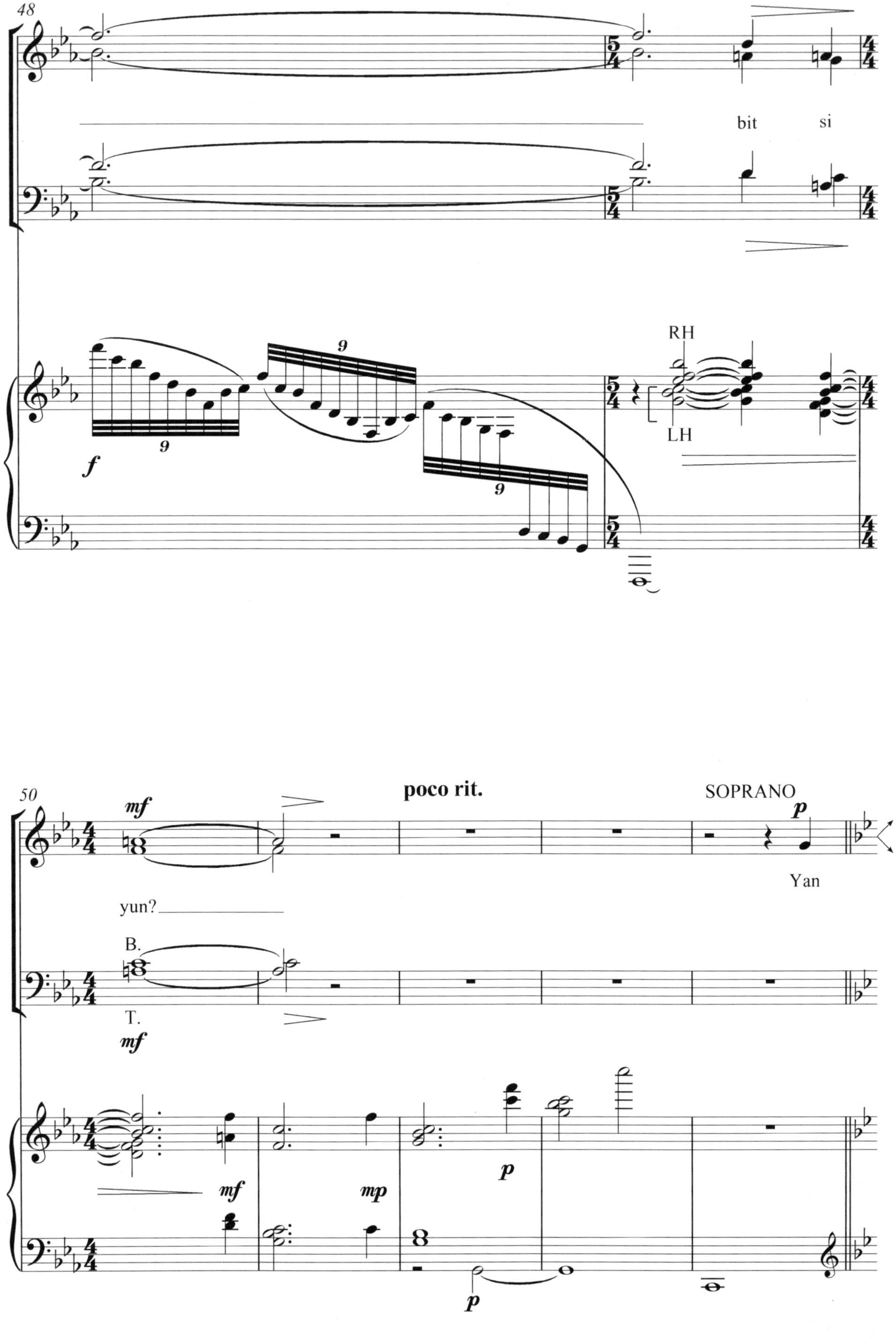

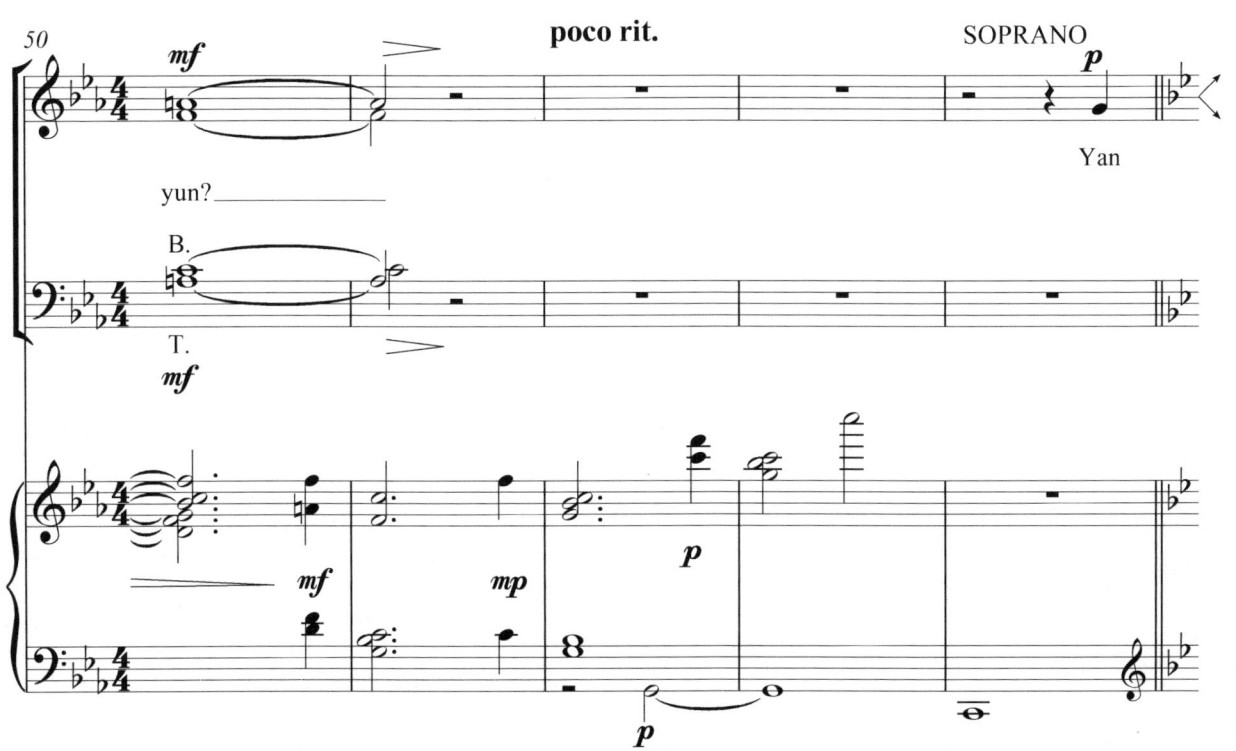

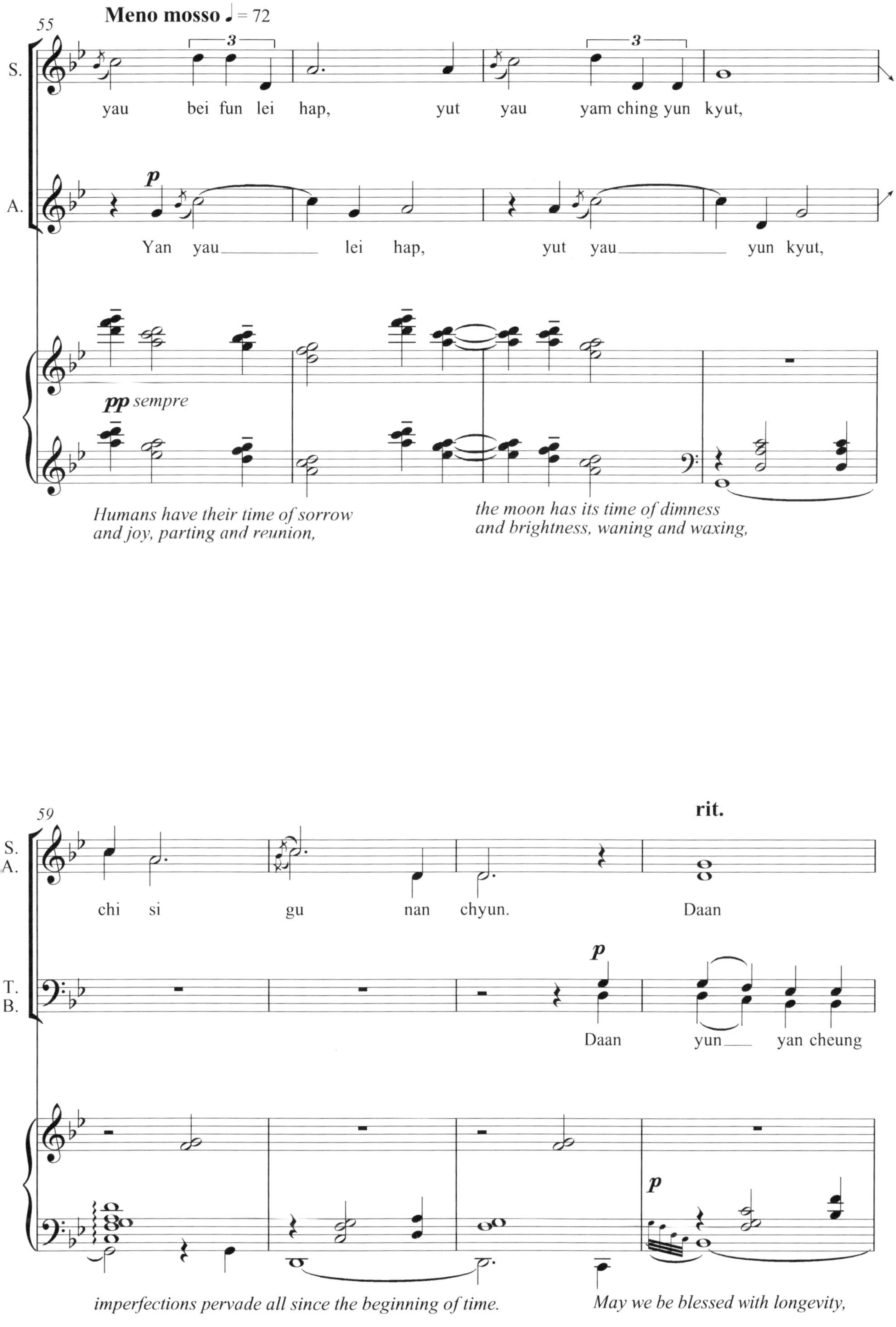

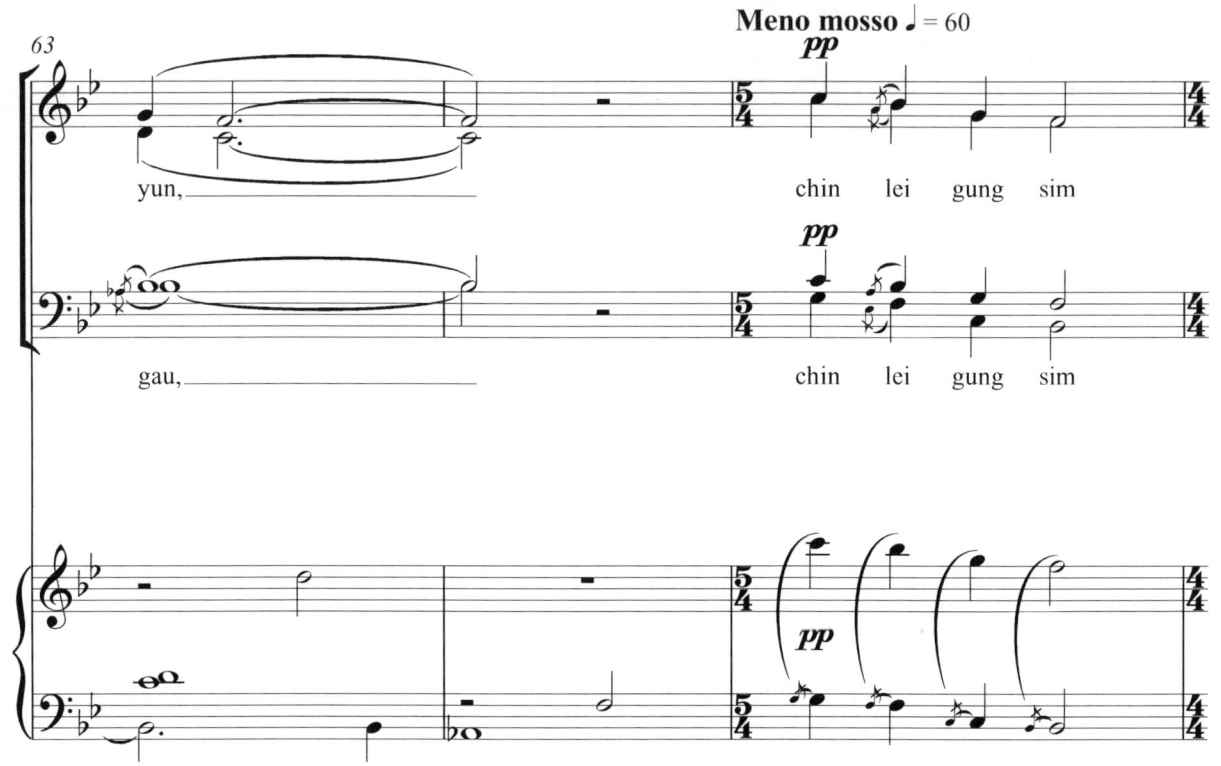

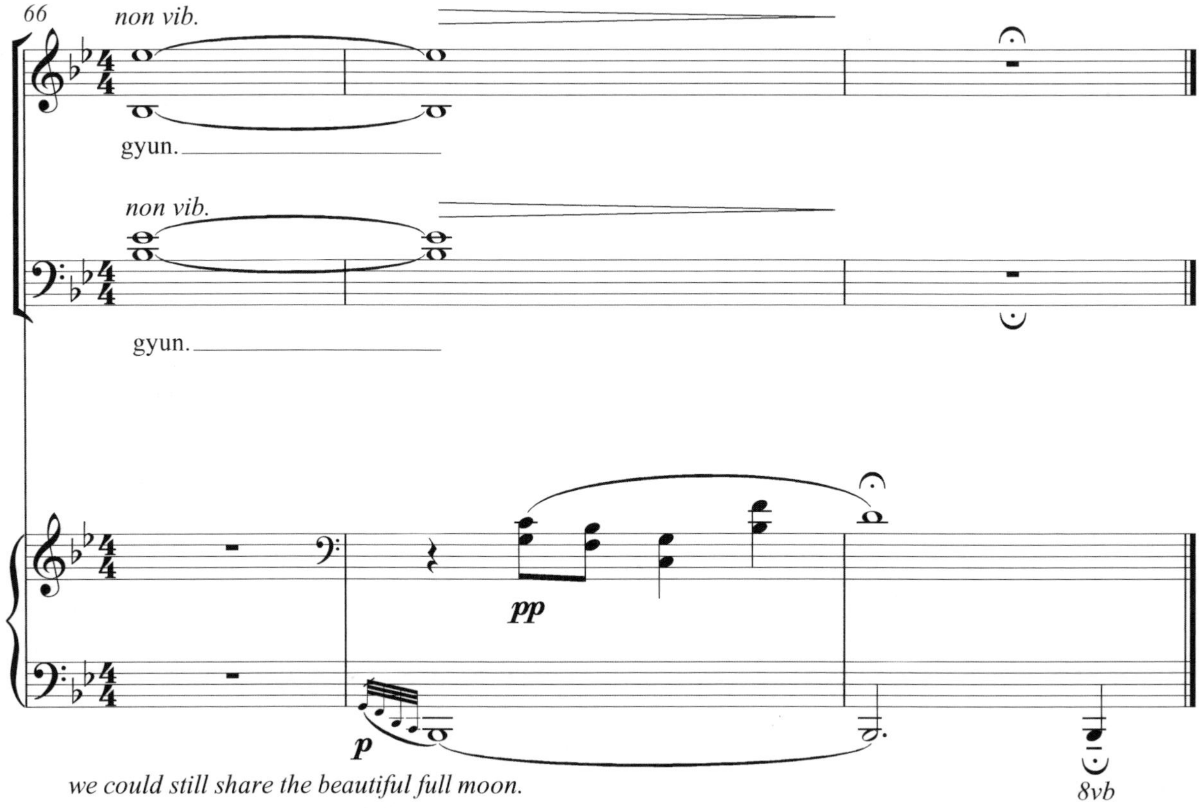

Shui Guang Lian Yan | Ripples Glisten Away...

Shui Guang Lian Yan is an unaccompanied choral setting of an ancient poem by Su Shi. It utilizes extended vocal techniques to depict the rippling water and exaggerated style of Chinese poetry recitation. **Language**: Mandarin.

Composer

Chen Yihan is originally from Changzhou, near Shanghai in eastern China. He is currently pursuing a Bachelor of Music degree in music composition and piano performance at Indiana University Jacobs School of Music. Among the youngest contributors to this anthology, Chen has already gained recognition as a composer and performer. He was the Grand Prize winner of the Concerto Division at the 2010 Cincinnati World Piano Competition and has won several composition competitions in the US.

Text

Like *Seui Diu Go Tau*, this work sets the text of the Song Dynasty (960–1279) poet Su Shi (also known as Su Dongpo, 1037–1101), a scholar-official and one of the foremost poets of his day. For part of his career, Su was assigned to an official post in Hangzhou, which is home to the West Lake. The West Lake has a great wealth of literature dedicated to its beauty and associated legends, and *Ripples Glisten Away...* is one such example. The poem has an introduction excluded from the choral setting, which — like many of Su Shi's poems — refers to the poet's reflections after imbibing: 'Drinking on the lake, first amidst sunshine and later in the rain.' Two poems follow: in the first, the poet welcomes guests to a festive gathering in the morning sunrise, only to see everyone scattering home intoxicated when the weather turns foul; in the second (set here), the poet is left to admire his natural surroundings in solitude.

The poem is short, with just four lines: the first two describe the glistening water in the sunlight and then the surrounding mountains in the rain; the latter two lines compare the West Lake to Xi Shi ('Xi zi'), who lived in the 5th century BCE and was a renowned beauty in classical China. She was said to be so beautiful that when fish saw her, they forgot to keep swimming and eventually sank to the bottom of the water. By comparing the two — both names begin with the syllable 'Xi' — the poet cleverly describes the clouds and sunlight as makeup for the West Lake and its mountain scenery, as well as the special skill needed to appreciate their unique charms.

This setting

This choral setting adopts a contemporary musical language to bring forth the poem's structure and imagery. First, throughout the introduction and opening two sections it uses an extended vocal technique of a hummed tremolo to depict the rippling water. The low-pitched hums, such as at bar 51 and later at 91, recall the distant thunder that ruined the social occasion of the first poem. It also includes accented grace-notes and *portamentos* on melodic leaps, partly for musical atmosphere and partly to imagine the exaggerated style of Chinese poetry recitation. Each poetic line has seven syllables, but the text is delivered freely among the different voices. The voice lines are pentatonic based, but different voices are built on different scales, and the middle two text lines have contrasting scales that add dissonance and emotional tension. Only on the fourth and climactic line 'both are always just as entrancing with makeup or without' do all voices come together, but even here they sing in irregular rhythms.

The final section is thin and quiet to express the poet's realization of his own loneliness. In this way, the piece captures the mixed emotions the poet must have felt — sunshine and rain, splendour and solitude — while writing the poem.

Performance notes

This work requires sufficient balance between flowing text delivery and vocal effects. Hummed tremolos marked with 'z' on the stems (as in bar 1) are to be performed as fast tremolos in the throat (not as melodic trills, but as early Baroque-style *trillo* — rapidly repeating the same pitch), with mouths closed. These can be done at different speeds among the voices, but keep the voices relaxed and focused on the tone, especially at the lowest dynamic levels. Bring out the sung text lines just a little above the hums until the sudden build-up from bar 69. Begin the grace-notes on the beat, rather than before. The accents are articulated on the grace-notes only and not on the primary notes that follow. *Portamentos* are expressive and should be only lightly weighted (not as much as *glissandos*), with primary focus on the two main interval pitches.

A step-by-step rehearsal process can help ease preparation. Because of the various textures and techniques in this piece, speak the text enough times in rhythm (monotone, without spoken tones) until each voice part is secure with the Chinese. Have choir members sing the pentatonic scales of each voice part so they get to know those relationships, then sing pitches on a relaxed monosyllable (later adding text) and humming without grace-notes, *tremolos* or *portamentos*. Later, try speaking the text with the embellishments first, before eventually singing the text with all the extended techniques. When preparing the text, give equal articulation to both vowels of diphthongs. The words 'shui guang lian', as well as 'zhuang' and 'xiang', all require adequate positioning of the first diphthong vowels while also gliding to the second vowels. On those syllables, form the internal mouth position for the glided vowels before articulating the initial consonants. Also, pay close attention to the special Chinese vowels on the syllables 'se' (of 'shan se') and 'zi' (of 'Xi zi'), both of which are sustained.

Literal translation

Shui   guang   lian yan qing   fang hao,
Water to glisten ripples sunshine side good,

shan   se   kong meng yu yi   qi.
mountain scenery empty mist   rain also wonderful.

Yu   ba   Xi   hu   bi   Xi zi,
To wish for to take West Lake to compare to Xi Shi,

dan zhuang nong mo   zong   xiang yi.
light makeup heavy to smear always suitable.

161

Shui Guang Lian Yan
水光潋滟
Ripples Glisten Away...

Words by Su Shi (Su Dongpo)
Chen Yihan

*) tremolo – fast, with throat

© 2015 by Peters Edition Ltd, London

their watery sparkle so charming in the sunlight,

*) tremolo – fast, with throat

mists veil the mountaintops . . .

their emptying haze so wondrous in the rain.

just as entrancing with makeup or without.

Shui Xian Hua | Narcissus Flower

Shui Xian Hua is an adaptation of the famous Chinese folksong *Mo Li Hua* (*Jasmine Flower*). The tune is commonly associated with China's coastal Jiangsu province near Shanghai.
Language: Mandarin.

Arranger

Lin Sheng-shih (1914–91), also transliterated as Lin Shengxi, was a native of Xinhui in Guangdong province, neighbouring Hong Kong in southeastern China. He was among the first generations of Chinese composers to adopt a Western musical language into their works. After studying in Shanghai in the 1930s, Lin lived in different parts of China during the war period before settling in Hong Kong around 1949, where he continued his work as a composer, conductor and scholar-educator until his death. He is highly regarded as an important figure in the development of new Chinese music.

Folksong

The folk tune on which *Shui Xian Hua* is based has a long and complex history, dating back to at least the eighteenth century. Previously entitled *Xian Hua Diao* (*Fresh Flower Tune*), the melody gained greater recognition as *Mo Li Hua* and has since assumed multiple versions in different parts of China, with each version having its own variation of melody and text. (This kind of variation on a common skeletal tune is typical of much of China's traditional music, and now extends to newer Chinese choral arrangements as well.) Two versions of *Mo Li Hua* appear in this anthology, with many more available, reflecting the high position this tune holds among the vast body of Chinese folksongs.

The main text theme of *Shui Xian Hua* and *Mo Li Hua* appears innocent on the surface — the spring-like enchantment of flowers in bloom. Lin wrote his arrangement around Chinese New Year, and the narcissus flower is often associated with this Spring Festival as a symbol of prosperity. Yet the two songs carry subtly differing subtexts. Whereas the jasmine flower of *Mo Li Hua* is a metaphor for unfulfilled romantic desire, the narcissus flower of *Shui Xian Hua* also represents the budding of nation and community. Its call for higher morals and peace is perhaps more indicative of sentiments expressed during China's turbulent decades of the earlier twentieth century. The melodic and dynamic intensification of the final bars could thus be interpreted as a resolute expression of peace, harmony and well-being.

This setting

Lin Sheng-shih set *Shui Xian Hua* for mixed chorus in 1960 with a text that departs from more common versions. Typically for Chinese composers who studied in the 1930s, Lin arranged the work in the style of the Romantic Art Song. Here, the composer maintains the original Chinese pentatonic scale for the melody, generally heard in the female voices, while the male voices and piano accompaniment harmonize using features reminiscent of nineteenth-century European music. The entire verse repeats, and the emotional nature of the piece intensifies when the melody leaps an octave the second time and the dynamic level increases. Lin's version is thus a rich combination of a traditional Chinese folksong blended with a Romantic piano-choral style. Such musical language was certainly not regarded as 'modernistic' in the West, but it represented a kind of 'modernity' to new Chinese music of the mid-twentieth century, at least until more experimental approaches became vogue from the late 1970s.

Performance notes

While the piece contains a number of Romantic features and musical gestures, the performance indication 'Simply and gracefully' suggests a restrained elegance and freshness throughout, without ever becoming heavy. The *crescendo* at bars 13–17 is only moderate and soon leads to *dolce* at bar 21. Variations in the piano part need to interact closely with the text and choral texture; for example, bars 13–20 can be seen as painting the phrase 'the flower that has fallen on my house'. Performers should aim for a sustained tone in the lower register in the first-time bars (bar 25) while saving the climax for bar 38, expressing perhaps a spirit of refined hope, rather than extreme dramaticism.

Lin Sheng-shih's arrangement relies on the strength of the melody and text for its more audible Chinese features, and so creating a 'native' vocal timbre — nasal, and with extremely forward tonal focus — is not a goal here. Aim for a warm vocal sound focused on blend and sing the text clearly within a *legato* style. Note that words which appear to be diphthongs in their Romanized transliteration, such as 'duo shui xian hua', are articulated more as glides unfolding toward their second vowel for primary emphasis. Take care also to distinguish between certain initial consonants that have similar formations, e.g. 'shui/xian', 'zai/jia' and 'qi/chang' (refer to the online Pronunciation Guide for detailed descriptions and audio examples).

Literal translation

Hao   yi duo shui xian hua,
Good a   Narcissus flower,

xian hua ya luo zai wo di jia,
Narcissus oh fall on my   house,

bang you dao,   min   an le,
nation has ethics, people peaceful,

jia jia   qi   chang tai ping ge,   tai ping ge!
everyone together sing   peaceful song, peaceful song!

Shui Xian Hua
水 仙 花
Narcissus Flower

Chinese folksong
arr. Lin Sheng-shih

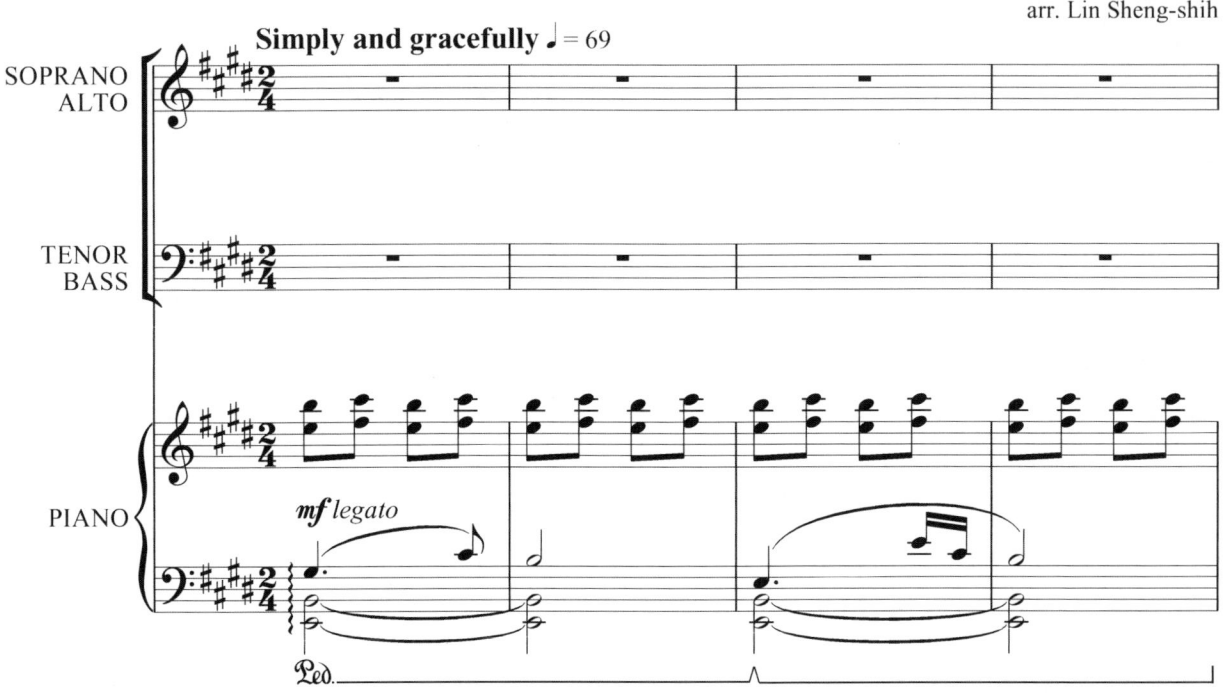

What a magnificent Narcissus!

© Lin Sheng-shih. Reproduced by permission of the Estate of Lin Sheng-shih.

Tin O O | Dark Clouds

Tin O O is an arrangement of a children's song from northern Taiwan. It tells a humorous story of a couple that argues over how to cook a fish. **Language**: Taiwanese.

Arranger

Tsai Yu-Shan is an arranger and pianist for the Formosa Singers in Taipei. Tsai received her Master of Music in Piano Performance from the Peabody Conservatory of Music before returning to Taiwan in the mid-1990s. Since joining the Formosa Singers, she has gained increasing prominence as a performer and arranger of folksongs that represent the island's many dialects and cultures. Her works are published and performed extensively in Taiwan and internationally.

Folksong

This song comes from the northern coast of Taiwan, an area known for its long rainy spells, and the words reflect daily rural life of the past. The opening line tells of ominous dark clouds that bring stormy weather. Grandpa is digging for taros and has the good fortune to dig up a mudfish, but he and Grandma disagree on how it should be cooked. So stubborn are both that they end up breaking the cooking pot. The pentatonic tune is in two parts. Each part has irregular phrases that combine strong beats into groups of two and three. Some of the words have meaning, while others are vocables. Just one vocable phrase '*yi ya he do*' repeats in both parts. In the last line, '*long dong chit dong chiang*' describes the sound of the cooking pot being smashed as it falls to the ground, and '*wa ha ha*' is the sound of children's laughter as they tell the story.

This setting

Most Taiwanese children — and adults — know this tune well. Tsai Yu-Shan arranged it for the Formosa Singers in 2001 (she also arranged a version for treble voices), and it has since been performed frequently by many groups in Taiwan. The choral setting is also in two main parts that contrast musically. The short introduction describes the darkening clouds — a humorous omen of the fight that follows. Bars 7–43 repeat the first phrase with variation. This section is arranged in $\frac{7}{8}$ metre, which departs from the original children's song, alternating with duple metre. The second part from bar 44 is playfully slow to represent the relaxed pace of life for the arguing couple. This part also repeats once with variation. The recurring '*yi ya he do*' phrase from the first part also marks a return of the faster tempo at 53 and 73. The coda from 69 concludes with a final burst of repeated laughter.

Performance notes

This arrangement is meant to be playful. The 'dark' $\frac{7}{8}$ theme and slow middle section should both carry humorous irony. Carefully prepare the $\frac{7}{8}$ metre with warm-up exercises and counting so that each final crotchet quickly moves to the next dotted crotchet downbeat. In the first section, practise speaking the text in rhythm so you can move effortlessly between $\frac{7}{8}$ and syncopated duple metre. Work towards an even *crescendo-accelerando* from bar 48, leading into the *f* Tempo I at 53. Relax the tempo again at bars 59–67, but not as slow as at 44. Bar 68 starts lively but is suddenly interrupted by the return of $\frac{7}{8}$ in 69. Bars 69–70 get increasingly agitated before an immediate slowing at 71. Each repeated '*long pua dia*' (69–71) and '*wa ha ha*' (75–8) needs to grow in intensity; if necessary, add a *crescendo* at 77–8 to emphasize the final laughter syllables.

As with *Diu Diu Dang Ah*, Taiwanese diphthongs should be very connected and have an almost exaggerated, nasalized sound, while monophthongs are more separately articulated. Taiwanese does not have a standardized transliteration system. The distinction between syllables that end in intoned or aspirated final consonants and those ending with vowels that are heavily nasalized or lead to stopped consonants is not always clear. Words with 'n' and 'ng' endings are often not fully intoned, but slightly stopped, while words like 'gia', 'jia' and 'dia' have implied, stopped 'ng' sounds at the end, as in 'gia(ng)'. The 't' endings on 'gut' are stopped, and initial 'b' consonants on 'be' have a slight 'm' sound before them. Refer to the online Pronunciation Guide for reference.

> **Literal translation**
>
> Tin o o be lo ho, a gong a gia di tao a be gut o.
> The sky black to want to drop rain, Grandpa to take a hoe to want to dig taro.
>
> Gut a gut, gut a gut,
> To dig and to dig, to dig and to dig,
>
> gut diou jit bwe suan liu go, *yi ya he do* jin jia tsu bi.
> to dig out a loach (mudfish) (vocables) genuine interesting.
>
> A gong a be dsu giam, a ma be dsu jia.
> Grandpa to want to cook salty flavour, Grandma to want to cook unsalted flavour.
>
> Neng e siu pa long pua dia,
> The two each other to hit to make broken cooking pot,
>
> *yi ya he do long dong chit dong chiang,* wa ha ha!
> (vocables), hah, hah, hah!

Tin O O
天 烏 烏
Dark Clouds

Northern Taiwan children's song
arr. Tsai Yu-Shan

© 2015 by Peters Edition Ltd, London

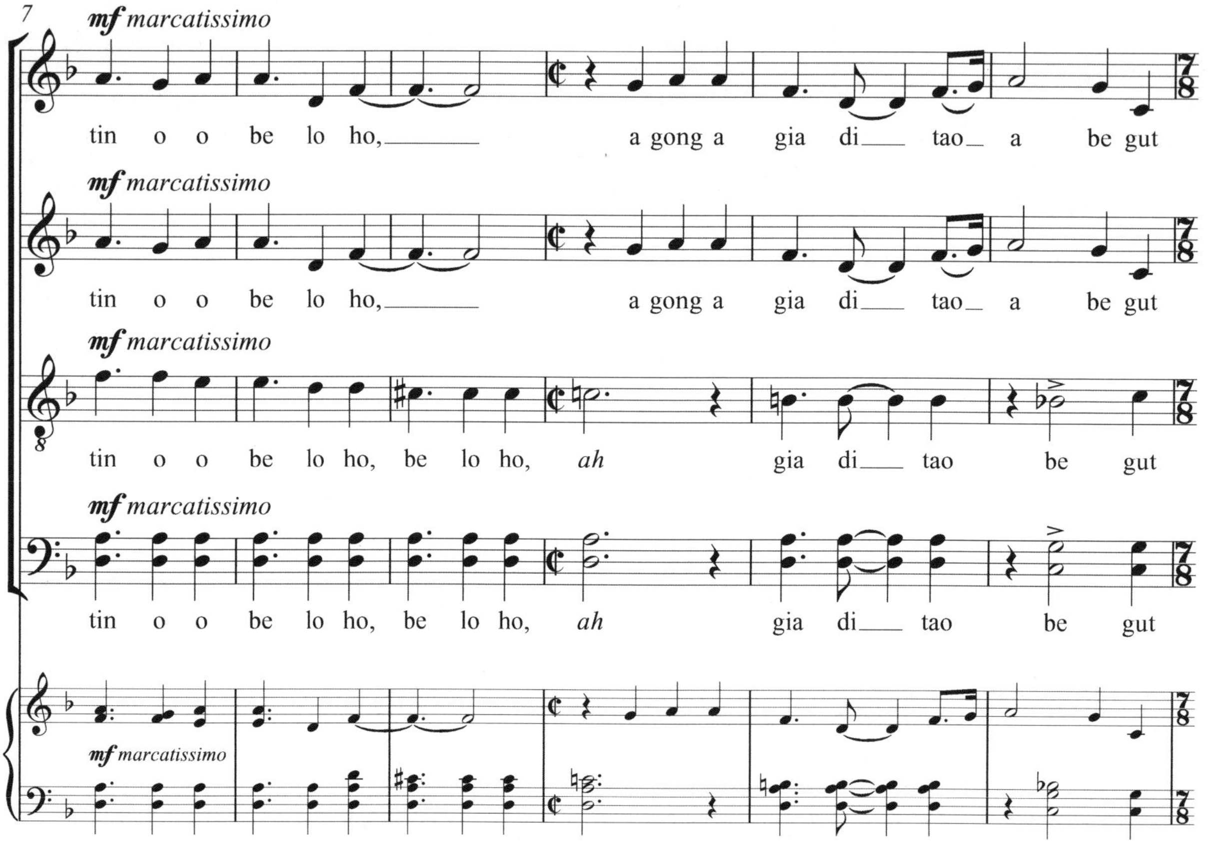
7
mf marcatissimo
tin o o be lo ho, a gong a gia di tao a be gut
mf marcatissimo
tin o o be lo ho, a gong a gia di tao a be gut
mf marcatissimo
tin o o be lo ho, be lo ho, ah gia di tao be gut
mf marcatissimo
tin o o be lo ho, be lo ho, ah gia di tao be gut
mf marcatissimo

the sky is dark and is about to rain, *Grandpa is digging for a taro with his hoe.*

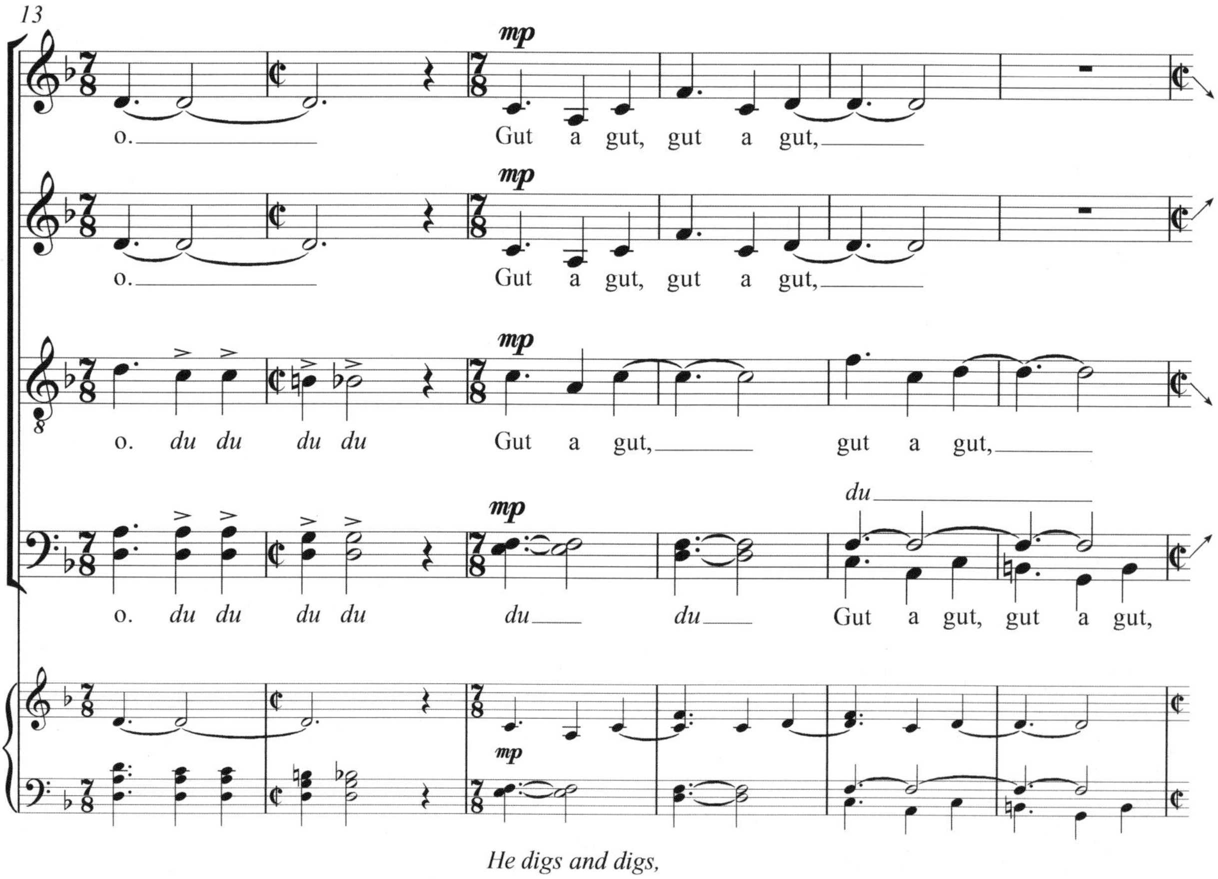
13
mp
o. Gut a gut, gut a gut,
mp
o. Gut a gut, gut a gut,
mp
o. du du du du Gut a gut, gut a gut,
mp
du
o. du du du du du du Gut a gut, gut a gut,
mp

He digs and digs,

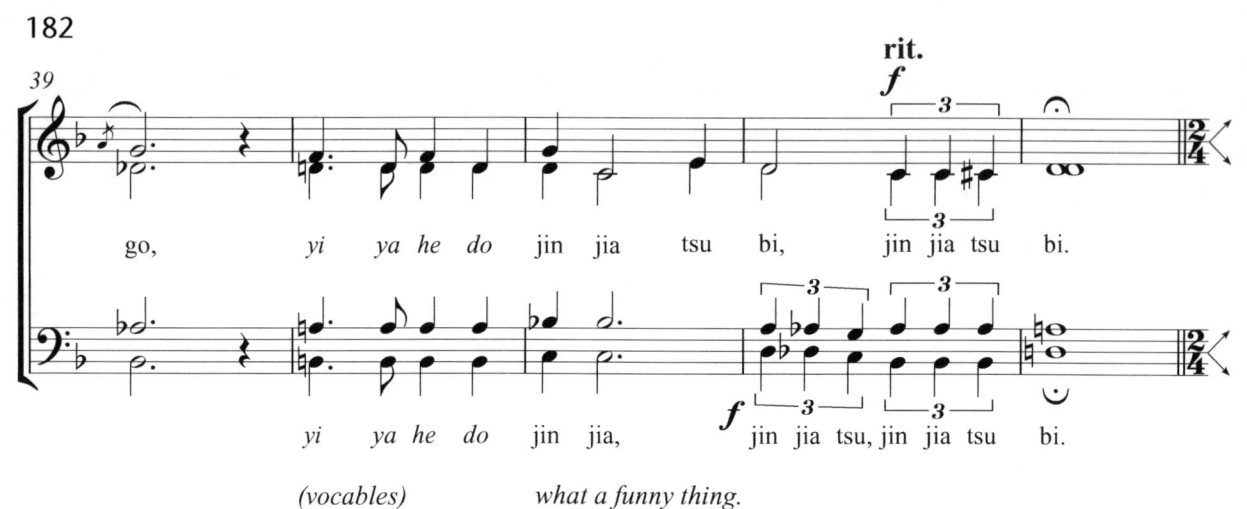

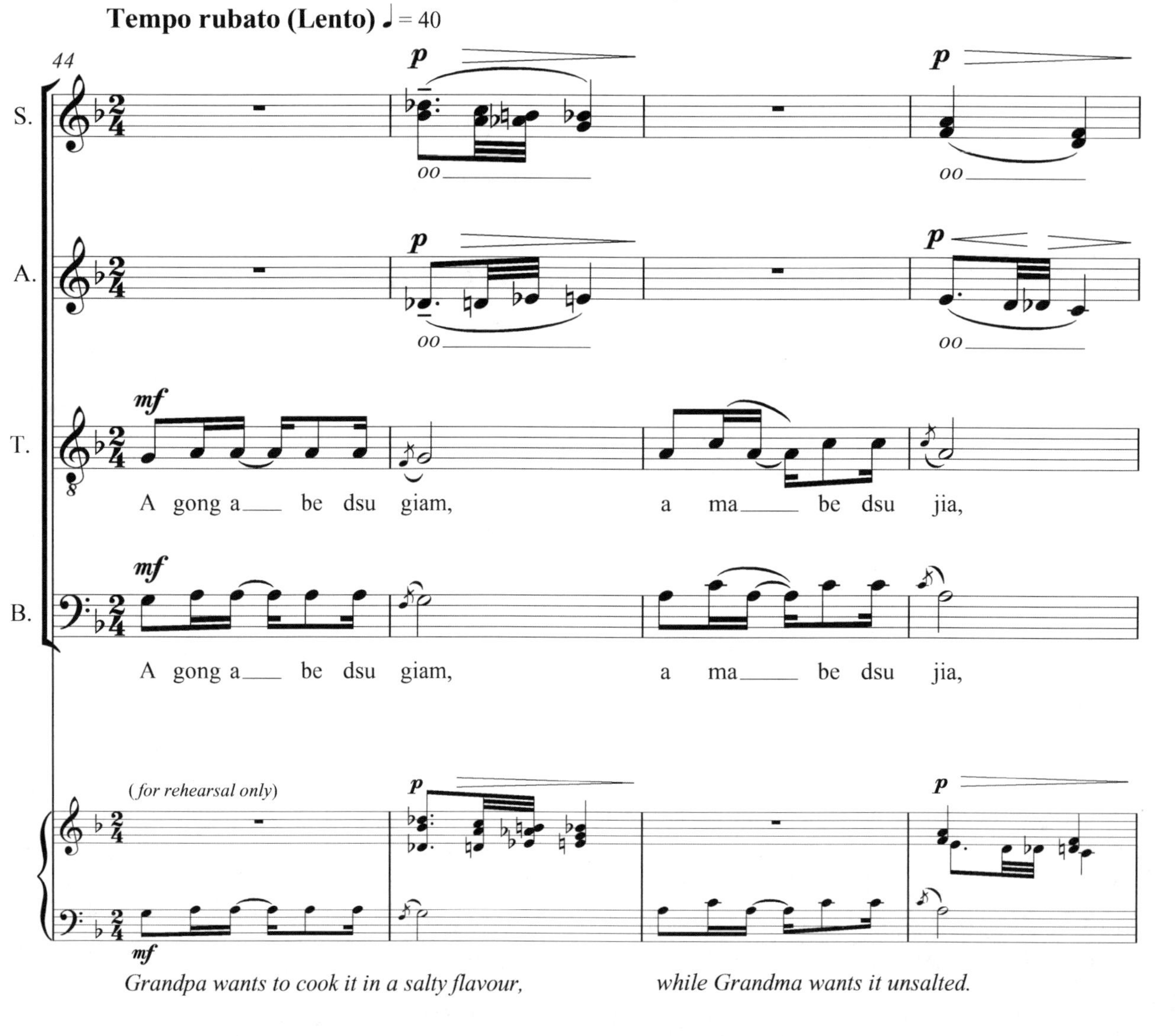

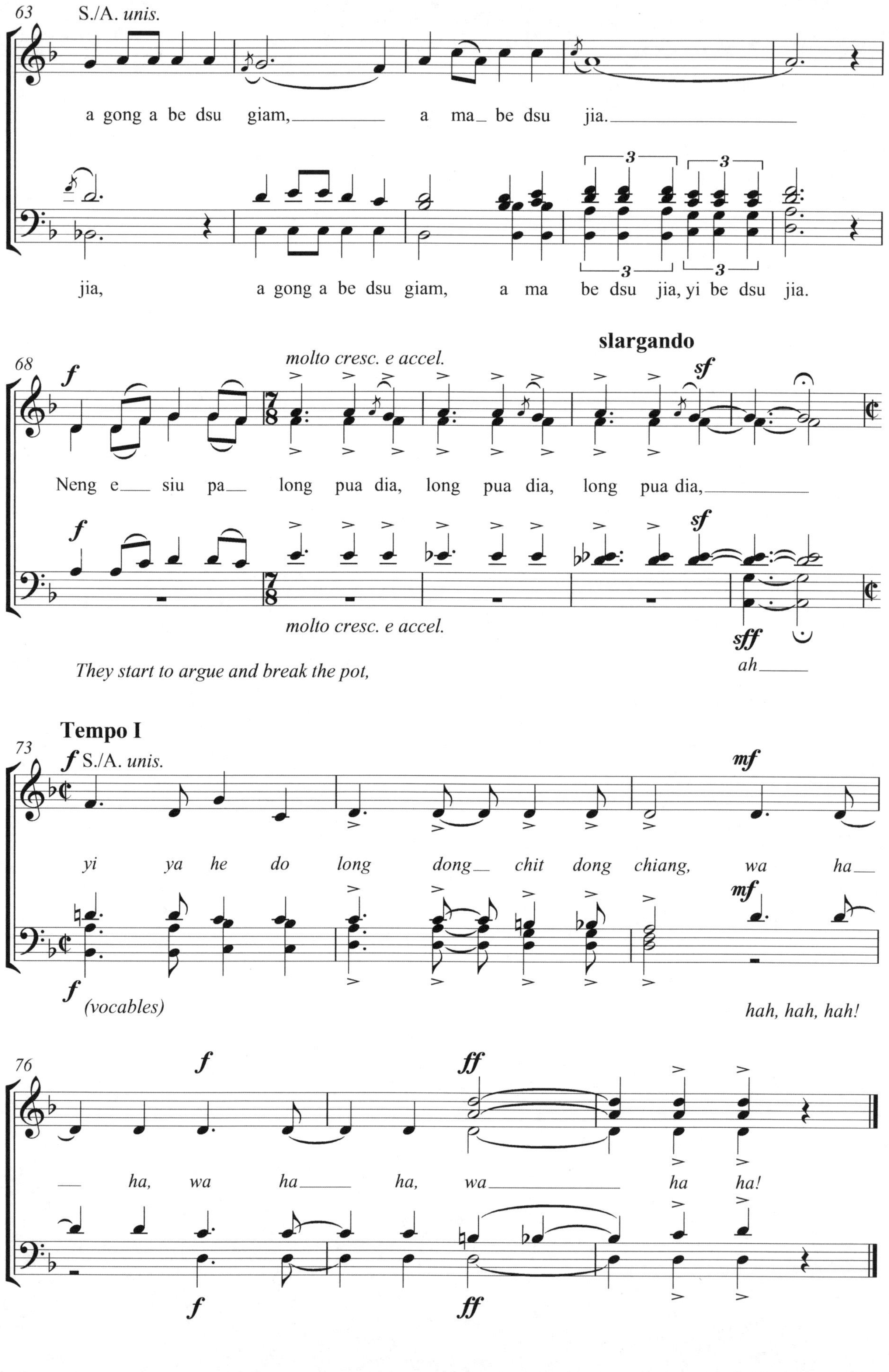

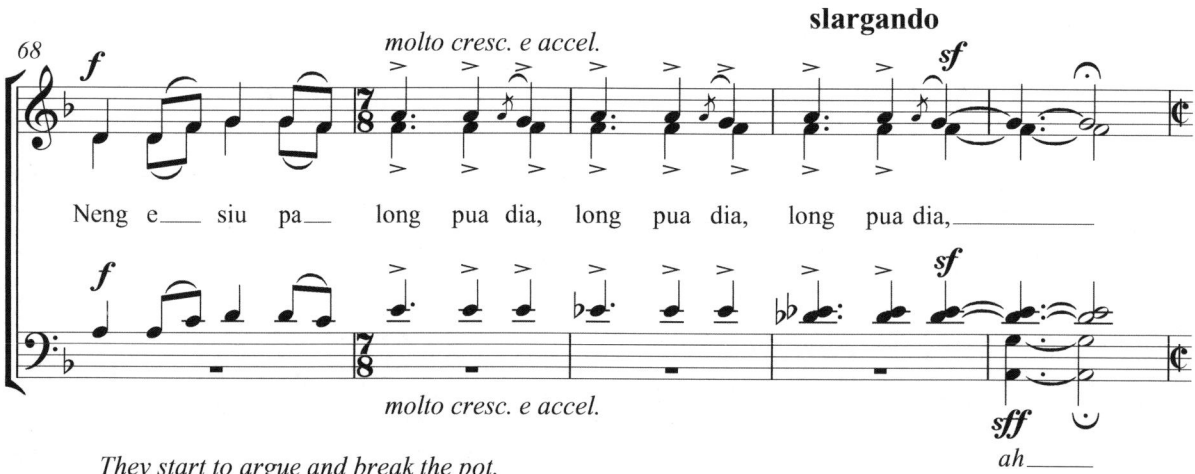

Xiao He Tang Shui | Flowing Creek

Xiao He Tang Shui is a tune from Yunnan province in southwestern China. It is sung from the perspective of a girl who yearns for her loved one in the mountains. **Language**: Mandarin.

Arranger

Ma Shuilong was one of Taiwan's most important composers and music educators of the late twentieth century. Born in northern Taiwan, Ma received his Bachelor's degree in music theory and composition at what is now the National Taiwan University of Arts in 1964. He received a full scholarship to study at the Regensburg Conservatory in Germany from 1972–5, and spent time in the mid-1980s doing further study in the US. He taught at Soochow University from 1975–81 and then worked in his main faculty position at what is now the National Taipei University of the Arts. Ma earned accolades for his various orchestral, chamber and vocal works, including compositions that mixed Chinese instruments with Western orchestra and chorus.

Folksong

Xiao He Tang Shui, from Yunnan province in southwestern China, has become one of China's more popular tunes. Yunnan is famous for its terraced rice paddies that extend down massive slopes, and against this backdrop *Xiao He Tang Shui* adopts the style of a mountain song, meant to express deep emotion. Its pentatonic melody actually assumes the contour of the mountain scenery with its many leaps, yet it also 'flows' with stepwise motion. Most characteristic is its long-sustained high notes, frequent embellishments and relaxed, flexible rhythm. The love song text expresses profound feelings of a young girl — traditionally referred to as 'little sister' in China — for her 'big brother' (male loved one) who is herding in the mountains. The serene text is full of scenic references, including the shining moon, flowing creek and cool breeze. The love entreaty is sung as if calling across the mountaintops: both verses have five text lines, with an 'echo' effect occurring in the first, third and fourth lines of each via repeated words like 'tian shang zou tian shang zou'.

This setting

Ma Shuilong arranged *Xiao He Tang Shui* for unaccompanied chorus in 1978 as part of a set of Chinese folksong arrangements. In the 1970s Taiwan pursued its own path of 'rediscovering' Chinese tradition as an alternative to events being played out on the Mainland. This arrangement weds Western compositional techniques to the original Chinese tune for this purpose. Originally arranged in three written-out sections, this version has the final section set as a *da capo* repeat. The two text verses thus create an ABA form, framed by a single-bar 'Ah' introduction, and a coda. The first verse is sung by paired soprano-alto voices, punctuated by tenors and basses in the first two lines, before all voices sing together. The second verse is set contrapuntally with the altos introducing the first line of the original melody in inversion (the same intervals 'mirrored' in the opposite direction). The following lines have different voices entering in succession and in varied combinations, again with all voices singing together on the final text line. The repeated first verse leads to a short coda with its dissipating 'A ge!' text.

Performance notes

The long, sustained pitches throughout can prove challenging for any choir. Gradually prepare the choir for efficient breath-tone connection through the rehearsal process. The entire piece, even the agitato segments, should be very *legato*; though lyrical, the tone should be pristine and not heavy. A lightly nasalized colour is appropriate in this style, but keep a focus on blend throughout. Add meaning to the repeated words either via a subtle mountain echo effect or an intensified emotion. Refer closely to the Pronunciation Guide for the special repeated syllables 'yue liang' and 'ge'.

The arrangement's numerous grace-notes have been written out in this score to help coordinate group singers. Conduct bars 1–14 with expressive rhythmic flexibility and not metronomically. Sing words like 'wang' in bar 3 and 'shan' in bar 7 with fluid rhythms and not too much weight on the first of the slurred pitches (they did not receive the metric weight of strong beats in their original context). The second section can be sung with greater forward motion and with the metric coordination of a Western contrapuntal passage. Carefully tune moving pitches of one voice in this section with other voices to bring out harmonic resonance alongside independent lines. Consider varying the dynamics on the repeat of the opening section, and vary the dramatic character of the sustained 'Ah' chords at bars 1 and 15.

> **Literal translation**
>
> 1.
> A! Yue liang   chu lai   liang wang wang liang wang wang,
> Ah! The moon out to come bright flourishing   bright flourishing,
>
> wo xiang wo di a ge   zai shen shan,
> I to miss my   elder brother in deep the mountain,
>
> ge   xiang   yue liang tian   shang zou   tian   shang zou,
> brother to be like the moon heaven on   to walk heaven on   to walk,
>
> ge   a! Ge   ya!
> brother ah! Brother ah!
>
> Shan   xia   xiao he tang   shui   qing   you you.
> The mountain under the creek to flow water clearly unhurried.
>
> 2.
> A! Yue liang   chu lai   zhao   ban po   zhao   ban po,
> Ah! The moon out to come to shine half slope to shine half slope,
>
> wang jian yue liang xiang qi   wo di ge,
> to spot   the moon to think of my   brother,
>
> yi zhen qing feng   chui   shang po   chui   shang po,
> a burst cool breeze to blow up   the slope to blow up   the slope,
>
> ge   a! Ge   ya!
> brother ah! Brother ah!
>
> Ni   ke   ting jian a mei   jiao   a ge.
> You to be able to hear   younger sister to call elder brother.
>
> Ai!   A ge!
> Alas! Ah brother!

Xiao He Tang Shui
小河淌水
Flowing Creek

Yunnan folksong
arr. Ma Shuilong

Ah! The moon comes out bright and clear,

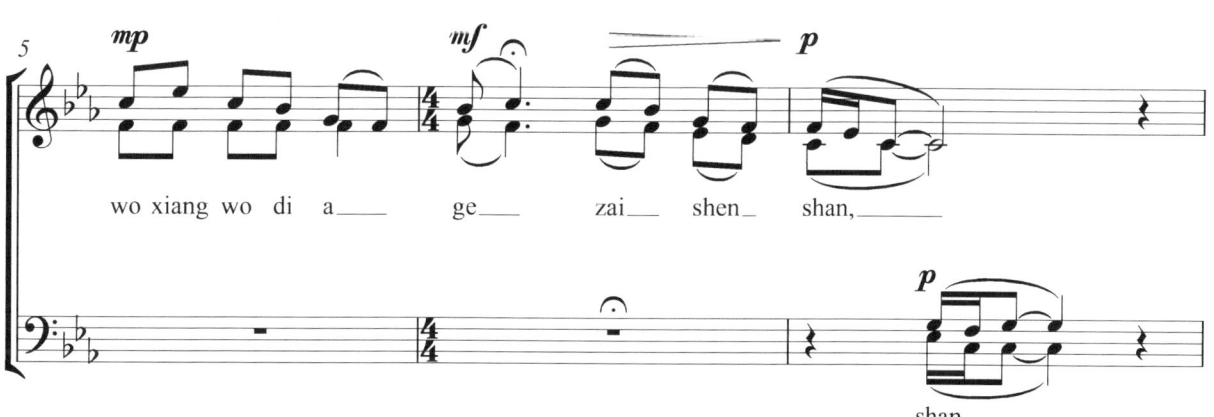

I yearn for my love deep in the mountains,

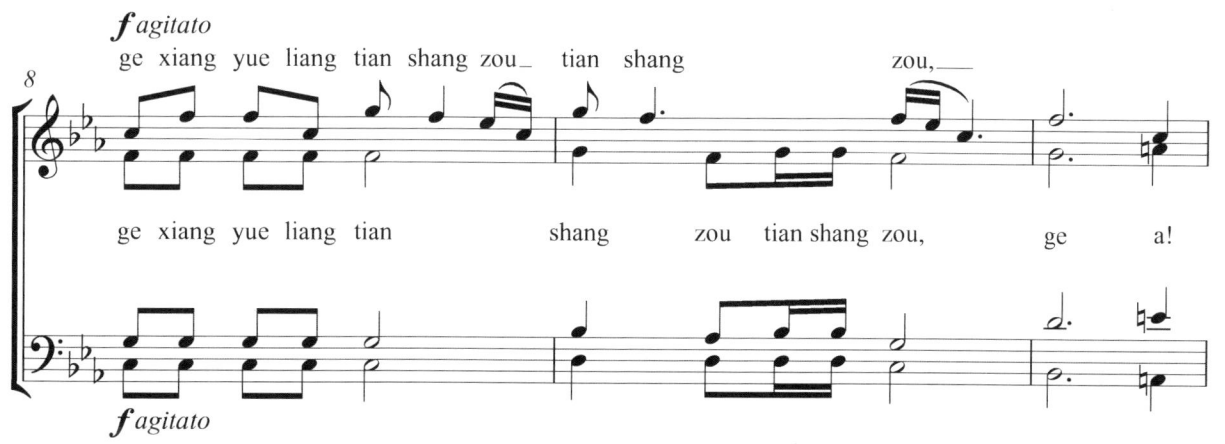

my love is like the moon walking in heaven, *ah, my love!*

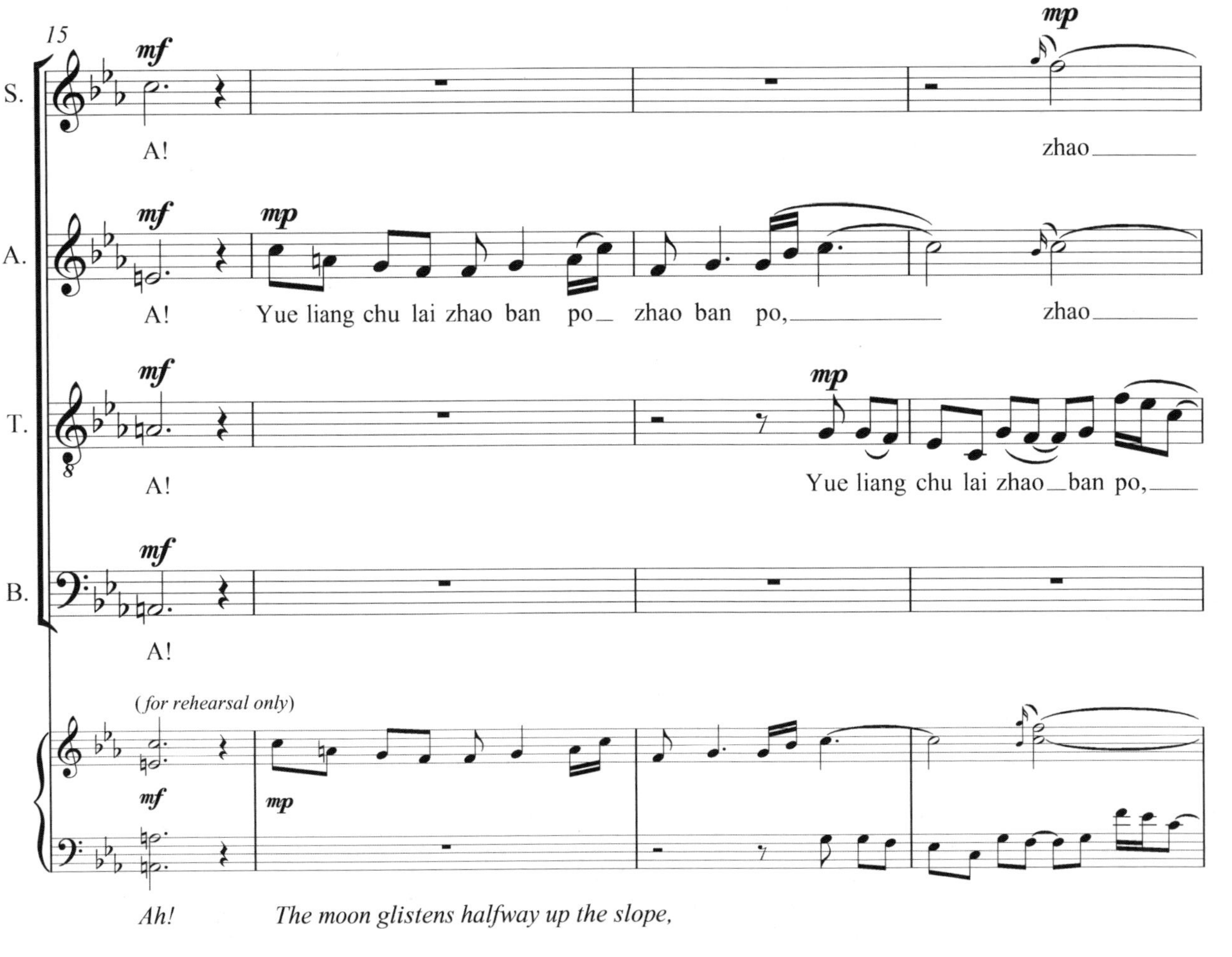

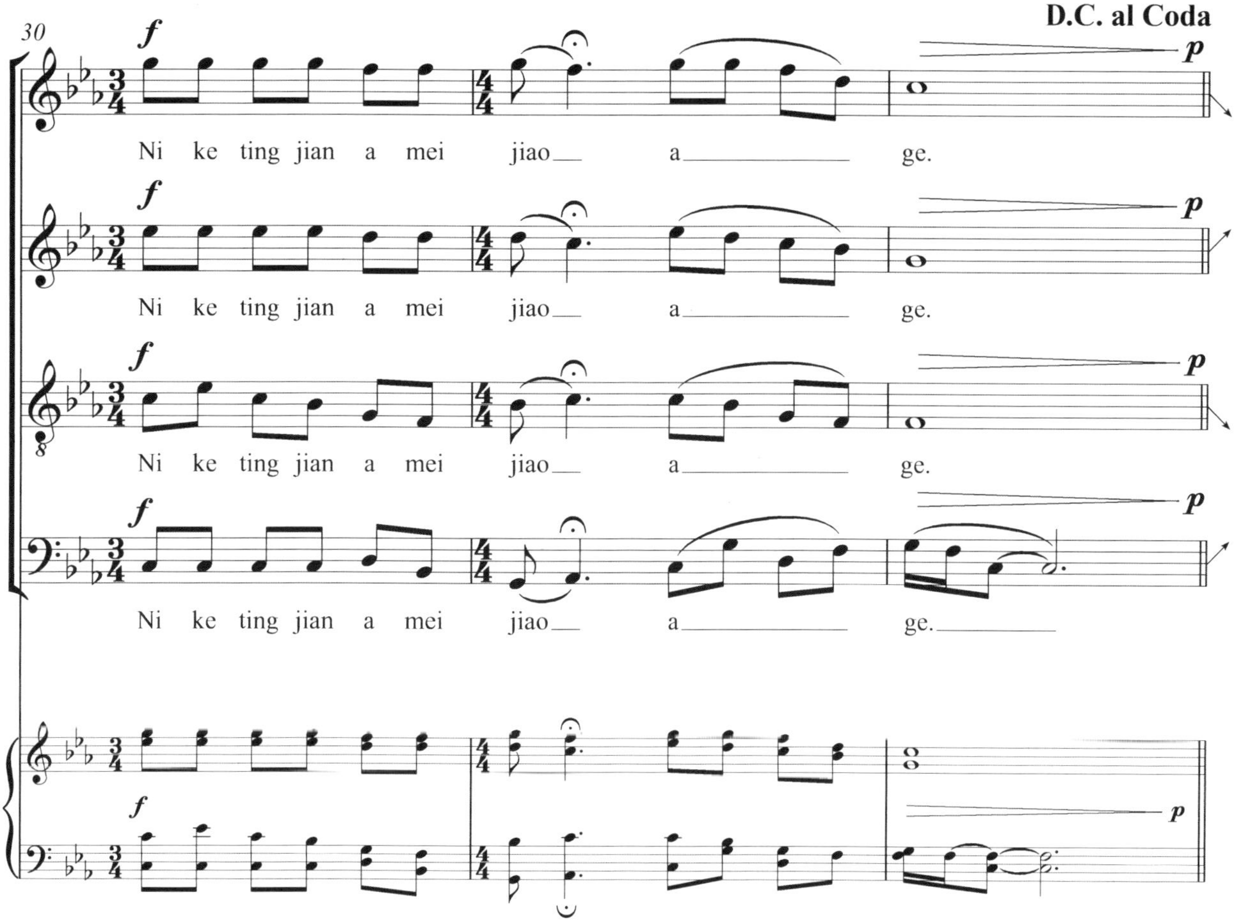

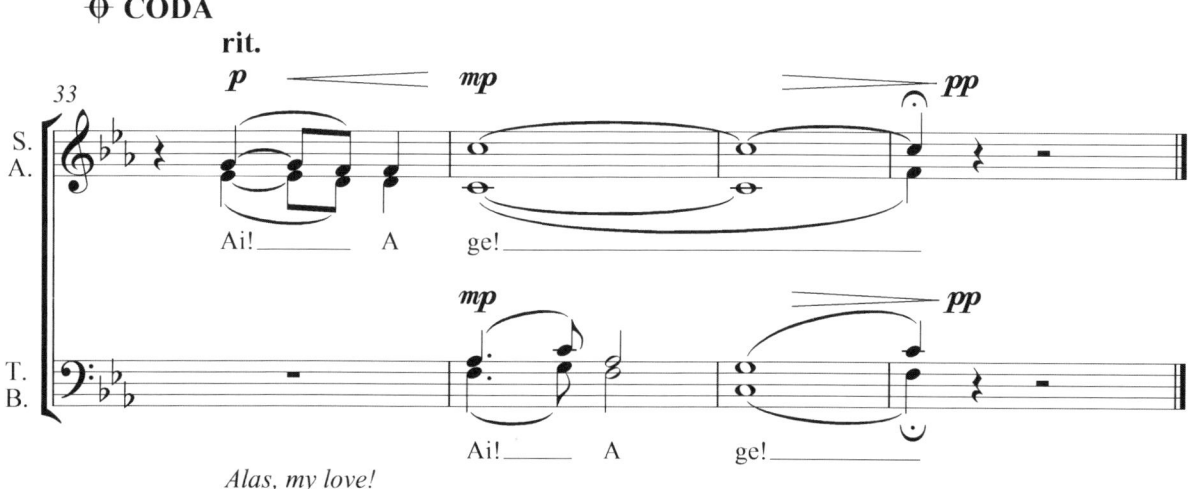

Xiao Huang Li Niao | Little Oriole

Xiao Huang Li Niao is a folksong from Inner Mongolia in northern China. It is a love song with nursery rhyme innocence. **Language**: Mandarin.

Arranger

Chan Hing-yan has gained acclaim for his style of blending Chinese and Western musical languages in his compositions, ranging from 'fusion concertos' to chamber works, dance dramas and vocal music. Much of his eclectic style comes from his advanced training on the Chinese *erhu* (two-stringed fiddle), as well as on piano and other Western instruments. Chan earned his Doctor of Musical Arts degree in composition from the University of Illinois, where he also minored in ethnomusicology. He is now Professor and Chair of the Music Department at The University of Hong Kong.

Folksong

Xiao Huang Li Niao is a love song in the style of a nursery rhyme. Here, 'Little Oriole' is a pet name for one's beloved. Although it seems like a children's song, it contains subtle features within. The love message is implied in the text reference to two, four and eight. All the even numbers represent the idea of love-struck pairs. The references to dragon and phoenix motifs on riding boots also point to the nomadic lifestyle on the Mongolian grasslands, where horsemanship is a feature of daily life.

The melody itself appears to be simple, but it has a wide range. First it moves to a low E, before ascending to a high G♯ just two bars later. Towards the end of the verse, the melody seems to prepare for another ascent to the high note, but then it suddenly drops an octave and settles on the low E again. Each verse has eight miniature musical-text ideas that mirror the idea of making 'a total of eight'.

This setting

Little Oriole was arranged for the Australian vocal ensemble The Song Company in late 2013. It premiered in Sydney in early 2014 as a concert-opener, where members of each voice part walked on stage at their first vocal entry (choirs performing this piece can similarly begin from offstage if they wish to use this as a processional).

Chan's inspiration for the choral arrangement came from versions of *Little Oriole* that he had learned in the style of a two-part invention on the piano during his student days. Hong Kong students of traditional Chinese music frequently interact with musicians who grew up in different parts of China, and Chan's Mainland composition teachers emphasized exercises in harmonizing folksongs. *Xiao Huang Li Niao* is one of the many Mongolian folksongs that has become popular in folksong collections and arrangements for voice and different instruments. This arrangement creatively develops some of the ideas Chan had encountered in these versions.

This setting plays with the love song theme. Like the folksong itself, Chan's arrangement shows clever simplicity. Through the three repeating verses, the melody is never completed stated by a single voice. Instead, the texture is staggered from start to finish, but the voices gradually build up in a pairing effect that reflects the song text. The unique harmony is produced partly by call and response and partly by voices that move at the same time but shift between wide open chords and octave or unison notes. The added dissonance in the coda section gives a flavourful final turn to the innocent love rhyme.

Performance notes

The first two verses are graceful, so *tenuto* marks should be effected without too much weight. The third verse at bar 39 becomes more passionate (*ardente*) as female and male voices sing together, but execute the *ff* dynamic markings from bar 43 with suitable expression that does not punch the *tenutos*. Maintain adequate forward motion while observing the *poco rall.* of the concluding phrase from bar 52; this will help keep the sense of the love song's juvenile innocence.

The wide melodic range can present challenges for choirs. Work towards seamlessly navigating downward leaps, especially when followed by continuous descending stepwise motion, by maintaining a high vocal position.

Give distinctive emotional expression to the different sub-phrases in each verse (signalled by punctuation marks), but allow the different voice lines to interact so that the folk melody flows without interruption. Pay special attention to tuning shifting harmony, such as bars 14–15 and 52-4. Properly balance the final open fifth at 61 after bringing out the tenor A♯ in bar 60. Allow the Chinese text to serve the *legato* folk tune flow by connecting diphthongs and triphthongs in phrases like 'xiao huang li niao' and 'liang duo hua'. Be careful to distinguish between initial consonants on 'xue' and 'shang', as well as 'cou' and 'cheng'. Focus the 'i' of 'si' high and forward, and form the 'uo' glide on 'duo' even as you articulate the initial 'd'.

Literal translation

Xiao huang li niao er ya, ni ke ceng zhi dao ma?
Small Oriole bird ah, you to be able already to know that?

Ma xue shang xiu zhe long tou feng wei hua.
Horse boots on to be embroidered with dragon head phoenix tail pattern.

Liang duo hua er ya xiu yi zhi xie ya,
Two individual pattern ah to be embroidered one single shoe ah,

gong you si duo hua.
total to have four individual flowers.

Wo he ni liang ge si duo cou cheng ba duo ya.
Me and you two unit four individuals to gather to make eight individuals ah.

Xiao Huang Li Niao
小黃鸝鳥
Little Oriole

Mongolian folksong
arr. Chan Hing-yan

© 2015 by Peters Edition Ltd, London

Two motifs are embroidered on each boot, totalling four motifs.

You and me, two fours make a total of eight.

Little Oriole, do you know?

Our riding boots are embroidered with motifs of dragon head and phoenix tail.

Two motifs are embroidered on each boot, totalling four motifs.

You and me, two fours make a total of eight.

Little Oriole, do you know?

Our riding boots are embroidered with motifs of dragon head and phoenix tail.

Two motifs are embroidered on each boot, totalling four motifs.

You and me, two fours make a total of eight.

Yang Guan San Die | Parting at Yangguan Pass

Yang Guan San Die is a choral arrangement of an ancient song. In traditional Chinese music, songs are frequently used for both instrumental and vocal settings. *Yang Guan* became famous as a standard piece for the Chinese *guqin* zither. **Language**: Mandarin.

Arranger

Mainland composer Wang Zhenya wrote this choral arrangement in 1954, just a few years after the establishment of the People's Republic of China in 1949. Whereas earlier generations of composers frequently set Chinese tunes to a predominantly Western musical language, composers of the 1950s were searching for ways to connect more closely with local traditions. Wang had developed a deep understanding of the Chinese zither through his close working relationship with *guqin* master Guan Pinghu. This led him to arrange numerous works from the instrument's repertoire for chorus and orchestra alike, and this arrangement of *Yang Guan San Die* is regarded as one of the most important.

Traditional song

The song was originally based on the Tang Dynasty (618–906 AD) poem *Song Yuan Er Shi An Xi* (*Sending off Yuan Er to Serve as Envoy to Anxi*) by eighth-century poet Wang Wei. *Yang Guan San Die* literally means 'three variations on Yangguan' because each instrumental verse was played differently. The *guqin* was long considered a highly refined instrument with delicate acoustical features. It was most commonly played non-professionally in intimate settings by members of China's social elite. The hands produce sound by plucking and pressing on the strings at various points and artfully shape the sound via highly ornate plucking, sliding, scratching, vibrato and embellishments. As a song-derived work, however, the technique for *Yang Guan San Die* is considered less ornate than in many *guqin* pieces.

Text

Parting at Yangguan Pass was also known as *Weicheng Song* and *Yangguan Song* due to its references to those ancient places. Yangguan was a gate at the western end of the Great Wall, near Dunhuang. This was the last Chinese outpost before entering what was considered 'barbarian' land to the west. Weicheng was the town from which the long journey to Yangguan Pass would begin. The text is from a type of Chinese poem on 'parting' — typically melancholic, bemoaning the imminent separation of a close good friend or lover. In this specific work, the poet urges his friend to have another cup of wine as he prepares to depart for his new duty at Yangguan Pass. The original poem included the four text lines (seven syllables each) that begin every verse. The additional verse lines after 'wu gu ren' were added later and greatly heighten the emotional intensity. The choral arrangement thus appears more like a lovers' parting than in the original.

This setting

Wang arranged *Yang Guan San Die* for the inauguration of the Music Research Institute of the Chinese National Academy of Arts in 1954. It was premiered by the Chinese National Song and Dance Ensemble Chorus for that occasion. The accompanied solo-choral setting allowed Wang Zhenya to experiment with *guqin* mimicry in the piano score at certain points and heighten dramatic tension throughout. Piano gestures like the upbeat to bar 1 and punctuation at bars 8 and 11 are drawn from the *guqin* model, although the piano plays a more Romantic style elsewhere. The choral texture frequently shifts within each of the verse variations, exploring dramatic possibilities. For example, the accented octaves on 'Gan huai!' are sustained through imitative entries at bar 28, before the voices come together at bar 29. Other imitative entries on 'Shui xiang yin' from bar 31 are an intensification of the corresponding point on 'li ku xin' at bar 12. They act as a middle climax at bar 34 that prepares for the solo entry in verse 3 at bar 36. The continued solo-choral interaction leads towards a larger climax at bars 53–4. The section from bar 64 leads to an apotheosis (high-note) ending by the soloist that was not uncommon for Chinese pentatonic-Romantic works of the mid-twentieth century.

Performance notes

Conductors, pianists and choir members are encouraged to listen to *guqin* recordings of *Yang Guan San Die* to facilitate preparation. Pianists may subtly shift between Romantic accompaniment and *guqin*-based gestures, maintaining careful attention to balance with the choir and soloist. Pedalling in some passages, such as the upbeat to bar 1, may be adjusted to reflect the overlapping pitches and natural decay of the *guqin*. Consider whether to play the accented piano figures at the end of bars 9 and 45 with a *diminuendo* to match the choir or to keep the accents strong against the voices as a reflection of the text. Keep the *crescendo* at bars 12–15 moderate to leave greater space to grow at 31–4. Special consideration is necessary for the passage at bars 49–57, in which interpretative flexibility of tempo between text sub-phrases is implied, rather than metronomic continuation. Chinese choirs often include a relaxed tempo from bar 49 to the downbeat of 51, followed by resolute, forward motion from 'Qian xun' to 'cun zhong' at the downbeat of bar 52 (with moderate accents on the solo line). This is followed by a *poco allargando* in bar 52 beats 2 and 3 and slight hesitation before the downbeat of bar 53, which is *a tempo* until the *ritardando* in bar 54. Choirs should strive for an even *diminuendo* in bars 61–3. Careful attention to balance is needed in the final passage from bar 66, where imitative entries in different voices need to be audible (especially basses and piano at bars 67–8) before dying away on the final pause.

Literal translation

1.
Wei cheng zhao yu yi qing chen.
Wei city morning rain moistens the light dust.
Ke she qing qing liu se xin,
The inn green the willow is freshly coloured,
quan jun geng jin yi bei jiu,
to encourage you yet one more drink,
xi chu Yang guan wu gu ren.
the west beyond Yangguan has no friends.
Chuan xing! Chang tu yue du guan jin,
Quickly go! Long journey pass cross gates waters,
li ku xin, yi zi zhen.
experiencing hardship, adequately yourself care for.

2.
Wei cheng zhao yu yi qing chen.
Wei city morning rain moistens the light dust.
Ke she qing qing liu se xin,
The inn green the willow is freshly coloured,
quan jun geng jin yi bei jiu,
to encourage you yet one more drink,
xi chu Yang guan wu gu ren.
the west beyond Yangguan has no friends.
Yi yi gu lian bu ren li, lei di zhan jin.
Reluctantly long for unbearably leave, teardrops moisten the cloth.
Gan huai! Si jun shi er shi chen.
Longing recollection! Miss you twelve divisions of the day (archaic).
Shui xiang yin, shui ke xiang yin, ri chi shen.
Whom to share with, whom can to share with, day and night to long for.

3.
Wei cheng zhao yu yi qing chen.
Wei city morning rain moistens the light dust.
Ke she qing qing liu se xin,
The inn green the willow is freshly coloured,
quan jun geng jin yi bei jiu,
to encourage you yet one more drink,
xi chu Yang guan wu gu ren.
the west beyond Yangguan has no friends.
Zhi jiu, wei yin xin yi xian chun.
Delicious wine, not yet to drink the heart is already intoxicated.
Zai chi yin, he ri yan xuan xuan lin,
To carry to gallop grey horse, when its sound to return carriage to sound,
neng zhuo ji duo xun?
to be able to drink how many rounds?
Qian xun you jin, cun zhong nan min,
A thousand rounds to have to exhaust the limits, tiny feelings to be difficult to vanish,
wu qiong di shang gan!
everlasting sadness!
Chi su shen, chi su pin shen ru xiang qin.
In letters to express, in messages often to express as if to be intimate.
Yi! Cong jin yi bie liang di xiang si ru meng pin,
Alas! From now apart two places lovesickness to enter a dream frequently,
hong yan lai bin.
the wild goose to visit.

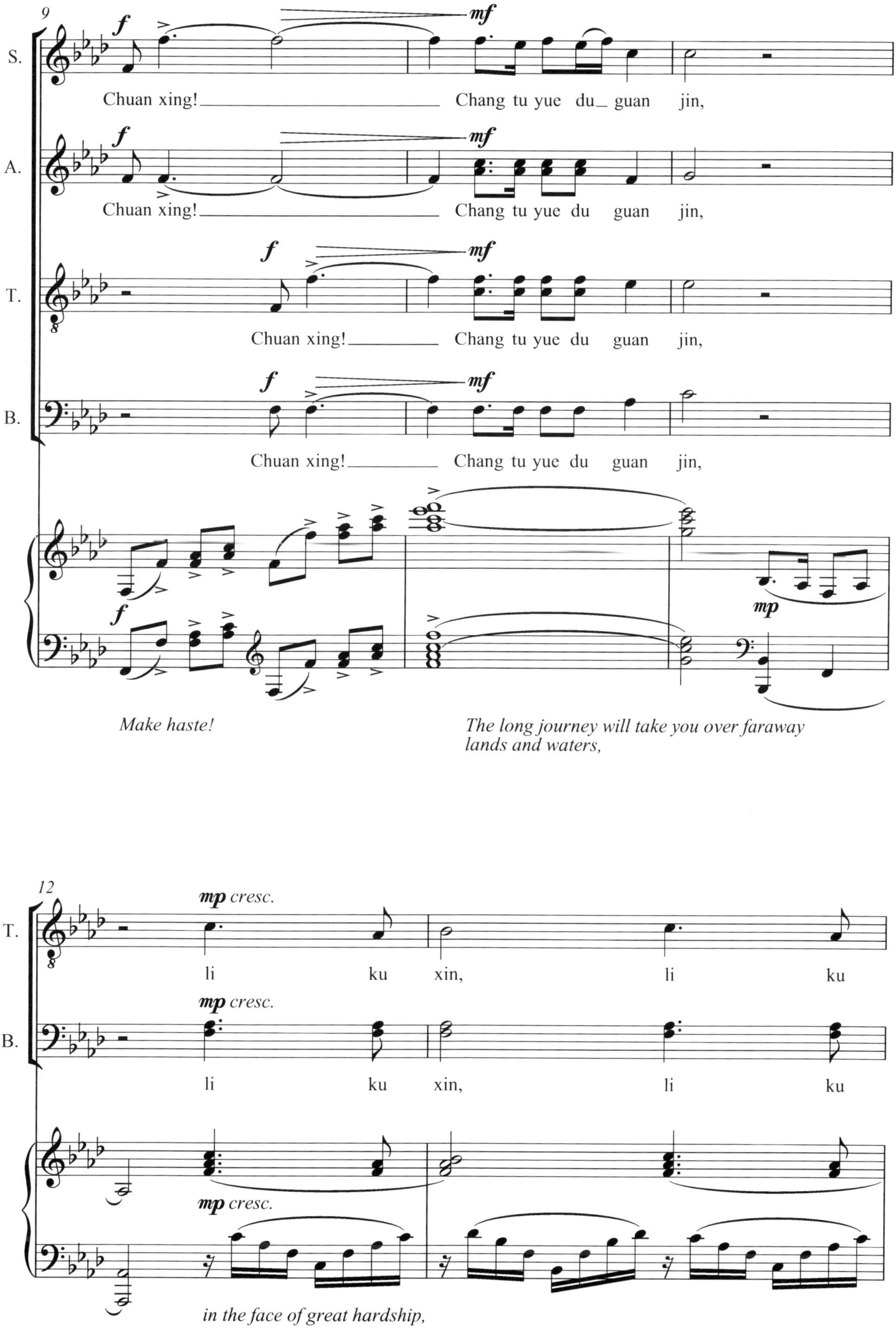

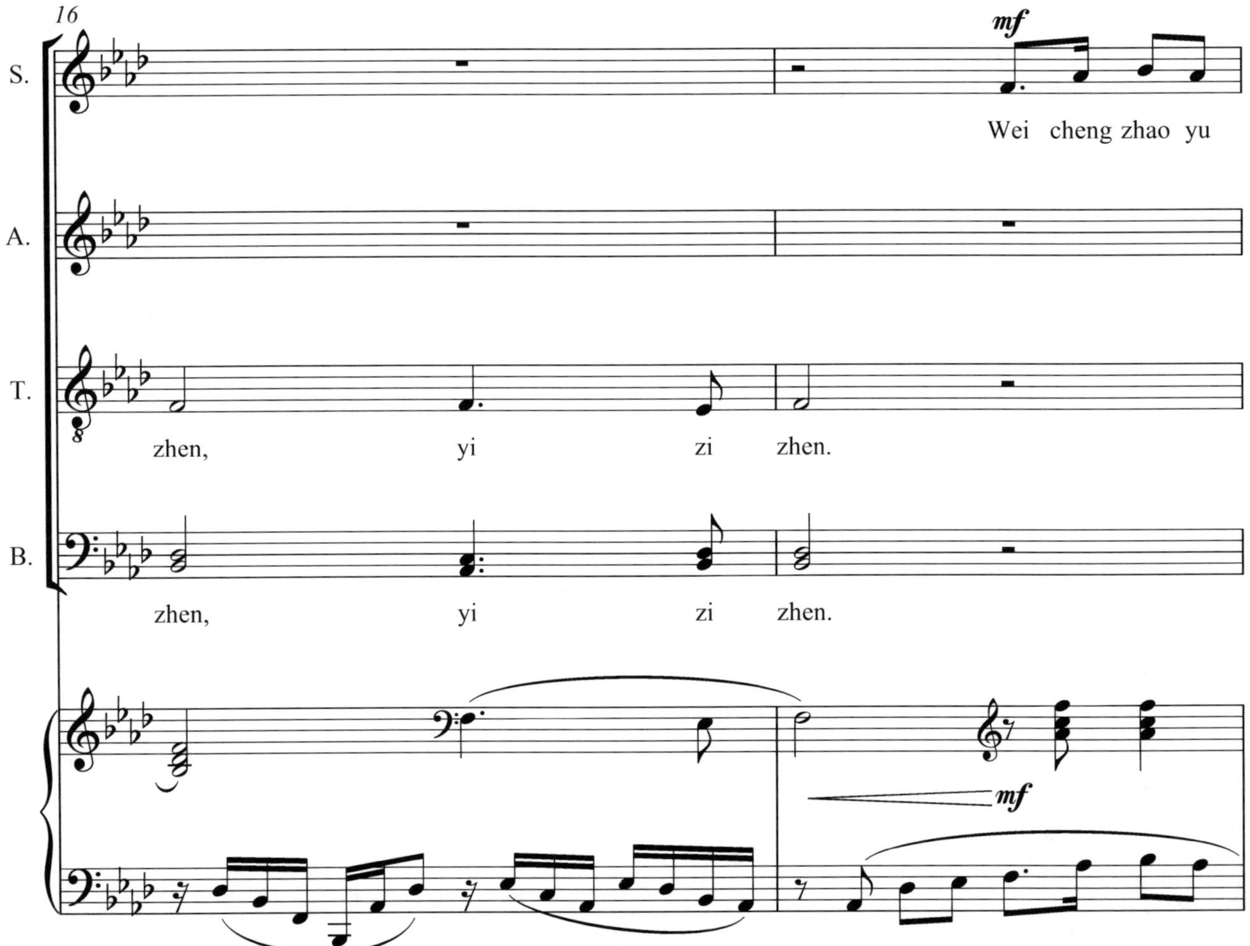

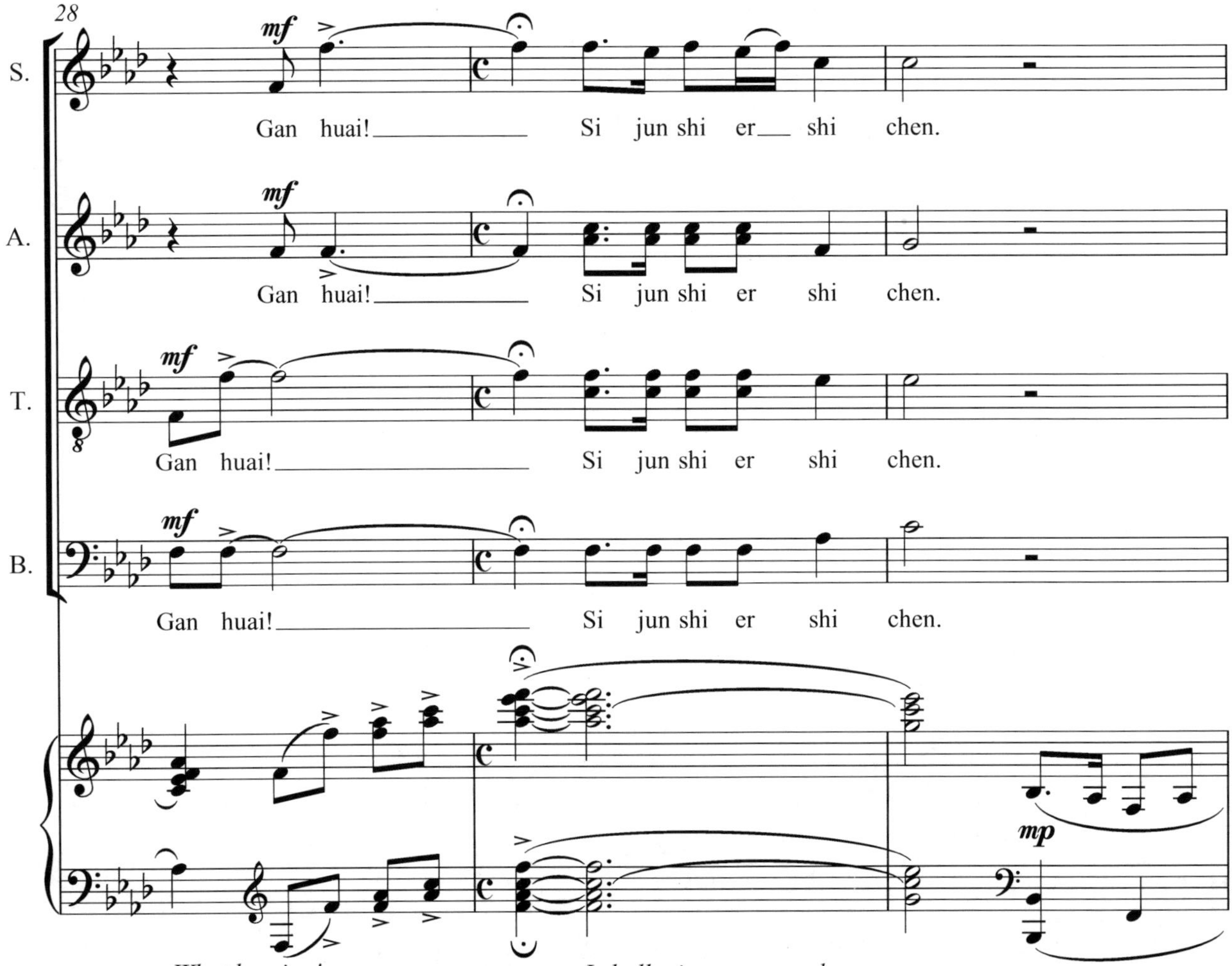

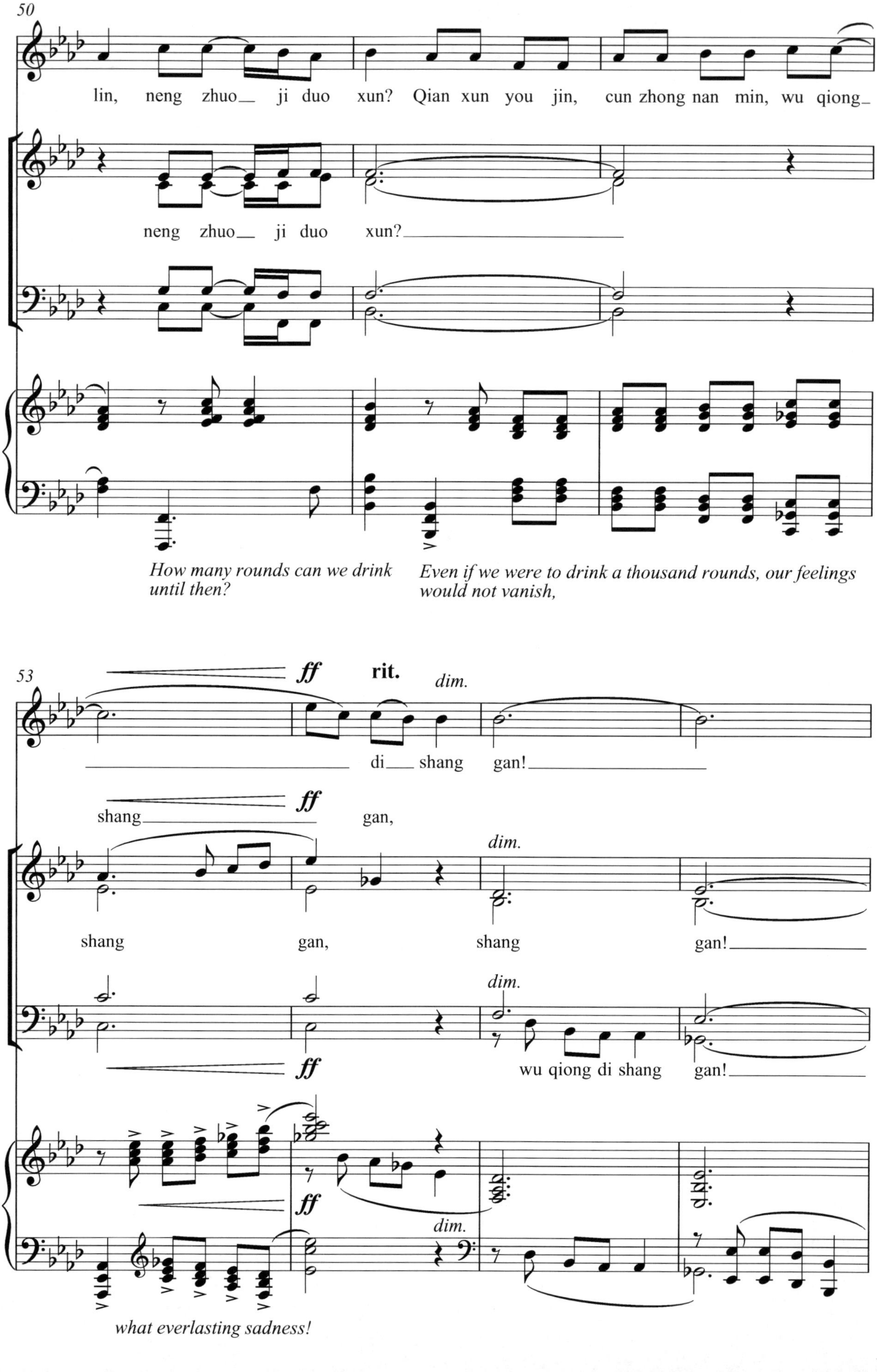

lin, neng zhuo ji duo xun? Qian xun you jin, cun zhong nan min, wu qiong

neng zhuo ji duo xun?

How many rounds can we drink until then? Even if we were to drink a thousand rounds, our feelings would not vanish,

di shang gan!

shang gan, shang gan, shang gan!

wu qiong di shang gan!

what everlasting sadness!

Yi Wang | To Forget

Yi Wang is an original work for SATB chorus, setting a mid-twentieth-century poem about the inescapable memory of heartbreak and forlorn love. **Language**: Mandarin.

Composer

Hwang Yau-tai (1912–2010; also written Huang Youdi) came from Guangdong in southern China. He received a Bachelor's degree in education from Zhongshan (Sun Yat-sen) University in Guangzhou in 1934 and immediately began his career as a music educator. He moved to Hong Kong in 1949, and in 1957 travelled to Rome for further study. After receiving a diploma in music composition, Hwang returned to Hong Kong in 1963. Composing over 2000 compositions, he gained recognition as a leading Chinese composer of school songs and choral works. Hwang moved to Kaohsiung in southern Taiwan after his retirement in 1987, where he continued to promote music education in the community.

Text

Zhong Meiyin wrote the poem in 1957. She and Hwang Yau-tai had previously collaborated in the early 1950s, and she asked Hwang to set *Yi Wang* to music in 1957, but his studies in Rome did not allow him to do so until over a decade later. *Yi Wang* is a poem of conflicted sentiments experienced from heartbreak. The multiple stanzas have varied patterns, lengths and rhyming schemes as the forlorn lover searches for solace amidst inescapable pain. The main text themes revolve around illusionary love stereotypes, passion's persistent memory and the dual metaphor of threatening wildfires and emancipatory clouds — both at an unreachable distance.

This setting

Hwang wrote *Yi Wang* in 1968. It was first written for solo soprano, piano and violin, then arranged for piano and SATB chorus; in this form, with the elevated importance of its piano part, *Yi Wang* adheres closely to the Romantic Art Song style. The work has six verses in an ABA form with both modified strophic and through-composed features. It is in the key of C minor with modulation through different keys and prominent, recurring semitone motives, including the added D♭ for the 'wander around me all through the night' theme. The piano-choral introduction, brief interludes and coda are all characterized by the recurring 'Yi Wang' theme. The first verse (A: 14–37) is repeated in the final verse with slight modifications (A': 130–53). The middle verses (B) are varied musically according to length and content. Verse 2 (42–65) is long and based on verse 1. Verse 3 (71–80) is short, in $\frac{6}{8}$ metre, and transitions to the long verse 4 (81–111), which moves through G major and E minor in varying tempos. Verse 5 (112–30) in G minor is agitated and transitional, leading to the reprise of verse 1 at 130.

Performance notes

Avoid starting too slowly so that later Andante and Moderato sections fit into a related tempo scheme. However, the indicated tempo of 100 is generally reserved for the most intensive moments and should not be strictly maintained. The piano should seamlessly shift between dramatic and accompanimental roles throughout. Play the moving right-hand slurs from bar 81 more as floating clouds than as virtuosic runs. Observe all dramatic *crescendos* with a character of helplessness rather than strain. Do not oversing the f and ff at 125–9. Give a musical shape to the recurring 'Yi Wang' motives, but always keep them at a ringing distance. The soprano soloist may interpret the length of the first and last notes of bar 129 flexibly, and there may either be a breath break with the choir before the downbeat of 130 or no caesura before that downbeat.

Literal translation

1.
Yi wang! Yi wang!
To forget! To forget!
Ruo wo bu neng yi wang,
If I not to be able to forget
zhe xian xiao qu ti, you zen zai de qi ru xu chen zhong you shang?
this delicate body, then how to carry on such heavy sadness?
Ren shuo ai qing gu shi zhi de zhong shen xiang nian;
People to say love story to be worth a lifetime longing;
dan shi wo ya, zhi xiang ba ta yi wang.
but I ah, only to want to take it to forget.

2.
Ge an di ye huo zai shao,
Far shore of wildfire is now to burn,
leng feng li shu zhi zai yao;
cold wind within tree branch is now to shake;
wo zhong ye zhi zhu di shang,
I all night to wander embankment on,
zhi wei zhui xun yi wang.
only to to seek to forget.
Dan shi ni ya, que si tian shang di xing guang,
But you ah, however to be like heaven above of starlight,
zhong ye rao zhe wo chang yang.
all night around me to wander.

3.
Ge an di ye huo yi mie,
Far shore of wildfire already to extinguish,
ye feng li chong sheng si qi;
night wind within insects sound everywhere;
lu shi tai hen, xing yue jiang chen.
dewy moss traces, star moon will to sink.

4.
Shui neng jiang fu yun hua zuo shuang yi,
Who to be able to take clouds to turn into a pair of wings,
zai wo xiang yi wang di gong dian fei qu?
to carry me toward to forget of palace to fly to go?
You shi wo hen zhe ke xin shi huo,
Sometimes I to hate this single heart is to live,
shi hui tiao yue, shi hui tong ku;
is to be able to leap, is to be able to hurt;
dan wo you pa yi wang di gong dian yo,
but I also to fear to forget of palace oh,
jiu lian tong ku yi fu que ru.
then even pain also to pay to lack to be as good as.

5.
Ying jie zhe tong ku ba!
To welcome this pain to let!
Sheng ming ru xiang yi piao qing shui,
Life if to be like a ladle fresh water,
wo ning yin xia zhe zhan ku bei.
I would rather to drink from this glass of bitter cup.

Yi Wang
遺 忘
To Forget

Words by Zhong Meiyin

Hwang Yau-tai

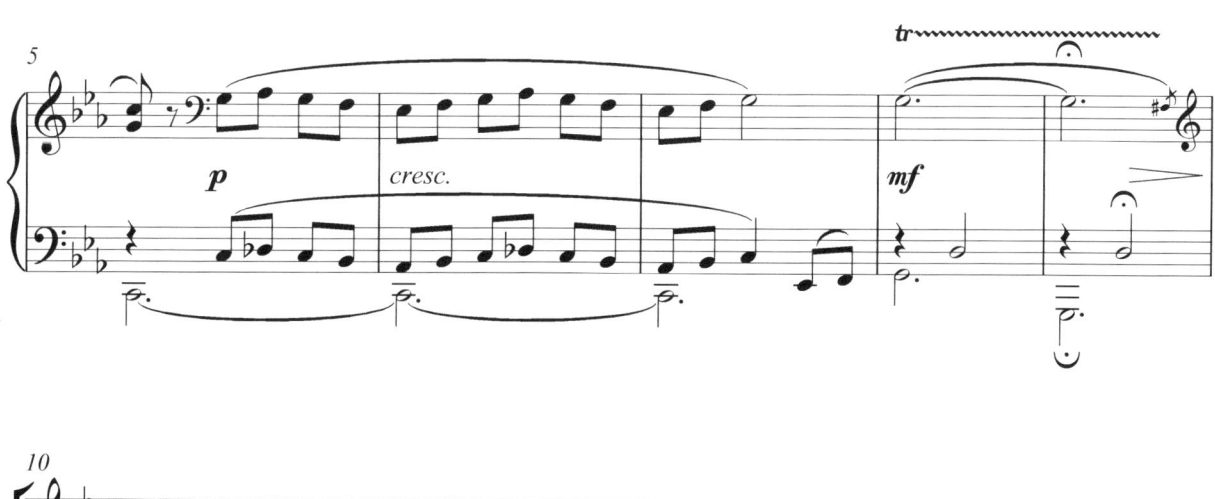

A simplified piano accompaniment is available to download at www.editionpeters.com/halfmoonrising

© Hwang Yau-tai and Zhong Meiyin. Reproduced by permission.

how can I carry such heavy grief within this fragile body?

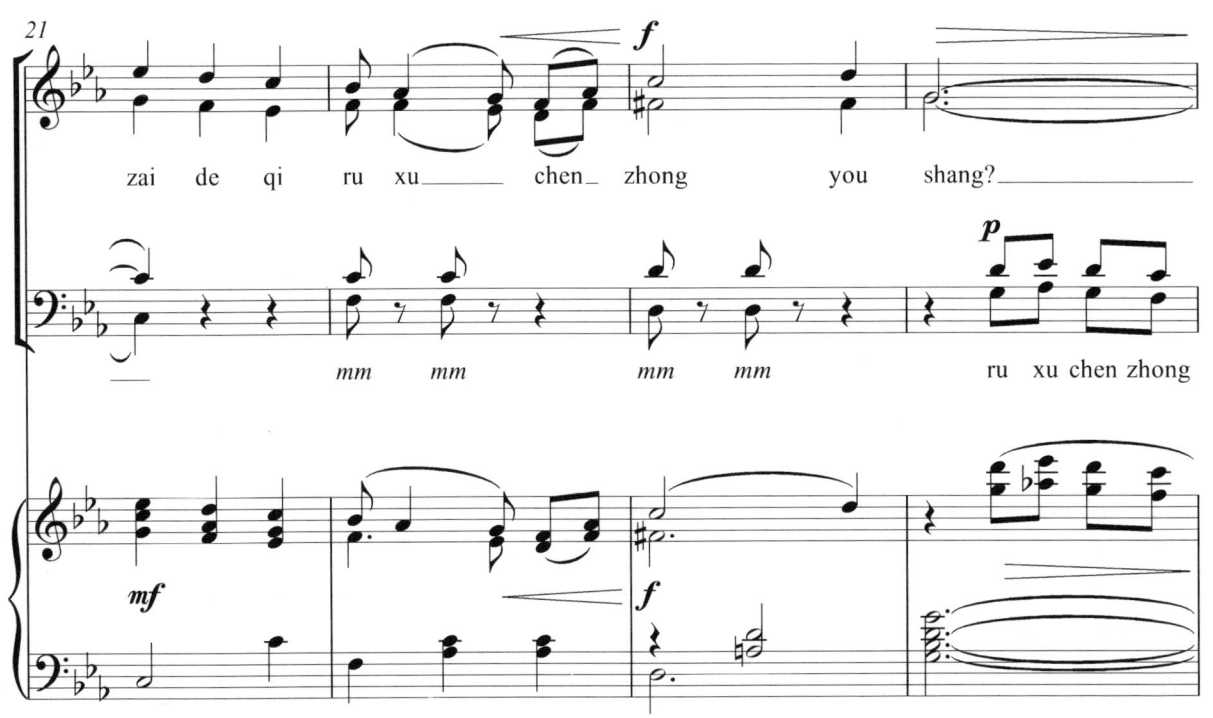

(such heavy grief?)

People say that a love story is worth a lifetime of longing;

(worth a lifetime of longing;)   but for me, I want only to forget.

but oh how I fear the forgotten palace,

that is even worse than the price of pain.

If life is like a ladle of fresh water,

I would rather drink from this bitter cup.   *(this bitter cup, I would rather drink from this bitter cup.)*

(such heavy grief?)

People say that a love story is worth a lifetime of longing;

and yet for me, I want only to forget.

To forget!